How to Buy a Great Business With No Cash Down

ARNOLD S. GOLDSTEIN

John Wiley & Sons, Inc.

New York   *Chichester*   *Brisbane*   *Toronto*   *Singapore*

*Dedicated to my wife Marlene for her
encouragement and assistance in the
preparation of this book, and
to those who helped me prove that money
is not a requirement for becoming a
successful entrepreneur*

Library of Congress Cataloging-in-Publication Data

Goldstein, Arnold S. How to buy a great business with
no cash down/Arnold S. Goldstein.
     p.   cm.
    Bibliography: p.
    Includes index.
    ISBN 0-471-61712-1   ISBN 0-471-54775-1 (paper)
     1. Leveraged buyouts. 2. Small business-Purchasing.
 I. Title.
HG4028.M4G58 1989
658.1'6—dc19   88-32125

Printed in the United States of America
10 9 8 7 6 5 4 3

Preface

It is ironic in this fabled land of opportunity, where so many dream of owning their own business, that so little is known outside sophisticated financial circles of what one uses for capital to achieve that dream.

The signs of quiet desperation are everywhere. Bored housewives, corporate serfs, ambitious dropouts and blocked executives, unhappy and frustrated people from every walk of life, are joined by the common goal to own their own businesses. They also share a common problem—too little cash to make it happen.

Certainly, buying a business with little or no cash down is far from an impossible dream since there are more than 14 million small businesses in the United States, with an estimated 20% actively for sale at any time. Many of these businesses soon will be owned by entrepreneurial mavericks who know the strategies you will discover in this book. These are the enterprising people who realize that lack of capital is their handicap but never their obstacle. So, armed with little more than hope, goals and a mountain of determination, they buck the odds, defy the rules and tweak the noses of conventional thinkers who stubbornly believe you really need money to make money.

How to succeed in spite of that handicap is what this book is all about. I want to show you how you too can become a successful owner of a profitable business using little or none of your own cash. As you turn the pages you'll share the experiences of those who safely traveled the road before you. It's through their experiences you'll find the workable techniques I speak about.

I've traveled the same bumpy road myself, buying 12 companies—from retail stores to a printing plant—using absolutely none of my own money. In recent years I've successfully counseled hundreds more with the same objectives and financial limitations. This experience furnished the insight for this book, and convinced me a book such as this was long overdue. Countless others undoubtedly want and need the same guidance as they strive for their own businesses.

Yes, there are many books that provide nothing more than inspirational pep talks about building castles in the air and magically going from rags to riches. Such books have their purpose; however, this book is designed to be more instructional than motivational. Cash shy but ambitious people need real answers to real questions and demand concrete advice if they are to buy and grow a business in the twilight world where creativity must take the place of cash. Still, "no cash down" is more than a technique, a mathematical formula or even a way of business. It's a state of mind.

After you finish this book you'll understand the techniques and strategies, but before you can successfully apply them you must first develop a no cash down mentality of your own. Without it you're the pawn, and the seller and his gang of advisers are the players. It's not simply what you know that counts. Whether you call it courage, daring, assertiveness or aggressiveness, it boils down to one thing: believing you too can make it happen!

I don't pretend it's easy or automatic for most people, because such a hard-hitting entrepreneurial attitude is not consistent with most personalities. However, confidence and experience can work wonders, and increased confidence will come with increased knowledge of how no cash down deals work.

No cash down business opportunities abound. It may take perseverance to find and put together your first deal, but it will happen if you keep trying. You may uncover ten deals with nine that otherwise suit your needs but fail to achieve your no cash down goal. It's the tenth that counts. Forget the nine "no deals" except for the experience and increased self-confidence they provide.

Every deal has its own unique blueprint for success. As we proceed through the book I'll ask you to set aside your opinions and misconceptions of what it takes to achieve 100% business financing. There are many ways to buy a good business using none of your own cash and I will give you the basics of most of them. But talk to other successful businesspeople, bankers, accountants and others within your industry. You'll be surprised at how they enjoy sharing their successes and failures and how willing they are to give valuable advice and further insights into the challenging world of leveraged buyouts.

Buying or selling a business is usually a once in a lifetime experience, and if you're like most people you're entering the marketplace for the first time. This essential guide will take you through each phase of the buy-sell process showing you proven ways to avoid the costly errors and dangerous pitfalls while obtaining the best deal possible.

Whether you are planning to buy or sell a small retail business, large manufacturing firm or a special situation such as a franchised company or turnaround opportunity, this book places years of my own experience and the experiences of many others at your fingertips.

Buying a business with no cash down requires a game plan—a financing strategy. But strategy alone is not enough. Your willingness and desire to reach your goal are equally important. Success won't come with the wave of the wand nor from the pages of a book. Just as others have discovered, you will find that success rarely comes without plenty of hard work, sleepless nights and a commitment to financial victory. Hopefully this book will make that task slightly easier.

ARNOLD S. GOLDSTEIN

Chestnut Hill, Massachusetts
March 1989

Contents

1

Who Needs Cash?

Directly across the road from my office is a large tire plant employing thousands of people. At precisely 8 a.m. each morning executives, clerical staff, and factory workers dutifully stream through the front door to punch a clock; and, like bees abandoning a hive, all stumble out the same door at precisely 5 p.m. each afternoon.

How many of these people are happy at their jobs? Truly happy? How many would achieve far greater happiness running their own businesses? You never know the answer. Some probably have never thought of owning a business, being content to punch a clock, pick up a paycheck and head home to enjoy a few beers before the television. Others harbor the idea but remain slaves to the illusive security of employment, afraid of the gamble and the inherent risks of being at the helm of their own businesses. Still others, the timid and the tired, lack the confidence to become boss of their own ventures as they mistakenly believe management involves a magic touch they lack. Whatever their reasons, these people wouldn't journey into business on their own under the best of circumstances. And they shouldn't even try.

In that endless stream of people faithfully marching in to work every morning, however, are the few who sincerely want their own business and have what it takes to be successful. There's only one thing holding them back—money.

Unfortunately, most will fall victim to their lack of capital and remain forever shackled to someone else's desk as the dream slowly drifts away. Yet, others with no more cash but far greater creativity and determination will somehow claw their way into business. These are the people who refuse to stay poor simply because they begin poor. They connive, beg, borrow and hustle to get it together and keep it together, and that's the thrill of it all. You want a business of your own so you go for it. In the process you thumb your nose at a world of nonbelievers, skeptics, pessimists and conventionalists with their words of wisdom of why you can't or shouldn't.

Who are these entrepreneurs? They come from every age group, background and walk of life. Women and others from minority groups increasingly are joining the ranks. What these people have in common is the dream of becoming independent and the opportunity to use their talents to build a better future.

When do they decide to go into business for themselves? When they get tired of the corporate rat race, or get fired, or are pushed into it by an ambitious spouse, or finally realize business ownership is the only way to reach their goals.

What will they buy? Every size and type business from pizza parlors to publishing firms, shoeshine stands to semi-conductor companies. Some businesses will be nothing more than part-time, work-at-home enterprises and others formidable corporations. The businesses acquired will be as varied as their new owners.

How do they go about it? The business may start with a vague idea, become a dream, progress through several stages and finally emerge a reality. Some entrepreneurs spend months, even years, learning, exploring, examining, researching and finally jumping. Others close their eyes and plunge right in. No matter how they go about it, virtually all will tell you that the decision to buy is at the same time exhilarating and frightening. You welcome the chance to build a better life, yet the future is uncharted. You have made the important decision that you want your own business, yet you realize this forces you to face countless other decisions. Why do I want my own business? What type business should I buy? Should I start a business instead? Do I need a partner? And eventually you come back to the one big question: *Where do I find the money*? Can I really find a good business to buy using little or none of my own money?

BUT THEY NEVER SAY "NO CASH DOWN"

You're a skeptic. You've read this far but like most people you just don't believe there are good, solid, profitable businesses you can buy with no money down. That's understandable, so let's see if we can explode the myth that it takes money to get into business.

First I want you to accept a small challenge. Put down this book for a moment and pick up your local newspaper. That's right, pick up the newspaper from any city and turn to the Business Opportunity Section. Scan the listings. There you'll see just about every type of business offered, from accounting franchises to zipper manufacturers. The ads describe the business, its sales and perhaps even the price. Read carefully. Do you see any offered businesses that say "no cash down?" Of course not. And I bet you never will. Over the past 20 years I have systematically scanned the Business Opportunity Section of the Sunday edition of the Boston Globe and never have noticed an ad that said "no cash down." Let's do some quick arithmetic. Since the Globe lists about 500 businesses for sale every Sunday, I have read approximately 500,000 ads during the past 20 years, not one of which advertised a no cash down deal.

No wonder you're skeptical. You should be, because no cash down goes contrary to your every experience. It's unlikely you've had a friend, relative or colleague benefit from a no cash down deal, and even if you have taken a hundred business courses you will have heard few professors explain how to get into business without cash.

Will you accept another challenge from me? Walk into any business brokerage office and tell them you are looking for a business but have no cash for a down payment. I once conducted that little experiment myself. One morning I discarded my lawyer-like business suit and briefcase for a pair of slacks and a sport shirt. Playing the role of a typical business seeker I innocently walked into five of the leading business brokers in the Boston area. My story was I had just completed a 20 year army hitch, took early retirement and wanted a small retail business. I would be interested in just about any type of retail business anywhere in eastern Massachusetts. My one problem was that I had no cash to put down.

The first broker literally laughed me out of his office. The others were somewhat more courteous but nevertheless escorted me to the door telling me that all their listings required a down payment.

And so it goes. Sellers want to sell and buyers want to buy and few know how to swing the no cash down deal. Don't let this discourage you. Soon you will learn not to take the Business Opportunity ads at face value and you will know how to convert many attractive situations to no cash down terms.

So what's the catch? If sellers are really willing to accept terms with no cash down, why don't they say so? Simply stated, sellers follow convention and do not know how to accomplish their own objectives any other way. That it takes cash to get into business is a myth that collapses when you show the seller how to accomplish his or her objectives without parting with a dime of your own.

Following is a discussion of some of the dangerous myths that can stand between you and a successful business.

Myth #1: You Need Money to Make Money

People say it and believe it. That explains why there are so many poor people. I agree that the rich may get richer, but that doesn't preclude a bit of success for the rest of us poor souls.

It's easier selling vacuum cleaners door-to-door than to sell people on the idea that they too can get started on a money-making venture with little or no money of their own. Bob Allen, best-selling author of *Nothing Down* (Simon & Schuster, 1982), had just this problem when he tried to convince his readers that they too could buy real estate with little or no money of their own. Now Allen was no fool. People could read, but would people believe? No, according to Allen. The skeptics were everywhere. So Allen threw out an interesting proposition: "Put me in any city," said Allen, "give me $100 for living expenses, and in 72 hours I'll return owning several properties without using a dime of my own money." The *Los Angeles Times* took the bait, handed Allen $100 and shipped him to San Francisco to turn his boast into proof. A few days later the triumphant Allen descended the plane clutching deeds to several choice Frisco properties.

Oftentimes I'm tempted to match Allen's challenge by boasting that you can land me in any city or town and within one month I'll have purchased a good, solid, healthy business without spending a dime of my own. But who needs another business?

Now what's the message? It's not boasting, and it's not about either real estate or buying a business. It's about money. You may need money to make money, but it doesn't have to be your money.

Myth #2: You Can't Buy or Build a Good Business without a Big Investment

How lucky we are that some people refuse to swallow this line. Thousands of sizeable companies are acquired every year as a leveraged buyout with the new owners investing little or none of their own money. In fact, buying or starting a business on a shoestring has spawned some of today's largest industries.

Could Royal Little predict back in 1923 that his $10,000 loan to start a small, humble, synthetic yarn processing plant would lead to today's Textron, worth over $3,000,000,000?

Did Frank Seiberling realize when he borrowed $13,500 to start Goodyear Rubber and Tire Co. that it would someday produce annual sales in excess of $7,000,000,000?

You wonder whether Atlanta druggist, Dr. John Pemberton, could have conceived that his $50 investment would become the mammoth Coca-Cola Company ringing up $4,000,000,000 in sales, when he concocted his first batch of syrup in 1886.

How could David H. McConnell foresee his $500 loan becoming the giant Avon Cosmetics?

What clairvoyance did George Eastman have when he scraped together $3,000 to begin the Eastman Kodak success story?

Can $40 in borrowed capital create a company valued at $4,000,000,000? It happened to Issac Merit Singer, founder of the Singer Sewing Machine Company.

What would the future be for Hewlett-Packard, when William R. Hewlett and David Packard scraped together their last $538 in 1939? It was a question these two budding entrepreneurs couldn't answer then.

Perhaps your goals are more modest. Perhaps you envision only everyday type businesses that commonly dot Main Street. But if giant corporations can be launched or acquired with such little investment, why should your more modest venture be more difficult to finance?

Myth #3: Too Much Debt is Bad

Yes, accountants, professors, bankers and a world of convention-alists warn against excessive debt. And they're often right. Too little investment can lead to an undercapitalized and overlever-aged business doomed to failure. But often the real reason these companies fail is not because the buyers invested too little of their own money but rather because the financing was improperly struc-tured. Moreover, even a well-capitalized business can stumble when cash flow is inadequate to satisfy debt commitments. While it is true that in a highly-leveraged deal you need exercise more caution in evaluating the capabilities of a business to handle financ-ing costs, the fact is that a business can safely be 100% financed provided it generates the cash flow needed to cover the debt service.

Myth #4: Only Wheeler-Dealers Need Apply

This is the biggest myth of all. Experience and watching hundreds of ordinary people bootstrap their way into business have taught me otherwise. You need not be a wheeler-dealer or financial whiz-kid to piece together a no cash down deal.

Face facts. While any idiot with money in his pocket can buy a business, it does require some skill to do it without cash. But it doesn't necessarily take a genius to do it. Ordinary people with absolutely no prior business experience achieve it every day. Wage earners who don't know the difference between a profit and loss statement and a balance sheet have done it. Housewives who have never written a check have done it. I've seen a group of high school kids do it.

Northeastern University researched which bootstrap entrepre-neurs were most likely to be successful. They discovered the best bets were people who were never in business before, had no business education and were cash poor. In plain language, ones that didn't know any better and couldn't do any better. It once again shows that what you don't know can't hurt you. To solidify the case, the researchers found the least likely people to even attempt to buy a thinly capitalized business were MBAs and buyers with extensive business experience. You'll find them still chained to their desks at some Fortune 500 conglomerates, believing business deals are done "by the book." They've been reading the wrong books.

Speaking of books, there are two more you may find helpful. The first is my own, *Starting On A Shoestring*, also available from John Wiley & Sons. This book is specifically for people with little money interested in starting (as opposed to buying) a business. John Storey of Storey Communications adds much to the subject with his own book *Starting Your Own Business*, also published by John Wiley & Sons. John's book, like my own, focuses on leveraged startups but is peppered with fascinating tales of how he bootstrapped his now highly successful communications empire using little cash of his own. As you'll read, John and I keep coming up with the same astonishing conclusion: *You don't need money to buy or start a business today; you only need knowledge.*

DEVELOPING THE NO CASH DOWN MENTALITY

No cash down is more than a technique, a mathematical formula or a financing strategy. It's a state of mind. I discovered this years ago when I began to search for my first business. Short on cash but high on hopes, I knew I had to change my thought process. Thought processes are habits that can be changed or altered. Most people have difficulty shedding their conventional thoughts on *how things are done* to *how things can be done*, and yet this mental transformation is necessary if you are to succeed.

This book can give you the tools to buy a good profitable business with no cash down, but the ideas mean nothing unless you are convinced they can work for you. The trick, of course, is to *substitute ideas for cash*. Creativity can be a far more powerful wealth-building tool than money in the bank. In fact, ideas and creativity are the backbone of all successful activities. You'll find this theme time and again when reading stories of how great entrepreneurs built incredible fortunes starting without a dime in their pocket.

I don't throw out this advice merely to mimic various "How To Get Rich" books but because it is absolutely true. In Napoleon Hill's famous book *Think and Grow Rich* I discovered that jewel of wisdom that is the cornerstone of creativity: "Whatever the mind of man can conceive and believe, it can achieve."

Looking back on my own no cash down deals I came to realize how very true that statement is. Whenever lack of cash stood between myself and my next deal I was forced to turn my own creativity one notch higher. Eventually I visualized solutions where none could be seen before. And with that vision in my mind I knew that perseverance would eventually turn that vision into reality.

But to become that creative thinker you must first understand the countless ways to put together no cash down deals. I read every book on business finance that I could get my hands on. I devoured books, scoured magazines for articles on leveraged buyouts and quizzed successful entrepreneurs until they were ready to throw me out of their offices. But I was learning. During this education, I kept coming up with the same nagging conclusion—*you don't need money to buy a good business; you only need knowledge*.

THE NO-FREE LUNCH THEORY

If it takes a large dose of creativity, perseverance and knowledge to get the keys to a business, it takes far more to stay in business and make it successful.

Precisely what does it take to go for it and succeed? I offer no long shopping list of personal attributes or personal skills. Lists don't work. Too many times we see the village idiot end up owning the largest and most successful business in town with the smartest kid on the block his bookkeeper.

But while there is no one profile of the effective business owner, I can tell you this—it will take far more effort to make a go of a leveraged acquisition than of a well-capitalized business. There's no such thing as a free lunch. In one way or another you pay the price for going it on a hope and a prayer. You may find yourself working 18 hour days because you can't afford more payroll. You will tread cautiously because you can't afford the luxury of costly mistakes. You will worry about any dip in sales because every nickel and dime in the cash register is precious. Cash flow will become king as you face the monthly challenge of meeting over-whelming note payments. Growth will come slowly because every available dollar is committed to paying for the business, leaving few dollars for expansion.

Several years ago *In Business* magazine contained a terrific article entitled the "One-Tenth Financing Principle." It aptly summed up what I say: You can buy a business with one-tenth the capital normally required (or even no cash at all) but in return you must work ten times as hard to make it succeed. Yes, it is still possible to go from rags to riches but the process is just a bit slower and the path a bit more bumpy when you rely on other peoples' money to get you started.

GET STARTED TODAY

Disraeli said: "Man is not the creature of circumstances, circum-stances are the creatures of men." This is perhaps the most impor-tant message of this chapter because the one great danger is not that you will try and fail, but that you will fail to try. How often the loftiest ambitions are stifled by procrastination!

Whenever I'm tempted to put off my plans for another day I need only swivel my chair. Behind my desk is a framed self-portrait of an elderly gentleman named Harold, poised with a palette in one hand and a paint brush in the other. It was not the great artistic skill with which it was obviously drawn, nor the deep personal relationship I had with the artist that compelled me to buy the painting. It was his smile. It carried an important message, and I wanted that smile to be my continued warning that hopes can grow old.

I met Harold while visiting a friend in a nursing home. He spent his days painting and smiling. Striking up a conversation with him, he confided the reason for his ever-present smile. "You know," he said, "when I was a young art student just out of high school, I wanted to open an art gallery. My father wanted me to be a dentist instead. I spent six years getting through NYU Dental School, hating every minute of it and wishing I owned my own art gallery instead. I wanted a career in art, not pulling teeth. But life plays nasty tricks. First came the depression, so I drilled teeth to make a living. Then came the war, and the Navy needed dentists. When I got back I had a wife and two kids to support, so I pushed aside my dreams of an art gallery and resumed my dental practice. When I hit 50 I figured it was time. My kids were on their own and I had money in the bank. My wife called it mid-life crisis and my kids thought I was insane to give up a lucrative dental practice to open an art gallery. So for the next 20 years I continued to push aside the idea of my own gallery and drilled more damned teeth. Well, now I'm 73 years old and too ill to start an art gallery so I paint instead. You wonder what happens to all the years and all your dreams." I never wanted to forget those words.

People always have reasons for pushing their ambitions into the future. Excuses come easy. If you really want to acquire your own business you'll face only one real enemy—procrastination. You can read this or any other book 56 times and memorize every word, but what good does it do if you don't put it into practice?

The procrastinator always has a reason. How many times have you heard someone say "the time isn't right," "the economy is bad," "money is too tight" or "I want to make certain there'll be no war in the Mideast." The list is endless. Year in and out the procrastinator reasons, while someone else makes the money.

One thing is certain, my friend. Nobody is going to knock on your door, lead you by the hand and do it for you. Nobody is going to give you the push to get started today. Why should they?

So let's face facts. Some of you will never own your own business. Your dreams are nothing more than fantasies. You'll hope for it, think about it and fabricate ten reasons why you can't do it. And you shouldn't. Whatever you want from your business your business will demand far more from you.

Then again, you may be one of the few who are ready. Perhaps you've been in business before and know what it's all about. Maybe it's your first time and you have kicked aside all your fears and doubts and are anxious to tackle it. Welcome to the club. Someday you'll look back at your first day at the helm of your own business. And when you do, you'll also stand tall and give yourself a hefty pat on the back. You'll deserve it. You made your own miracles.

KEY POINTS TO REMEMBER

1. There is no need to stay chained to your job because you don't have cash to buy a business.

2. Overlook the fact that businesses are never advertised on no cash down terms.

3. An undercapitalized business is not necessarily a risky business.

4. Substitute ideas for cash; they can be far more powerful.

5. There is no free lunch, so expect to work considerably harder when you buy on leveraged terms.

6. Don't wait—you will be neither younger nor wealthier next year.

2

Building Your Financial Pyramid

LEVERAGE: THE TOOL THAT MAKES MILLIONNAIRES

Archimedes once said, "Give me a lever long enough and a prop strong enough, and I can single-handedly move the world." Such is the power of leverage!

Leverage is one of the best ways a "small" guy or gal can make a million dollars. Leverage is basically a method used to control an asset with little or no money. Using leverage to control a profitable business without using any of your own cash is called "infinite leverage" or "creative financing."

Investment experts don't mind going into what I call creative debt, if they smell fat profits. Creative debt is a further refinement of OPM (other people's money). You borrow money and pay the going interest rate for that money—let's say 15 percent. I call these "equity-confiscation" loans. You use that money, if you're wise, to find a good business that will yield a financial return far in excess of 15 percent.

The no cash down approach I am advocating here refines the OPM philosophy by using knowledge to avoid borrowed seed money to acquire a business. You create the ideas, and the cash necessary to close the transaction inevitably follows. The money will come to you when you provide the proper incentives to attract the partners and lenders necessary to complete the no down payment deal.

Of course, if you're making sufficient money on the borrowed funds, the interest rate is meaningless. But watch out! Leverage is a double-edged sword. You can lose any investment or equity you have if you can't handle the mortgage payments or other debts you incurred to purchase the business. Follow this prudent rule: Before you leap into deep debt to acquire any business through leverage, thoroughly do your homework. Be certain the business will earn adequate profits to comfortably handle the debts.

You'll be amazed to discover it can be as easy to buy a business without cash as it would be if you had a pocketful of money to hand a seller. So buckle up! In this chapter you'll learn the basic formula you need to start on the road to financial freedom and wealth with the seven essential lessons of a successful leveraged buyout.

LESSON #1: PRICE IS ONLY A NUMBER

An asking price can intimidate the untutored buyer who erroneously believes the business is beyond his reach. Scan the want ads and you'll encounter numerous businesses sporting astronomical price tags. Whether $50,000 or $100,000 or $1 million, you might as well proceed to the comics, you mumble, because you can barely scrape together $20 to take the family out to dinner. But don't be intimidated by numbers on a newspaper page. Price is only symbolic. A $100,000 price does not mean that $100,000 must come out of your pocket. As you will see in this chapter, none of it need come out of your pocket.

In reality, a price tag should send you an entirely different message. Interpret it as "Mr. Buyer, I want to receive the equivalent of $100,000. My business can generate the cash, and your job as the new owner is to see that it does."

Let's take a sample ad and test it in this light:

Restaurant for sale. Sales over $500,000. Price $140,000.

How would you get the seller $140,000 from his own business? That, of course, is always the challenge. Let's start with zero (where you always begin when piecing together no cash down deals) and gradually build the $140,000 while making use of somebody else's money.

How many ways can you stack your financing blocks to reach $140,000? Too many to count if you are creative. Perhaps you can achieve it with one giant financing block, persuading the seller to lend you the entire $140,000. On the other hand, you could theoretically borrow $1 from each of 140,000 different people, in which case you would accomplish the same goal with lots of small financing blocks. Chances are your successful strategy will involve a blend of different sized financing blocks which in the end total $140,000. There is no one right formula. Five different buyers competing to buy this same restaurant on no cash down terms might construct five very different financial pyramids to reach the same goal of $140,000.

Let's see what their formulas might look like:

Buyer #1

$ 75,000	Bank loan secured by the business
40,000	Seller financing
10,000	Assumption of seller's liabilities
15,000	Loans from suppliers
$140,000	**Total**

Buyer #2

$ 90,000	Seller financing
30,000	Bank loaned secured by the business
20,000	Investment by partners
$140,000	**Total**

Buyer #3

$ 60,000	SBA loan
20,000	Seller financing
20,000	Assumption of seller's liabilities
10,000	Loan from business broker
10,000	Supplier financing
20,000	Borrowed from business cash flow
$140,000	**Total**

Buyer #4

$100,000	Seller financing
40,000	Investment by partners
$140,000	**Total**

Buyer #5

$ 60,000	Bank financing secured by the business
30,000	Seller financing
5,000	Loan from business broker
10,000	Sale of certain business assets
10,000	Personal loan
5,000	Borrowed from business cash flow
10,000	Supplier financing
10,000	Assumption of seller's liabilities
$140,000	**Total**

While each method is different, what do the methods have in common? Each raises 100% of the purchase price using capital from sources other than the buyer's own checkbook. In the following chapters you'll learn where to find the needed building blocks and how to use them to put together your deal. But for the time being focus on what every smart no cash buyer knows: The total is only the sum of its parts, and the possible parts are so numerous you need only a bit of imagination to find the ones for your deal.

LESSON #2: BUILD FROM THE GROUND UP

Build your no cash down financing pyramid one careful step at a time. Start at the bottom using the largest financing blocks first, and gradually climb to the top by adding a small block here and there. Let's turn again to the case of the $140,000 restaurant as I show you how one of my clients actually negotiated the financial pyramid needed to successfully buy the business.

After the usual buyer-seller dickering, Barry decided the restaurant was a perfect acquisition for him and the $140,000 price was fair, so it was time to start building his financial pyramid using everybody else's money.

The seller, an elderly gentleman who we will call Conroy, was a typical seller—reasonable and willing to listen, but also concerned about getting his money. Here's how our negotiating session went, as Barry piled his financing blocks in place one by one.

I started by asking Conroy what financing was available if we agreed to pay $140,000. Conroy sat back, pondered the question and replied, "I suppose I could finance about half the price." Immediately we had our first $70,000 building block through seller financing. My next question upset Conroy at first. I said we needed to know about the restaurant's existing debts. Conroy sharply answered, "None of your business! It's my responsibility to pay my creditors from the proceeds of the sale." I countered that Barry might assume the debts as part of the purchase price. "Wouldn't you, Mr. Conroy, wind up with the same amount of money if the buyer assumed your debts and deducted them from the down payment?" Conroy had to agree, handing us another financing block—existing liabilities totaling $30,000. Deducting liabilities from the seller's price, we immediately locked the "assumed debt" financing block into place. Now we had commitments for $100,000—$70,000 through seller financing and $30,000 through assumption of liabilities. We still had $40,000 to go to reach the top of our no cash down pyramid.

I knew no bank would lend the last $40,000 on the business because the restaurant's assets already were tied up as collateral to secure the seller's $70,000 loan. But what if I could persuade Conroy to subordinate his $70,000 note to a bank loan that would have priority on the collateral? I asked Conroy if he would object to our obtaining a $40,000 bank loan with his $70,000 note second in line behind the bank if Barry defaulted. Conroy objected. He obviously wanted to be first in line in the event of default. Though I could hardly disagree with him, it was nevertheless time for a little give and take. I reminded Conroy that we were willing to pay the $140,000 asking price. "Mr. Conroy, you probably expected us to haggle the price down to $130,000, maybe even $120,000. But we'll pay the full $140,000—if you'll let us secure a $20,000 bank loan by a first mortgage on the business. If Barry defaults you'll admittedly have to pay the $20,000 to take back the business but in reality that $20,000 merely represents the difference between $140,000 and the reduced price you were probably willing to accept." Conroy agreed. It would be no trick to get a bank to lend $20,000 with a $140,000 business as solid collateral. Our financial pyramid began to take shape:

$ 20,000	Bank loan secured by a first mortgage
70,000	Seller loan secured by the second mortgage
30,000	Assumption of seller's liabilities
$120,000	**Total**

We had negotiated for about half an hour and already had secured $120,000 of the $140,000 price. The top of the financial pyramid was within easy reach.

But where would we find the final $20,000? Typically the no cash deals involving the big dollars which finance 60 to 70 percent of the price fall into place quickly. It's the last few dollars that can be the hardest to find. Fortunately there are scores of sources you can tap.

To start the ball rolling we approached the wholesaler who supplied produce to the restaurant. He willingly loaned $5,000 to be paid back within the first year leaving only $15,000 to go. The restaurant had two cigarette machines provided by a vending company which earned Conroy $8,000 a year in commissions. If the vending company would advance Barry $5,000, he would extend a two-year concession lease and the vending company could repay itself from commissions due Barry's restaurant. Rather than risk losing the location, the company agreed. The financing gap narrowed further. We had $130,000 in place without Barry committing a dime on his own.

Barry figured out several possible ways to raise the final $10,000, but one method was all we needed. Quickly calculating the business grossed about $10,000 a week in sales, Barry gave Conroy an interesting proposition. "Look, I'm only $10,000 short. Why don't you take an additional $5,000 out of next week's receipts instead of paying it to creditors on current bills. That will increase my assumed liabilities from $30,000 to $35,000. For the final $5,000 I'll give you my personal check if your attorney will hold the closing papers in escrow for a few days until the funds clear." Barry knew he could "borrow" the $5,000 needed to cover his check from sales once he took over ownership.

So the deal was struck! Within two weeks Barry became his own boss and now proudly reports record sales for his new restaurant. He draws a hefty $60,000 a year salary and continues to build equity as he pays those who provided the money for his no cash pyramid.

Now let's review Barry's financial pyramid:

$ 20,000	Bank loan
70,000	Seller financing secured by the business
35,000	Assumption of seller's liabilities
5,000	Supplier financing from the produce wholesaler
5,000	Advance commissions from cigarette company
5,000	Business cash flow, to cover Barry's check
$140,000	**Total**

Follow Barry's example. Once you realize that price is nothing but an objective to be reached by pyramiding individual financing blocks, you'll never again be intimidated by an asking price.

LESSON #3: IGNORE DOWN PAYMENT DEMANDS

Forget down payment demands. Pretend the words "down payment" don't exist, because in reality they have absolutely no meaning when it comes to structuring your 100 percent financial pyramid. Here are two reasons why:

1. A seller quotes a down payment demand based on his perceptions of what is needed to finance the deal and the "financing blocks" available to finance the deal.

2. A seller quotes a down payment to tell what he wants to walk away with from the closing, not to tell where your financing blocks will come from.

These are the only interpretations you can give the words "down payment."

Now let me show you why the words "down payment" mean positively nothing. If you accept the first interpretation you immediately see that the seller is dictating what must come out of your pocket to satisfy his or her idea of what your financing pyramid will look like. For example, a seller may put his business up for sale for $150,000. He does some quick calculations and concludes that a buyer can obtain a bank loan for $50,000 and he'll finance another $50,000. That being the seller's idea of the financing, the buyer obviously needs $50,000 to reach the $150,000 price. To the seller that's simple enough—the buyer needs a $50,000 down payment to easily finance the business.

But once you know the many financing blocks at your disposal you can build your own financial pyramid without blindly accepting the seller's financing design. Analyze your own possible position in the above example. To begin with, the seller did hand you some valuable building blocks—$100,000 worth to be precise. You must be your own architect for the remaining $50,000. Without even knowing the numerous methods the following chapters uncover, some obvious answers will come to mind if you recall how Barry achieved his 100% financing. Try it out. You could, for example, attempt to negotiate larger than a $50,000 bank loan. That would give you a larger financing block to start with. Chances are the original loan on the business was higher and has since been reduced. Why shouldn't a bank favorably consider a loan higher than one-third of the price then? You also might convince the seller to increase his financing from $50,000 to a larger amount. It's always negotiable. If you can increase the seller financing to $60,000, an additional $10,000 is reduced from the required down payment. Don't overlook accounts payable. That's a commonly available financing block sellers forget. It can effectively be used in the vast majority of business takeovers. Suppose the liabilities are $15,000 and would have to be paid by the seller from your down payment. Try to assume them as a building block.

Perhaps you now have $135,000 to $140,000 of the purchase price firmly in place. For the other $10,000 to $15,000 you might use some of the methods Barry employed, or any one of the other methods described in this book. When you're through the deal may possibly look like this:

$ 70,000	Bank loan (increased from $50,000)
60,000	Seller financing (increased from $50,000)
15,000	Assumption of liabilities
5,000	Business cash flow
$150,000	**Total**

At this juncture you may ask, What if the bank *won't* increase the loan to $70,000? What if the seller *won't* agree to finance more than $50,000? What if the seller *doesn't* have liabilities to assume? Then what happens to that hypothetical pyramid we just built? I have a simple answer: We design another financing pyramid using still other financing blocks that *will be* available. There are literally thousands of possibilities and combinations available to you. Perhaps another bank will lend $70,000 if the existing bank won't.

Whittle away at the price using smaller financing blocks. A loan from the business broker? Can the seller create liabilities for you to take over? Can you exploit some hidden assets? Can you cultivate some supplier financing? The list is endless. Your job is to know the alternatives and decide on the financing blocks most likely to work for your deal.

The fact is that most sellers do not know the most creative ways to finance the business they're selling nor do they strain themselves to find the best ways. For these reasons sellers should never be counted on to properly engineer your 100% financing pyramid. Don't forget—it's much easier for a seller to simply say you need $50,000 for a down payment.

Now we come to the second subliminal message in down payment demands—the seller sees your down payment as his "walk-away" money. That, of course, is sheer fallacy. In real life what the seller puts in his pocket at closing bears no direct relationship with what comes out of yours.

Let's go back to our seller's demand for a $50,000 down payment on the supposition that if you have it, he will get it. If instead you're that imaginative buyer who raises $50,000 from sources other than your own pocket, the seller still receives his $50,000!

The average person takes the term no cash down to mean that the seller must end up with no money at the time of closing. Nothing could be further from the truth. Of course, with many no cash down deals a seller will agree to finance 100 percent of the purchase price, with no closing money in his pocket. Yet, it's certainly not a requirement when building your financial pyramid. It's entirely possible you will finance 100% of the price, while the seller is paid at closing every dime of the purchase price.

Remember Conroy who sold out to Barry. What if Conroy had said "I need all cash, period." Such a demand is not unusual. True, Conroy would have deprived Barry of seller financing as a handy financing block, but we could have found others in structuring our no cash deal. A bank, for instance, might have financed $70,000 to $80,000 against the business. We could still have assumed $35,000 in accounts payables. The produce wholesaler and cigarette company would still chip in their $10,000 and Conroy would probably still agree to hold your $5,000 check for a few days. To raise the small balance would simply require a little more creativity. But as you can see, a seller should never require a down payment to come from your own pocket when so many enticing alternatives are available.

LESSON #4: YOU MAKE YOUR OWN MIRACLES

Creativity is what helps you discover the financing blocks that give you a 100 percent financed pyramid. As we all know, the human mind is complex and can be amazingly creative if you work it hard enough. Pose to the less creative buyer the problem of buying a $140,000 business and you might hear the typical answers: Borrow from a bank, ask the seller to hold some paper, try the Small Business Administration, or call your mother. But shopworn, conventional answers won't help if you want the business on no cash down terms. Sure, such textbook strategies may get you 50 to 80 percent of the purchase price, but how do you raise the other 20 to 50 percent? That's where creativity can indeed work miracles.

I showed you Barry's solution. Although his story does not necessarily represent the most creative of all possible solutions, nothing more was needed to successfully reach his 100 percent financing goal. You may need far more imaginative ideas to find those last few illusive dollars needed to cement your deal together.

In Chapter 1, I described the no cash down mentality. In subsequent chapters we will explore more examples of creative no cash down strategies. Some of the cases in this book may appear contrived to make a point, but I assure you that's not the case. The solutions you see are proven solutions, and yet they too only scratch the surface of no cash down possibilities.

Barry and I tried brainstorming as we pondered his $140,000 restaurant before the actual financing finally fell into place. We knew we could raise $100,000 from the seller, banks or other more obvious sources, but we were less confident about the final $40,000. We let our imagination run wild as we fantasized where that money might come from, throwing ideas back and forth. Some ideas were practical, others ludicrous. But even a crazy idea may sow the seeds of a creative and workable solution.

Barry hit me with a barrage of possibilities. "Let's sell stock in the company. No, wait. Let's lease out the basement for a disco and collect the year's rent in advance. Hold it, how about this? We'll ask Conroy to become a silent partner if he knocks $40,000 from the price." On and on he went, one idea springing from another. Barry was in a frenzy when he blurted his ultimate crazy idea. "Why not sell 'dinner memberships' to everybody in town? For $10 a member would be entitled to one free dinner for each dinner purchased." Barry loved his idea. "Imagine, if I sell 4,000 memberships, my customers will buy me my own restaurant!"

Barry will never have trouble closing no cash down deals because he has the creativity to find solutions where other people see only obstacles. If one idea doesn't work, you can count on Barry to have two more ready in its place.

Remember, it can be those last few dollars that stand between you and your business. Every deal offers its own creative solutions to find those dollars if only you use your imagination!

LESSON #5: THE DEAL DICTATES THE FINANCING

This book contains all the financing blocks needed to achieve 100 percent financing for your business. Which blocks you use will largely depend on the deal. Your financing strategy therefore depends on what financing is most readily available and the financing blocks that will provide you the greatest economic benefit. While there are many ways to finance a deal, some are more obvious and preferable than others.

The characteristics of the deal offer valuable clues as to the financing blocks that will be most readily available. As you turn to Chapter 8 and learn how to take over troubled companies with no cash down, you will find that your obvious financing block will be the assumption of the company's liabilities. It would make no sense to consider borrowing $50,000 from a bank to pay $50,000 to creditors when the debts owed already represent "built-in" financing.

In Chapter 9 you'll see how suppliers can help you finance your business. It is possible that you can advantageously combine supplier financing with some larger financing blocks such as seller or bank financing as discussed in later chapters.

Perhaps you'll locate a business with excess inventory or other disposable assets. By learning the techniques in Chapter 11, you'll be able to grab hold of yet another financing block that can create your pyramid as you see how to turn these surplus assets into cash.

If you keep your eyes open, you'll find financing blocks everywhere.

Once you are fully familiar with all the ready sources of money that can take the place of your own cash, you may find that the available financing blocks will actually exceed 100 percent of the purchase price. It may sound farfetched but it's absolutely true. Experience will not only let you design a 100 percent financed pyramid, but in many cases those financing blocks can buy the business and put money in your pocket!

LESSON #6: BUILD A STRONG FINANCIAL PYRAMID

Build your pyramid choosing financing blocks that provide the greatest financial strength. Every source of financing has its own special characteristics, advantages and disadvantages. As you proceed through this book you'll see the various strengths and weaknesses that each financing block offers. However, the best financing blocks:

- Provide the longest payback period,
- Carry the lowest interest rates,
- Require little or no collateral, and
- Demand no personal liability.

No one source of financing, of course, will display all these characteristics. Bank loans may offer you a long payback period, but require personal liability on your guarantees. Taking over the seller's debts ordinarily avoids personal liability but may require a fast payback and hence strain cash flow. Partnership funds overcome each of these unfavorable points but require you to give up equity in the business.

So as you look around for your building blocks, go first for those that meet your specific requirements. Building that perfect pyramid may require financial and legal guidance, so be sure you have professional advisers to help you.

Achieving 100 percent financing must be more than a mere mathematical exercise. Obtaining it through financing blocks that give you a strong financial pyramid will allow the business to survive and grow, which is the real objective of financing.

Give your pyramid these acid tests. Can the business pay the obligations? Is the level of personal liability acceptable? Can profits be increased through lower interest rates offered by other financing blocks? Can the business be more favorably refinanced in the future? Ask the important questions and remove your rose-colored glasses. Don't fall victim to a faulty design!

LESSON #7: CAN IT REALLY WORK FOR ME?

Every approach to no cash down deals outlined in this chapter can work for you. Every case you'll read in this book proves this point, because each is a true story of how others with no unique talent bought a successful business without cash. There are thousands of others who have landed their own businesses without a dime of their own by following the same no cash down formula. In fact, most businesses can be purchased without cash of your own given the necessary know-how, creativity and perseverance.

But the most important lesson in this chapter is that you have to believe it can work for you. Possibly not in every deal, but in more than enough deals—in any line of business—it can work to get you just the opportunity you want sooner than you think. You'll see how others have effectively used financing building blocks to put them in a business of their own; and perhaps one day you too may say: "Who needs cash?"

KEY POINTS TO REMEMBER

1. Anyone can buy with no cash down once they know how.

2. Price is only a number—you reach it with creative financing.

3. Build your financial pyramid one step at a time using everyone else's money.

4. No two deals are alike—match the financing to the deal.

5. Design your own pyramid—sellers do not think in no cash down terms.

6. Always start from the ground and work your way to the top.

7. The seller can receive his money with no cash down deals.

8. Use creativity to find your building blocks.

9. The no cash down formula does work if you believe in it and effectively use it.

3

Prospecting for No Cash Down Deals

LOOK AND YOU WILL FIND

Good businesses for sale are easy to find. Why shouldn't they be? Every business is for sale for the right price.

No matter how many deals you come across, the trick is to hunt for opportunities that both make sense and will put money in your pocket with no cash down financing. You need to develop a search and screening process that brings deals just right for you. I have found good no cash down deals from just about every source. There are indeed diamonds in every coal pile.

While there are countless businesses for sale, however, as you will discover, very few are right for you. Therefore, to find your best opportunity you will need plenty of determination, time, patience and the help of the strategies found in this chapter.

HOW TO PREPARE FOR THE SEARCH

To properly search for your business keep these seven points foremost in mind:

Be Patient

Don't get discouraged if you don't find quickly what you're looking for. It frequently can take a year or more and the investigation of hundreds of businesses before you locate the right opportunity.

Develop Experience

The search should be a learning experience where you look at as many businesses as possible to sharpen your judgement and develop a feel for the market. Don't rush in and buy until you have checked sufficient opportunities to determine comparative values.

Think Competitively

You are not the only buyer in search of a good business. In fact, there are many more qualified buyers than there are good, reasonably priced businesses. Therefore, as a no cash down buyer you will need a comprehensive, innovative and aggressive strategy to be the first to reach the best deals.

Explore Every Source

Don't rely on only a few sources for leads. You will discover many valuable ways to find businesses for sale. While some sources tend to be more effective than others, you never quite know where or how you will find your perfect deal so leave no stones unturned.

Be Flexible

You'll start your search with a reasonably good idea of the type of business you're looking for, but stay flexible and keep your options open. You may come across an opportunity far better than what you hoped to buy if your vision of the ideal business is not too fixed.

Be Organized

A systematic, well-organized search is essential. Start by setting goals. How many leads will you obtain each week? How many businesses do you plan to visit or investigate? Develop and stay with your action plan. Keep a notebook and record the information on each lead so you'll have the data on each business at your fingertips. Searching for a business requires a consistent and thorough effort.

Have the Deals Come to You First

Don't look for diamonds after everyone else has sifted through the coal. You must be first in line if you are to latch onto the most worthwhile deals. That's why conventional sources of leads such as newspaper and broker listings usually feature the "no-go" deals. The very best deals don't have to be advertised. They're quickly grabbed up through word of mouth without being advertised or listed.

COLD CANVASSING FOR HOT LEADS

The best way to find no cash down opportunities is to directly approach owners of the type of business you are interested in. This is precisely how business brokers obtain listings; yet very few buyers consider using this direct search strategy for themselves. The obvious advantage of the direct approach is that you are likely to find the best opportunities before they are actively placed for sale. There are quite a few owners who have an interest in selling but for one reason or another have not yet advertised or listed the business with a broker. Your inquiry may be both timely and profitable.

Use a dual approach to reach owners. Start with a direct mail campaign and follow up several weeks later by telephone. You can obtain mailing lists through yellow pages, trade associations or mailing list brokers. Personalize your inquiry letter to draw increased attention. The primary message of the letter is to let the owner know you are a ready and able buyer for his or her type of business.

An owner may not respond to your letter but may be receptive to discussing the possibility of selling once you phone. Don't press for information over the phone. Inquire only whether the owner has an interest in selling. Obtaining further information should be left for a follow-up meeting.

If you are too timid (or don't have the time) to make hundreds of phone calls to prospective sellers, consider a telemarketing firm. These professionals are expert in the art of telephone inquiry and can generate a surprising number of leads at a nominal cost.

ADVERTISING FOR RESULTS

A second way to reach prospective sellers is to advertise your interest in buying. Most advertising, of course, is undertaken by sellers, but it can be even more effective for buyers because there are relatively few buyers who advertise. Advertising also helps reach the many prospects who can't be reached by mail or telephone, and continuous advertising might reach owners at the moment they decide to sell.

Where should you advertise? Newspapers of general circulation are most suitable when advertising for businesses in broad categories (retail, manufacturing, financially troubled, etc.). Trade journals, association publications and other media targeted to your specific industry, however, will bring far better results when you have a specific type of business in mind.

What could be better than sitting behind your own desk while an anxious seller tries to sell you a business? You can then reverse the intimidating games sellers play on you. A simple newspaper or journal ad can bring them knocking at your door if you know the right strategies.

A friend of mine wouldn't approach it any other way. He buys all kinds of run-down businesses, gets them on their feet and quickly sells out at phenomenal profits. He has but one unshakeable rule—he never uses his own cash. Here's the ad that John uses to reel in deal after deal:

> I want to buy any type retail business in Boston area. Immediate cash available.

John has it all figured out. He knows the "down and outers" will come calling. The lure of "cash available" is intriguing. Once John lands the seller in his office he invariably finds a way to do the deal without cash. You can easily modify this same ad to attract your specific type of business.

A simple ad can work! One $15 ad a week in the Sunday classifieds draws 20 to 25 calls. John's preliminary screening is by telephone and he usually ends up investigating five to six deals a week. John tells me that he only closes about one deal every three or four months because that's all he can handle. According to John, "There are plenty of good no cash down deals that I have to turn away. And to think there are still people out there working for a living who believe it takes money to buy a good business!"

SUPPLIERS SUPPLY LEADS

Suppliers always seem to know who the likely sellers are within their industry. Credit managers know of customers who may be having problems and want to sell out, while sales people develop strong relationships with customers and are often the first to hear when a business is ready to go on the market.

How can you convince suppliers to furnish you these valuable leads? Suppliers feel an obligation to give their best leads to valued customers, to build good will and assure continued patronage after the sale. Unless you happen to be an existing account, you're at a decided disadvantage when seeking supplier leads. For that reason you should convince the supplier you too will become a valued customer should you buy one of his leads.

Ask people in the trade which suppliers sell to your target industry, and don't overlook even the smallest suppliers or local firms as they often are closest to their customers and thus in the best position to know who soon will be for sale. Don't forget to follow up. Out of sight is out of mind. Make it a point to call once a month to remind suppliers you still want to become their customer.

Developing your own referral network can bring you leads. What kind of referral network would you develop to buy, for example, a liquor store? Liquor wholesalers should be your first stop. Tell them what you're interested in and follow up. They know the industry and usually know what stores are up for sale. The best way to really get leads is to stay close to the salespeople who call on the retail accounts. They're in the best position to know the scuttlebutt as they frequently develop close relationships with their customers.

Believe me, it works. For example, I can call any one of ten salespeople for hardware wholesalers and find out anything I need to know about any retail hardware outlet store in the state, including who is for sale. So cultivate a few key salespeople in your industry. Offered a small incentive they'll keep you more than busy with leads.

A BUYER'S GUIDE TO BUSINESS BROKERS

Since 60% of all businesses are sold through brokers, this valuable source can hardly be overlooked. However, the typical broker has ten buyers for every good listing, so you must motivate a broker to work hard to find you the right business. Try the following:

1. Convince the broker you're a serious qualified buyer. This is the key. A broker can't waste time with dreamers, lookers and perennial "tire-kickers."

2. Act like a successful businessperson. Call for an appointment. Don't walk in cold. Brokers are professionals and appreciate buyers who treat them as professionals. Don't forget that dress and appearance count; impressions help convince the broker you are a qualified buyer.

3. Prepare a portfolio with your resume and business criteria. This quickly tells the broker who you are and what you are looking for.

4. Avoid telling the broker you have limited cash. Always let the broker think you can raise the required funds for the right deal. It's all part of being a "qualified buyer." You can negotiate your no cash down terms later.

5. Create the impression that you're relying on that one particular broker. Brokers work best if they believe you are looking exclusively through their office. Nevertheless, you should check available opportunities with every broker. You can't afford to rely on one broker unless he in turn will contact other brokers on a co-brokerage arrangement.

6. Review your business criteria with the broker. As a professional in marketing business opportunities the broker is best qualified to tell you if the business you are looking for can be found readily.

7. Check out every listing conceivably of interest to you. Don't ignore a listing because sales appear too low, price is too

high or other terms seem out of line. Neither you nor the broker know whether a business is for you until you inspect it, or whether terms are acceptable until you negotiate.

8. Let the broker know why you decline a business, so he can obtain a clearer idea of what you are looking for.

9. Stay in constant communication with the broker. A phone call every two or three weeks reminds him you are an active buyer. And don't forget—new listings come in every day.

10. Always work through the broker on any listing he presents to you. It is the broker's role to be the intermediary between you and the seller. Brokers provide a valuable professional function and rightfully expect their commissions to be protected.

Many buyers hope to buy businesses at lower prices by avoiding brokers whose commissions they believe inflate prices. It's false economy. In very few cases does the broker's commission materially affect what you pay for the business. In fact, the existence of a middleman in the negotiations can often offer considerable benefit. Most brokers negotiate well, and can mediate deals that wouldn't come to pass through direct confrontation between buyer and seller. So don't look at the broker as a needless expense. The broker plays a role far more important than merely showing you a business.

Approach all brokers in your area. Don't limit yourself to the largest or the most active. You never know which broker has the right listing hiding in his or her files until you inquire. Bear in mind that brokers advertise fewer than 10% of their listings. Generally, brokers use newspaper ads to promote easily saleable businesses and ones with wide appeal. A less attractive opportunity may be your best deal.

Start with brokers who specialize in your type of business. Firms specializing in specific businesses such as restaurants, liquor stores, taverns, motels, food stores, drugstores and greeting card shops are commonly found in most major cities. For example, the firm Restaurant Brokers of America handles only restaurants and related businesses in New England. Interested in a country business in New England? You'd be wise to choose a firm such as Country Business Brokers in Brattleboro, Vermont. If you want farm property anywhere in the United States, consult United Farm Agency. Glance at your own metropolitan newspaper or yellow pages to find the specialists in your area. Specialty brokers know their industry well, can help you establish values, can arrange financing and will bring you a wide selection of opportunities.

Franchised or networked business brokers usually have multiple offices within your area or even throughout the country. Like multiple listing services in real estate, each affiliated office benefits from the listings of every other office, offering an unusually broad selection. For example, VR Business Brokers has offices throughout Massachusetts and in most other parts of the country as well. If you visit any VR office, you can draw upon listings from their other offices. Like specialty brokers, they can offer you valuable professional assistance because their size permits them to employ specialists in all phases of business acquisitions.

Smaller independent business brokers have their own advantages. You'll find wide variation in abilities and approaches, so start with brokerage firms that advertise most actively in your area. The results you obtain from business brokers may, in fact, depend more on the specific broker you work with within the organization than on the agency itself. Business brokers are like other professionals. Some are quite active and some exceptionally lazy. The active broker may not have precisely what you want but he'll diligently search for it. Therefore, if you contact a multiple broker office try to spot and work with the most aggressive broker within the firm.

Real estate firms occasionally include business brokerage as a sideline. In rural areas, where usually a full-time business broker can't be supported, businesses are frequently sold by real estate offices. However, don't spend time with urban real estate firms unless you're looking for a motel, car wash, nursing home or other business considered a real estate investment, or unless you luckily spot an ad by a real estate agent who just happens to have a business closely matching your requirements.

Fish around. The more lines you drop in the water the better chance to land your ideal fish. If you can't visit all brokers in your area, send detailed letters reciting your specific needs. Periodic follow-up letters are essential to let them know you are still interested.

TURN A BROKER INTO A BLOODHOUND

Can you turn a broker into your bloodhound? That will depend on whether he sees you as a serious buyer, which means a ready, willing and able buyer. Nothing irritates brokers more than the perennial shopper who wastes their time. You must convince them that you are serious, know what you want and are ready to buy.

Business brokers typically work for the seller, but there's no law that says they can't work for you. Properly motivated they can be persevering bloodhounds who can save you a lot of legwork as they scout out your ideal opportunity. A friend of mine really knows how to motivate brokers to bring him the best deals first. Studying his strategies is time well spent.

Hal selects only one broker in an area. He doesn't necessarily select the biggest brokerage firm, as he knows big does not necessarily mean better. But his broker bloodhound must be aggressive and devoted to the task. Hal has a simple approach to insure just that. He tells the broker precisely what he is looking for and he always candidly put the cards on the table: It must be a no cash down deal.

Hal routinely gives the broker leads to follow up. That's a switch, of course. But Hal has a refreshingly different technique. He knows that with furnished leads the broker is set on his path and can easily follow up. At the end of each week Hal meets the broker and reviews the facts of each deal based on information uncovered by the broker.

Hal told me about one buyout where this routine really clicked. Hal, at the time, was interested in buying dry cleaning shops. Hal already owned several shops and figured additional acquisitions would help him build a more successful chain. He scanned the newspapers and trade journals for dry cleaner listings while his ears were cocked to pick up rumors of people in the industry ready to sell. One fine day Hal heard of a thriving dry cleaner who had just been divorced and was thinking of moving to Florida.

Fed this information, the broker immediately went to work. The broker of course disclosed to the seller that he represented a buyer but he never revealed Hal as the buyer. The broker met several times with the seller and easily obtained information that Hal as a principal was not likely to have learned on his own. This seller, for example, confided he was anxious to sell in a hurry. The broker negotiated that one fact into a lower price. Over dinner the broker deftly convinced the seller his down payment demands were far out of line. On and on, the broker kept working on the seller. What started as a $50,000 asking price with a $20,000 down payment was finally offered to Hal for $32,000 with only $5,000 down. The broker had indeed proved valuable for "priming the pump" and thus helping Hal land the best deal possible.

Hal didn't use the broker the way most buyers would. Obtaining leads is the easy part. Hal knew that the broker would be looked upon by the seller as an objective neutral, perhaps even a confidant. When the broker told the seller the price was out of line, the seller listened. Nothing Hal could have said to the seller would have been as convincing.

You can turn brokers into your bloodhounds. Have them work and negotiate for you—not the seller. If a good broker is on your side he will earn his commission many times over.

GOOD OPPORTUNITIES ARE ADVERTISED

Contrary to popular belief, plenty of good opportunities can be found in the newspaper classifieds. Sellers often first try to sell through newspaper advertising before turning to brokers. Very small businesses with small price tags can't afford the $5,000 to $7,500 minimum commission charged today by most brokers, and newspaper ads provide a practical alternative for finding buyers. And, of course, you'll notice that brokers place many ads. Brokers don't spend advertising dollars on losers. Yes, there are plenty of winners to be found in your daily newspaper if you know how to read between the lines:

1. Try to obtain back issues of the Sunday paper. Observe whether a particular business of interest appeared over several weeks and whether there's a decrease in price or other sign of desperation that can lead to a no cash down situation.

2. Look for words that provide clues. "Owner must sell" or "Illness forces sale" are usually designed to attract interest but don't necessarily signify a bargain. "Financing available," "Terms negotiable" or "Low cash down" are usually signs of a highly motivated seller.

3. As with broker listings you should ignore quoted price and terms. If a business is of interest, investigate.

4. Be analytical. Today's ads include businesses advertised last week, last month and the month before. But notice how the terms change as the business becomes stale. Prior ads allow you to track seller anxiety and can provide a valuable negotiating tool.

LOOKING FOR A FRANCHISE?

There are an estimated 2,000 franchised businesses to choose from if you know where to look. With a long list of ready buyers, many successful franchisors such as McDonald's and Holiday Inn have no need to advertise. However, you will find many new and worthwhile franchise opportunities through these sources:

1. The International Franchise Association, 7315 Wisconsin Avenue, Washington, D.C. 20014 will send you a roster of their member firms.

2. *The Franchising Opportunities Handbook* is an excellent guide compiled annually by the Department of Commerce. Write the U.S. Superintendent of Documents, Washington, D.C.

3. The *Wall Street Journal* and Sunday *New York Times* are usually used by national chains for advertising franchise programs. You can find regional and local systems in your own metropolitan paper.

4. Three magazines that heavily feature franchise opportunities are *Venture, Inc.* and *Entrepreneur*, all available at many newsstands. *Entrepreneur* publishes an annual franchise directory worth reviewing. Write for their most recent edition.

5. Business/Franchise opportunity shows are held once or twice a year in every major city. Sponsored by different groups, these shows exhibit hundreds of distributorships and franchises. Check your local exhibition halls for a show schedule.

Franchised opportunities acquired directly from a franchisor are seldom suitable no cash down candidates as franchise companies usually require substantial cash in the venture. But an owner of an existing franchised business may be more than willing to consider a sale on highly advantageous terms. You can find these opportunities much as you would find non-franchised businesses. However, it may be worthwhile to contact franchise companies direct for a listing of franchisees within their organization that may be for sale.

WHO WANTS A TROUBLED COMPANY?

Many no cash down buyers are interested in a company with problems that can be picked up at a bargain price, turned around and operated or sold at a profit. If you want to try your hand revitalizing a near-bankrupt business you will be a step ahead of the competition by using the following sources:

1. Check the public records for companies with tax liens against them. Professionals dealing with insolvent firms consider this a surefire sign of financial crisis.

2. Contact auctioneers. As liquidators of an insolvent firm, perhaps they can arrange the sale of an intact business before publication.

3. Court appointed receivers and Bankruptcy Trustees are certainly prime sources to contact. Check with the Bankruptcy Court for a list of attorneys routinely appointed as Trustee. You can also contact the Commercial Law League, 222 West Adams Street, Chicago, Illinois 60606, for a membership roster. Most bankruptcy specialists are members of this organization.

4. Dun and Bradstreet national credit reporting service will sell you lists of companies with poor credit ratings. Contact your local Dun and Bradstreet office for details.

5. There is at least one brokerage firm that handles only financially troubled companies: Galahow & Company, 850 Boylston Street, Brookline, Massachusetts 02167. Their phone number is 617-277-4165.

6. Don't overlook commercial banks and other lenders. They may have problem accounts that they will encourage to consider a no cash down deal if they think you can solve their loan problems.

While these are excellent sources for finding financially troubled companies, don't overlook the traditional prospecting sources. You'll find plenty of distressed situations both in newspaper ads and in broker files.

Keep your eyes open, particularly if you are looking for a retail business where signs of near-failure are easily visible. There are signals that a troubled business may be for sale, even if the owner hasn't placed it on the market. Look for distress signs: low inventory, sloppy store, lack of promotion and advertising, ineffective sales staff. These tell-tale signs show that an owner has lost interest and may be willing to sell at an advantageous price and no cash down terms. All you have to do is ask.

FIVE MORE SUREFIRE SOURCES

In your search you should not overlook five more valuable opportunity sources:

1. Trade or professional associations oftentimes maintain a buyer/seller file as a membership benefit. Don't forget to check association newsletters and journals for ads. For a listing of trade associations in your field of interest check Gales Directory of Associations, available at most public libraries. National trade associations can lead you to local associations within their industries.

2. Schools or colleges that train people in your target industry may list opportunities for new graduates. Pharmacists, beauticians, barbers and even physicians and dentists attempting to sell their professional practices are prime examples.

3. Accountants and attorneys usually know when a client is planning to sell. Try to locate the professionals who specialize in your field.

4. The Business Opportunities Journal monthly lists hundreds of businesses for sale nationwide. If relocation is no problem, the journal is definitely worth scanning. Write them at: 1021 Rosecrans Street, San Diego, CA 92106.

5. Business Owners Multiple Listing Service is a new concept in marketing opportunities. For a nominal listing fee they will add a business for sale to their computerized listings. You can obtain a free copy of over 15,000 businesses for sale by phoning 800-327-9630.

DON'T OVERLOOK YOUR BOSS

Almost 20% of all buyers end up buying their employers' businesses. So your perfect no cash down opportunity may be right under your feet. First, consider whether the business that employs you meets your criteria. It can be a costly mistake to buy a business simply because it's conveniently available or easily found. Judge the business by the same standards as any other prospective acquisition.

If the business does satisfy your needs, keep your ear close to the ground for telltale signs that the business may be available. Your employer's age and health and business conditions are important clues. If you think your boss may be interested in selling, don't be too shy to discreetly inquire.

I know one sales manager who worked for several years for a wholesale meat firm owned by a larger corporation. He considered it the one business he'd most like to own, but of course his employers never knew of his interest. Anxious to sell for tax reasons, the company was quietly sold to an outside firm, much to the surprise of the sales manager. Storming into his boss' office he stammered, "Why didn't you tell me the business was for sale? I would have bought it in a minute!" Peering over his glasses, his boss quietly answered, "Why didn't you ask?"

That's what the hunt is all about. Asking!

KEY POINTS TO REMEMBER

1. To get the best deals you must be first in line to spot them.

2. Be patient but persevering. Finding a good business can be like finding a diamond in a coal pile.

3. Why not start your own advertising campaign? Let sellers knock on your door.

4. Don't overlook suppliers. They might lead you to the best deals in town.

5. There are hundreds of sources of good business opportunities. Try them all. You never know where you will find your perfect deal.

4

Beware of Booby Traps

The woods are full of booby traps and so are many available small businesses. To succeed, smart buyers must learn to avoid the snares. Dishonest sellers and deal killing attorneys abound. So too are businesses too far gone to save, and even seemingly healthy companies often can turn your dream into a nightmare. If you know what to look for, you often can save time, effort and money. Beware! You don't want a booby trap deal at any price or on any terms, including no cash down!

Sellers peddling booby traps will do most anything to get you on the hook, and then paint pretty pictures to reel you in. Remember P.T. Barnum's famous saying, "There's a sucker born every minute." Don't be that sucker.

Expect to encounter your share of booby trap deals. Once you announce you're in the market for a business, sellers will waltz out of the woodwork proclaiming, "Have I got a deal for you!" And they will. No one can protect the gullible from their own foolish fantasies.

BEWARE THE ROSE-COLORED
GLASSES SYNDROME

Unfortunately, some people need a guardian angel. Never seeming to learn from previous lessons, their lives consist of stumbling from one booby trap deal to another. What an expensive disease! Those afflicted suffer from its chronic symptoms—seeing only what they want to see and failing to see what they should see. Any deal can appear attractive if viewed through rose-colored glasses.

Consider the tale of an old army buddy of mine. Jack fantasized about a business of his own and decided to pursue a health club which had an asking price of only $100,000. Blindly, Jack ignored the whopping $40,000 a year rent. Since the business grossed only $80,000 a year and had little prospect to enroll more members, the $40,000 rent represented an astronomical expenditure. Not surprisingly, the health club lost $30,000 its first year of operation and promised even greater losses in its second. The seller, desperate to get out, would have snapped up a no cash down offer. Ignoring the facts, Jack walked right into the trap. I remember my entrepreneur friend's customized T-shirt emblazoned with "Jack's Health Club" on the front and "Have a new body overnight" displayed on the back. The few who joined on the ad's promise could not say it was misleading, because that's about all the time one had to develop that new body. Predictably, the trap sprung shut and Jack went broke within two months.

The wounds on Jack's ankles barely healed when Jack next stumbled into the direct mail business selling books. It was a simple proposition. Jack could buy $20,000 worth of "how to" books for $10,000. All he had to do was mortgage his house to secure the payment. The seller, a midwest promoter, convinced Jack that if he advertised his books in leading journals the money would roll in quickly. But if this was such a super moneymaker, why didn't the seller place his own ads and rake the money in himself? Jack's enthusiasm prevented him from asking this obvious question. You can guess the result. Two months later, Jack was flat broke and buried beneath his pile of books.

It's no sin to try and fail. In fact, it's the American way. Everyone makes mistakes and inevitably makes more as time goes on. Giant corporations can fall into traps, too. Remember how 200 MBA's at Ford Motor Company decided every American would want an Edsel in his garage?

But people like Jack are seldom the victim of the educated guess gone wrong. Rather, they are victims of their own rosy outlook, which blinds them to obvious facts. Don't allow eagerness to be your own boss blind you. Emotion can obscure logic. Remove your rose-colored glasses and whip out your magnifying glass. Know beforehand what you're getting into and give the deal the acid test.

WEIGH BENEFITS AGAINST RISKS

Every single business decision you ever make should provide benefits which outweigh the risks. When you picked up this book at the bookstore you spotted the price. Didn't you subconsciously quantify the risk in terms of the price? You next glanced through the book to see what you might learn and how it might, benefit you. Once you perceived that benefit might exceed risk, you decided to buy.

But what if the book had been on sale for half price? The benefit to the reader would be the same, yet the risk in terms of cost would be reduced 50 percent. How many more copies of this book would people then buy? Of course, this is precisely the thought process that propelled publishing into the new-age paperback boom.

Now suppose instead I offer to sell you a perfectly good and healthy business from which you will earn $50,000 year after year. Suppose further you need no investment or down payment, and will incur no personal liability on notes or other obligations. Moreover, you will seldom have to vist the business for it to nicely hum along making money for you. Interested? Of course. You see an attractive $50,000 a year benefit with no corresponding risk. How can you lose?

The answer is easy. You couldn't lose. Unfortunately, such deals don't exist in the real world. If you ever encounter an all benefit/no risk deal, stick it under your microscope. Chances are you'll spot a costly booby trap. The phrase, "There's no such thing as a free lunch," is alive and well even in the world of no cash down deals. Everything has its price.

Since we play in the real world your deal will offer both benefits and risks. Determine that the potential benefits exceed the risks by a comfortable margin before you proceed.

You cannot always define the "benefits" you will receive. If you make $20,000 a year at your present job but find a prospective business will give you $30,000 for the same work, you would define your "benefit" as $10,000 a year. Suppose instead you build the business and in ten years sell with a $100,000 profit. Now you have reaped a $200,000 benefit. Still, regardless of the financial rewards, not everything in life can be conveniently measured in dollars and cents, even in business.

That financial rewards are not everything can be learned best from a young chap with a constant smile and easygoing manner. For several years Paul worked as a copywriter for a high-powered Madison Avenue advertising agency and earned $50,000 with prospects for far greater financial rewards. I helped Paul purchase an art gallery on Cape Cod, though I could not understand why he'd abandon his $50,000 position for a small business that barely would generate a $20,000 income.

Two years later I had my answer. Paul was exceptionally happy as his own boss, and since he loved art he turned his avocation into a full time vocation. Although Paul knew he'd earn much less in his art shop, the satisfaction and reduced stress of doing what he most enjoyed were all the "benefits" he needed. Paul's story is hardly unique. In his small village you'll find other shopkeepers, artisans, teachers and writers who have chosen an alternative lifestyle. Money represents only a small part of what these content people consider important.

Perhaps you're the opposite of Paul. The challenge of growing a business spurs you on, not for the sake of money alone, but because the hustle and bustle of succeeding makes you happy. For such people money eventually becomes the yardstick by which to measure success, but success in terms of accomplishment remains the real goal.

So add up the benefits. What can your business realistically offer you both in monetary and nonmonetary terms? Underscore the word "realistically." Be conservative when evaluating financial rewards. Don't foolishly believe a business that historically earned its owner $30,000 a year will earn you $90,000 unless you have a track record to support that belief.

What about "risk"? Risks also take many forms. You must carefully evaluate the cash investment; debts and obligations that may create personal liability; and lost time and effort, including lost opportunity elsewhere.

Cash Investment. If you adhere to the no cash down methods described in this book you can, of course, ignore this factor, because you will hopefully take over your business with no cash down.

Personal Debts and Obligations. Hope for the best but prepare for the worst. What if the business fails? Eighty percent do fail within the first five years. What personal liabilities will you face should business assets not satisfy obligations? Quite often you can accurately quantify this risk.

If you find a no cash down deal for $50,000 and the seller holds your personal note for the $50,000, your potential loss on the obligation is, of course, $50,000. If the seller holds a mortgage on the assets of the business and could realize $20,000 upon the liquidation of the business, you still face a $30,000 liability. For risk to be acceptable you must have confidence the business assets can cover the obligations on which you are personally indebted. Now come the crucial questions. Can the risk be reduced? Can you readily absorb the loss? What are the chances of failure? Remember, startups are considerably riskier than taking over existing businesses. In a typical no cash down deal, personal liability is the only financial risk, but it can be a considerable one.

Lost Time and Effort. If you're presently idle, time and effort pose no risk. If you sacrifice a $40,000 a year position hoping to earn $50,000 from your business, and wind up earning only $30,000 a year, then you have "lost" $10,000 a year. As obvious as that appears, many people have trouble understanding it. Ask Carl, for example, who operated a toy store for over three years. All Carl could afford to pay himself was $300 a week, although as a skilled programmer any employer gladly would have paid him $600 a week. Since his business showed a meager profit, Carl was satisfied. Yet in reality, Carl subsidized his business by $15,000 a year by drawing an inadequate salary. Surprisingly, Carl could not understand that he unwittingly invested $45,000 in his toy store over three years with slim chance he would ever recover it. Time and effort can spell high risk, for time is money. Can the business pay you adequately? Anything less than an appropriate salary is a hidden investment added to the risk side of the equation.

Analyze your benefit/risk ratio on a prospective deal. Be conservative when assessing what you may gain and pessimistic about potential loss. Weigh one against the other. Are the odds in your favor?

THREE DEALS YOU DON'T WANT AT ANY PRICE

In my travels I've observed thousands of business deals, and hundreds of no cash down acquisitions, From three decades of experience I've learned to avoid certain types of deals because they produce nothing but headaches.

The High Risk/Low Benefit Deal. As I already warned you, you can't afford to gamble on deals that expose you to risks greater than the potential benefit.

The No Profit Business. Whatever your business, it must eventually show a profit. If it can't, walk away. Even if no risk exists, avoid the temptation to buy, for if you cannot develop a credible plan for producing profits, your business will monopolize your time and energy and sidetrack you from deals that can produce profits. Don't forget that profit is what the business game is all about.

The Negative Cash Flow Business. Thousands of businesses do or can generate a profit and yet have money going out faster than it comes in. They thus face inevitable insolvency despite profits. Ask a bankruptcy attorney how many businesses earn profits and still go bankrupt because of insufficient cash flow. Cash flow analysis therefore becomes all-important. A business with a $25,000 annual profit may not be able to pay $45,000 a year on loans. Loan payments are not reflected in the profit and loss statement, but the business must pay $20,000 a year more than it earns. After a period of time that $20,000 cash drain takes its toll. You may drain inventory or build up unpaid bills, but eventually it becomes a business killer. This problem can be particularly severe with no cash down deals. A seller without large notes to pay may survive on modest profits. But you will likely have note payments. Be

certain the cash will be there when needed. If you cannot comfortably handle the financing with a positive cash flow, either
restructure the debt or leave the deal behind. Getting into business
with no cash down is only the first objective. The more important
objective is to stay in business so you can make money.

HOW TO QUICKLY SCREEN A BUSINESS

Since you will be constantly exposed to a large number of businesses for sale, quickly screen each prospect to determine whether
further pursuit and investigation is justified. Proper procedures
help to determine quickly whether prospects qualify for more
"in-depth" evaluation, allow you to avoid premature rejection of
businesses that could be suitable acquisitions, and prevent needless effort on opportunities that are not suitable.

A business should qualify for further investigation if three initial
conditions are met:

1. The business is located in an acceptable geographic area.

2. The business can produce satisfactory profits.

3. An acceptable lease is available.

The business should not be rejected hastily because existing sales
or profits are low. You may, for example, consider $500,000 sales
acceptable. Should this eliminate the business now grossing only
$300,000, but with the hidden potential to gross that $500,000? Can
this lower volume business generate the same profits as a higher
volume business? The answers to these essential questions require
more than a superficial glance at the business.

Equally important, an unfavorable asking price, down payment or
even financing should not discourage you from pursuing the business if the business otherwise qualifies, as these terms are best left

for negotiation. You never know the deal you can strike until you try, and the time to try is *after* you know you want the business.

THE BUSINESS ANALYSIS—AN OVERVIEW

The importance of a thorough analysis of the seller's business cannot be overemphasized. A carefully planned and comprehensive business investigation will help you to:

Verify the seller's representations about the business;

Determine the true value of the business;

Detect serious problems and pitfalls;

Forecast the true potential and future of the business;

Negotiate, by pinpointing problems the seller may have with the business;

Finance the acquisition through analysis of the legal and financial structure;

Protect yourself by uncovering items requiring special attention in the purchase agreement; and

Plan the future business by highlighting areas of operational weakness and strength.

Investigation procedures vary greatly depending on whether the business is a manufacturing, retail or service operation. Other factors also influence the scope of investigation: the age and reputation of the company, reason for sale or acquisition, required investment and your prior familiarity with the business.

Obtain Assistance. Unless you have solid experience in the type business you are about to buy, you definitely need outside help. Never try to evaluate a type business you know little about as there are too many pitfalls you may overlook. Hire a consultant who does know this type business. For best results, look for an owner or manager of a successful non-competitive business operating within your industry.

Coordinate With Your Advisors. Map out an investigative strategy with your accountant and attorney. Your accountant can pinpoint operational areas to focus on based on his preliminary financial evaluation while your attorney may require additional legal information to protect you on the contract.

Protect Confidentiality. Sellers are rightfully concerned about confidentiality and this must be respected. Ask in advance whether you may approach sources such as suppliers, customers and employees. Bear in mind, the seller may hesitate to allow you access to trade secrets or other proprietary information unless you sign a non-disclosure agreement.

Check Outside Sources. Evaluating a company can seldom be accomplished only through analysis of the seller's records, plant inspection or other disclosures by the seller. While this information is important, look to outside sources to confirm facts. If allowed, talk to suppliers, customers and employees. Ask about the reputation of the company within the trade. Check with credit reporting bureaus. No information source is too unimportant to be overlooked.

Work the Business. The one best way to evaluate a business is to work it. Checking books and records alone won't show you the real inner strengths and weaknesses of the business. However, by working within the business you'll see first-hand how loyal customers really are, what the employee morale is like, how efficient the operation is and the countless other tricks, gambits and secrets that are part and parcel of every business. A seller may readily agree to your request to work within the business once convinced you are a serious buyer, particularly if there is basic agreement on the terms of sale and you agree to keep confidential the true reason for your "employment."

Demand Complete Disclosure. A final word of caution—never buy a business unless the seller is willing to disclose fully information fairly needed to evaluate the business. Should the seller refuse full disclosure, try to find ways to solve any concerns he may have, but never buy unless you have had access to all the information you and your advisors need.

THE BUSINESS ANALYSIS— A MASTER CHECKLIST

How do you check out a business? To seriously investigate the business prepare to sift through a mass of information in twelve key areas, probing the following questions to the extent applicable.

1. *Product Analysis*
   - What is the description of each product line?
   - What is the relative importance of each product line?
   - What is the market share for each product line?
   - What are the growth trends for each product line?
   - What is the anticipated longevity for each product line?
   - Who are the principal competitors for each product line?
   - What is the market share held by each of seller's competitors?
   - Are the product lines complete, or are additional or "tie-in" products needed?
   - Are seller's products licensed or subject to license rights?

- What product planning is in process by the seller?

- How stable is each product line?

2. *Customer Analysis*

  - Who are the major customers?

  - What is the aggregate dollar amount of sales to each major customer?

  - What percentage of sales is allocable to each major customer?

  - How long has the seller sold to each major customer?

  - Are customer dealings subject to contract, and if so, what are the terms of contract?

  - Are customers likely to remain with a new buyer?

  - What percentage of sales is sold to foreign, governmental or military customers?

  - How financially stable is each of the major customers?

  - Is repeat business increasing or decreasing?

  - Is repeat business comparable to industry averages?

  - Is there evidence of any threatened loss of a major customer?

  - What pending or future orders exist or are anticipated?

3. *Sales Analysis*

  - How are seller's products marketed?

  - What percentage of total sales is allocable to each sales or marketing method?

  - Is the external sales organization well organized?

  - Is the internal sales organization well organized and sufficient in size to handle present business? Projected volume?

- Are total sales and marketing costs comparable to industry averages?

- Is the selling organization performing effectively both in terms of cost and in relation to sales?

- Are sales personnel on salary or commission?

- Does the sales compensation program provide sufficient motivation?

- Are territorial allocations proper or are new territorial allocations needed?

- Is the sales staff adequately supported by advertising?

- Are the sales produced by each sales personnel acceptable, and if not, why?

- What changes in sales approach are needed to handle new products or markets?

4. *Advertising Analysis*

- Does the seller have a formal advertising or promotional program?

- Does the advertising program feature institutional or product advertising, or both? Is the advertising mix appropriate?

- How does the seller's advertising costs compare as a percentage of sales to industry averages?

- What is the ratio of advertising costs to sales for each product line?

- Is advertising handled internally or by an outside agency, or both?

- Is the advertising agency under contract, and if so, what are the terms

- How long has the advertising agency represented the company? How effective has the relationship been?

- Are additional advertising expenses required to bring sales to an acceptable level?

- Are extraordinary expenses foreseen or planned to launch new products?

- What changes in advertising approach will be needed by buyer, and at what additional cost?

5. *Management Analysis*

- Does the seller have a formal organizational chart with clear delineation of management function?

- Are the lines of authority and responsibility adequately defined?

- Is the organizational structure appropriate for the size and nature of the business?

- Will the organizational structure require major revision under the buyer's management?

- Are the seller's major administrative departments understaffed or overstaffed?

- Are corporate executives rated on performance?

- Are key management personnel on employment contract and if so, what are the terms?

- What fringe benefits and perquisites are available to executive and management personnel?

- Do compensation and fringe benefit programs compare favorably to industry averages?

- Does the total management compensation bear a favorable relationship to sales?

- Will key management remain with the organization after sale?

- Will any increased compensation be required to retain management personnel after sale?

- What is the morale among the management personnel?

- What is the reputation in the trade of seller's management?

- Is management centralized or decentralized? Does one person run the organization or is decision making reasonably balanced?

- Will additional or replacement management personnel be required? Are they readily available?

- Can management personnel be terminated without considerable difficulty or expense?

- Are key personnel bound by non-compete agreements?

6. *Employee Analysis*

- Is the company unionized?

- Is there a threat of future unionization, or history of prior collective bargaining attempts?

- Is the business or industry vulnerable to unionization attempts?

- Would a unionization attempt be successful?

- What is the nature of the compensation structure?

- Are wages competitive within the industry or market?

- What percentage of employees are highly skilled?

- Can replacement or additional personnel in each job category be readily obtained?

- Can size of employee force be varied to meet production or sales needs?

- Do working conditions compare favorably to industry standards?

- Does seller have an apprenticeship or training program?

- What are seller's hiring policies and other personnel procedures?

- Does employee turnover compare favorably to industry standards?

- What employee changes are contemplated or required upon acquisition?

7. *Research and Development Analysis*

    - What is the nature of research and engineering development?

    - What is the amount of research and engineering time spent on each of seller's major products?

    - What are the short and long term objectives of the seller's research and development program?

    - How much does the seller spend on research and development? Do the costs compare favorably to product revenues and industry standards?

    - What projects are presently being handled by the seller's R & D department? What projects appear promising?

    - How many persons are employed in R & D? How are they allocated between supervisory, technical and non- technical personnel?

    - How productive has R & D been in developing successful new products?

    - What is the reputation within the industry for development of innovative new products?

8. *Market and Competitive Analysis*

    - What are the demographics of the seller's market?

    - Is the market growing? Stable? Declining?

    - Is the market existing or emerging?

    - What share of the market has been captured by the seller? Is market share growing or declining?

- What internal factors will influence future market share?
- What external factors will influence future market share?
- Who are the major competitors?
- What strengths and weaknesses does the company have against competitors?
- What future competitive changes are foreseeable?
- Are there any pending or threatening legal enactments to influence product demand or competitive advantage?
- What contemplated or required changes are required to maintain market share and competitive position?
- What are the short term and long term growth prospects for the company?
- What expenditures are required to achieve possible growth? Required growth?

9. *Facility Analysis*

- Is the location stable?
- Is the location advantageous to reach the market?
- Does the plant have proper space for present needs?
- Can the plant be expanded to accommodate future growth?
- What immediate renovations or improvements are required to improve efficiency?
- Is the plant adequately served by public utilities, transportation and shipping?

10. *Lease Analysis*

- Are facilities leased or owned? If owned, is the property included in sale?

- Is there a possibility of a sale and leaseback if premises are to be acquired?

- If property is leased, will the available lease have a sufficient term to justify investment?

- If lease term is unacceptable, can the business be readily relocated at reasonable cost?

- Will the proposed lease have a reasonable rent on a square footage basis and as a percentage of sales?

11. *Material and Equipment Analysis*

- Is there a list of equipment, machinery, furniture and fixtures?

- Is equipment owned or leased, and if leased, what are lease terms?

- Is equipment in good working order?

- Is equipment suitable to manufacture different or other nonrelated products?

- Is new equipment required, and if so, what is the anticipated additional cost?

- What is appraisal value of equipment and other capital assets included in sale?

12. *Inventory and Purchasing Analysis*

- Is there a list of present and past supplies to the company?

- Are inventories adequate, overstocked or depleted?

- What additional inventories are required to bring business to full potential?

- What percentage of inventory is shopworn, obsolete or otherwise unsalable?

- Is inventory of the appropriate mix? Does the company buy on advantageous terms?

- Does the company have open credit or restricted credit?

- Is the company obligated on purchasing requirements or vendor contracts?

- How long have vendors done business with the company?

- Are vendor relations considered satisfactory?

- Are alternative sources of supply available on equally advantageous terms?

- Does the company rely on any one supplier, and if so, can the continuity of supply be assured?

- Are suppliers related to the selling corporation?

- Do supplier prices compare favorably with prices paid by selling corporation's competitors?

- Are purchasing procedures well organized and functioning properly?

THE BUSINESS ANALYSIS—EVALUATING THE FRANCHISED BUSINESS

The analysis of a franchised business can usually be made with with greater precision than of an independent business, as accounting records are usually more detailed to comply with the franchise requirements. Nevertheless, you must investigate the franchisor of an existing business with the same thoroughness as any other operation, as there is no lack of shaky franchise companies. That's precisely why so many franchised units are re-sold, often on most attractive terms. The present franchisee, disenchanted with the franchisor or sensing inevitable failure of the franchise system often attempts to pass the problem on to an unwary buyer. Unless the franchise is very well established, approach the acquisition of a franchised business with caution because better franchises are usually repurchased by the franchisor or quickly grabbed by other franchisees within the system. How can you check out a "franchise"?

Review the Disclosure Statement

Begin with a review of the disclosure statement required by the Federal Trade Commission to be issued to all prospective franchisees (including transferees of existing franchises). (Many states have even stricter disclosure requirements.) This disclosure statement contains twenty points on the background and performance of the franchise system, but seven are particularly important:

1. Identification and experience of each of the franchisor's officers, directors and key management personnel.

2. A description of any lawsuits involving the franchisor.

3. Prior bankruptcies of the franchisor, or its officers or directors.

4. Information on the number of existing franchisees, projected franchisees and terminated franchisees, including the number repurchased or not renewed.

5. A projection of franchisee profits and the number of franchisees achieving those profits.

6. A list of names and addresses of existing franchisees.

7. The franchisor's financial statements.

Although disclosure of these and other items are mandatory, no governmental agency verifies accuracy. Therefore, you should independently investigate these key items. The nature of existing lawsuits is an important area to probe. While lawsuits against even the best franchisors are to be expected, determine whether litigation is excessive or based on a recurring complaint.

Closely study the growth of the franchise, paying particular attention to the number of franchises renewed or terminated. Does the attrition rate exceed industry averages for this type franchise? Many franchisors experience rapid growth initially only to fail within several years.

Next, study the franchisor's financial statements. Where financials appear reasonably strong, determine whether income comes primarily from the sale of new franchises or from royalty income. Solid franchise systems survive on royalties.

Check Outside Sources

No investigative technique is more important than inquiry to other franchisees, who can objectively report the strengths and weakness of the franchise system. Seek answers to these questions:

When and why did you buy the franchise?

Why did you select this franchise over others?

How effective was the training program?

Did the franchisor fulfill its obligations in setting up the franchise?

What do you buy from the franchisor? Are deliveries on time? Quality acceptable? Prices competitive?

How adequate is the supervision?

Do sales and profits compare favorably to projections? Are sales and profits increasing?

Has the franchisor honored the franchise agreement?

What specific problems do you have with the franchisor? Are they being resolved?

Are you generally satisfied with the franchise?

Poll a number of franchisees selected at random to obtain a fair
assessment. Follow the advice of the International Franchise Association and make inquiry to suppliers and franchisees who have
terminated affiliation as well as The Better Business Bureau and
regional office of The Federal Trade Commission.

Analyze the Franchise Agreement

If the franchise appears worthwhile from a business viewpoint,
review the franchise agreement:

Franchise Fees

> What are the fees to effectuate transfer?
>
> Is there a new franchise fee upon renewal?
>
> What are the on-going royalties?
>
> How are royalties paid?

Controls

> Does the franchise allow for absentee ownership?
>
> Are there salary limitations?
>
> Who controls hours of operation?
>
> Who controls product selection?
>
> Are sources of supply limited or controlled?
>
> Is pricing policy controlled?
>
> Is there an operations manual that must be followed?

Support

> Will training be provided the buyer?
>
> What are the details of training? Location? Cost?

Will the buyer have start-up or takeover assistance?

What continuing supervision is provided?

Are legal or accounting services provided? Are they mandatory?

Are there additional charges for these services?

Is inventory control provided?

Advertising and Promotion

What are the local/national advertising plans?

Must the franchisee participate in all promotional programs?

Can the buyer undertake its own advertising? Is prior approval required?

Is there a separate advertising charge?

Non-Competition

Is the territory exclusive?

If non-exclusive, are competitive franchises planned within the geographic area?

Can the franchisor own and operate its own units?

Transfer

Can the franchise be sold, mortgaged or transferred?

What are the transfer provisions upon death?

What are the restrictions on transfer?

Does the franchisor have a repurchase option? A right of first refusal?

Duration and Termination

What is the franchise period?

Is the franchise renewable? On what terms?

What constitutes a default or breach? Is there a "cure" provision?

Financing

Are there restrictions on the buyer's ability to finance the franchised acquisition?

Does the franchisor offer financing assistance?

Guarantees

Are the franchisees' obligations under the franchise agreement personally guaranteed?

What are the limitations and terms of the personal guarantee?

INTERPRETING THE RESULTS

The business investigation will invariably result in mixed findings. Every company features a blend of strengths and weaknesses and there's no such thing as a "perfect" opportunity.

Summarize your findings of the business under review. Weigh the relative advantages and disadvantages against each other and against comparable businesses for sale. Be objective! Is this the right business for you? Does the business pose any insurmountable obstacles? Can it provide you the income or growth potential you seek?

There is no need to settle for a poor opportunity because you plan creative financing. You can find the best and buy the best even with a pauper's pocketbook.

KEY POINTS TO REMEMBER

1. Any business may have its booby traps. Your job is to find them.

2. Don't view a business through rose-colored glasses. Be objective and thorough.

3. Weigh potential benefits against risks. This is how the pro's make business decisions.

4. Learn to quickly screen all opportunities and thoroughly investigate the best.

5. Ask the important questions before you decide to buy.

5

What Is the Business Worth?

While many questions accompany the purchase of a business, few are as important as accurately determining what the business is worth. Both you and the seller share the same problem—you each need to value the business. What are the various methods for evaluating the business and how do they differ? When should each method be used? Is the business being sold or acquired at too high or too low a price?

Small business valuations are exceptionally difficult. Valuation is not a precise science, as no one valuation formula can deal with the many diverse factors that must be considered. Valuation is ultimately a blend of many subjective and objective considerations which, if a sale is to occur, must be shaped into a perceived value closely shared by buyer and seller.

THREE VALUATION OBSTACLES TO OVERCOME

Unlike the publicly traded company whose value is easily determined by the reported trading value of its stock, the small privately-owned business is difficult to appraise for three important reasons.

Lack of Accurate Records. Small businesses notoriously suffer from lack of records essential to portray the true financial performance of the enterprise. In fact, the seller may be the only person able to judge the value of the business as an income producer and will likely value the business on the earnings, including the many hidden benefits and perks he realizes. However, if the seller is unable to prove a profit history the business deserves a lower valuation, consistent with the profitability shown on the books.

The Emotional Element. Small businesses are an extension of their owners, and a seller frequently has developed an emotional as well as a financial relationship with a business. This psychological bond is particularly true when the seller owned the business for many years and relied upon it for his primary livelihood. Since the seller may have started the business and nurtured it to maturity, it obviously is difficult for her to objectively measure its true value in strict economic terms. This perhaps explains why so many small businesses are grossly overpriced and remain unsold even when the seller offers the most lenient terms. The subjectivity of the human factor does not, of course, alter the actual value of the business; and when a seller refuses to sell at a reasonable price because of a faulty mindset, it presents an obstacle to reaching agreement on price.

Projecting the Future. The true value of a business is largely based on how much the business will earn under the buyer's management. But accurate forecasting is difficult. Small businesses as income producers are exceptionally unstable. The business is often built on the talents of one or two owners and the success of the business is therefore the result of its owner's personality, effort and management skills. A successful pattern of business operation may or may not be duplicated by you. You must look realistically at what you can achieve with the business. The small business field is loaded with examples of companies that quickly doubled or tripled sales and earnings under new management. Others have seen their business fortunes dramatically shrink. To the extent you are buying an economic future, the financial forecast must translate into an accurate portrayal of that future.

FIVE COMMON VALUATION TECHNIQUES

Because small businesses can be so difficult to value, frequently formulas are used that are at best "rule of thumb" techniques. These conventional yardsticks are easy to use but fall short as accurate valuation methods as they do not consider adequately future earning power.

The Sales Multiplier Approach

Every industry has a rough formula that somehow translates sales into an approximate valuation. Supermarkets, for example, are said to be worth the cost of inventory plus one month's sales. Luncheonettes and small restaurants are popularly priced at 3-4 month's sales. According to industry reports drug stores should sell for approximately 100 day's sales. Obviously, no sales multiplier method alone can logically place a value on the business because it disregards profits.

The sales multiplier can make sense when the profit of a business is always proportionate to its sales, but, of course, that is seldom the case. Examine a number of small businesses within a particular industry and you will see little correlation between size and profits. Some businesses inevitably show substantial sales and more substantial losses, while some small volume enterprises produce enormous profits.

Sales are an important factor when valuing the business, but only when you can project your expenses falling into line to produce those proportionate profits. Absent that projection, the sales multiplier remains a faulty valuation technique to be avoided.

The Comparison Approach

To many buyers, valuations are nothing more than a crude attempt to compare the price asked for target business against prices asked for comparable businesses. This is not necessarily a poor approach since the value of any item is based on prices for comparable items. And because market conditions certainly do influence value, both buyer and seller should have a clear idea of prices for businesses.

The major difficulty with the "comparison approach" is that unlike other commodities, few businesses can be accurately compared. As an economic entity there are far too many variables to consider. Since earnings depend on the individual characteristics of the business—volume, expenses, loan terms, competition and future potential—you will find within your given industry few businesses with sufficient economic similarity to allow credible comparisons.

When comparisons are made, your comparison is likely to focus primarily on sales, and thus the approach will be similar to the sales multiplier method. This may not be true with buyers granted the opportunity to adequately investigate the financial affairs of similar ventures, but it will be so with sellers confined to a competitor's sales and selling price.

Franchised businesses are one notable exception. Franchising is based on a high degree of operational uniformity and therefore franchised businesses with equivalent sales should show near equivalent profits because profit margins, expenses and other operating data closely conform to chain standards.

The "Asking Price" Approach

Another common but erroneous valuation technique is based on the strange belief that value is related to or can be determined by the seller's "asking price." It may from the seller's viewpoint, but seldom from yours.

Unwary buyers usually do rely on asking price as a threshold from which to bargain. These buyers wrongly believe that if you can reduce the asking price by 15-25% you have gained "value." It is dangerous to assume that the seller's asking price has any rational relationship to value. A seller is the least qualified individual to determine "value." This helps explain the reality that 90% of all small businesses are overpriced. After the business sits unsold for a year of two, a seller gradually may lower price until it finally enters the reality zone and becomes closer to true value.

Rather than start at the top with the seller's asking price, it is preferable to assume the business has no value, and then weigh every dollar you agree to spend against the profit potential of the business.

The Asset Valuation Approach

The most common method for valuing the small business is to separately value each asset being sold. This approach is particularly useful for retail businesses.

A seller, for example, may believe his business is worth $100,000 based on $50,000 for inventory at wholesale costs, $25,000 for fixtures and equipment at replacement or fair market values and $25,000 for good will. Any other assets to be sold would also be valued and added to the price.

Valuing a business by the sum of its assets also has serious limitations. The tangible assets can be accurately appraised. Inventory can be precisely tabulated at cost and replacement value for fixtures and equipment can be readily obtained by professional appraisal. The difficulty, however, is computing a value for "good will," that intangible asset which is an important part of most small, profitable businesses.

The value of good will frequently is equal to or even greater than all the tangible assets combined. The validity of the overall valuation then necessarily depends on an accurate appraisal of good will. Yet, since good will represents nothing more than the future profitability of the business, you still are forced to develop a profit orientation when adopting an asset valuation approach.

The business selling for the value of its tangible assets alone does not always represent an easier situation. A seller may bargain, for instance, to sell a retail business for the combined value of inventory and fixtures alone. If those assets cannot produce future profits, however, they are worth nothing more than their liquidation values.

Book Value Approach

"Book value" is an accounting term which reflects the owner's equity in the business as reflected in the financial statements. If total liabilities are deducted from the depreciated tangible assets (excluding good will), the difference is the book value of the business. Larger companies are frequently sold by the transfer of corporate shares at a value based on book value.

There are, however, two problems with using "book value" to value a smaller business. Again, this valuation method does not consider the profitability or earnings potential of the business. Further, the fixed assets (real estate, equipment, etc.) normally are shown at depreciated value rather than fair market value. Because there can be a considerable difference between the two values, the stated book valuation can be easily distorted and not reflective of the worth of the business when measured against more rational economic yardsticks.

MEASURE THE EARNING POWER

How then can you best value a business? Professional appraisers recognize that earning power is the most logical and best value indicator. Under this technique, commonly called the "capitalized earnings valuation," we primarily look at the return on investment the business will produce. Three basic steps are necessary.

Calculate Present Profits

Reconstruct the seller's income statement to determine the accurate current pre-tax operating profit. One key item to adjust for is the owner's salary, which often is inflated to minimize taxes. Similarly, other owner perks may be buried in other expense categories and should be evaluated. Depreciation should next be adjusted to reflect the actual decrease in asset value each year, which may be considerably different than the depreciated amount. You see the idea. Review each line item until *present* earnings have been accurately recast.

I underscore *present* earnings because many buyers mistakenly use projected profits under their management as the basis for determining value. This approach is wrong because "value" is what the business is *currently* worth, not what it will be worth after *you* invest time and money building the business. Potential can and should influence value but it should never control value. Be willing to pay the seller only for the profits *he* delivers.

Set an Acceptable Return on Investment

After present profits have been defined with the greatest possible accuracy, the task is to translate those earnings into a reasonable value. This forces you to consider the minimum return on investment acceptable to you. For example, if the business shows current profits of $20,000 and you require a 25% return on investment, the business justifies a price of $80,000.

This is a central question—what should you demand as a satisfactory return on investment from a small business? Since small businesses generally are neither a secure nor "liquid" investment, you likely would want a return somewhere between 25 to 40 percent. But clearly understand your investment objectives. If you are planning to buy with the objective of rapidly building the business for quick resale at a sizeable profit, you will insist upon a far higher return and expect to earn that return on the profits from the sale rather than through operational profits.

Establish a "Valuation" Range

The "capitalized earnings" approach provides a broad valuation range. Obviously, asset values must still be considered to some extent. A service business with virtually no assets and a retail store with $100,000 in tangible assets may each generate a $20,000 profit, yet you would logically expect to pay more for the retail store because it has assets of value, whereas the service business has none.

Leverage is another consideration, and one that points out the problem in defining the "investment" against which profits should be measured. With some logic, many acquisition consultants argue that you should consider only your down payment as the true investment and then measure profits (after the financing costs) against that investment. Others suggest the total price is the best yardstick of "investment," as it is what remains invested after the debt financing is paid. When you are buying a business with no cash down, just think how few dollars profit is necessary to give you an excellent return on your investment.

NINE FACTORS THAT INFLUENCE VALUE

In strict financial terms, return on investment *controls* the value of a business, but many other factors *influence* what you will end up paying for it. So far we have been speaking of "value" as the appraisal of what the business is worth. Value, of course, is not synonymous with price, as the latter simply reflects what the seller wants for the business or is willing to sell it for. Therefore, value remains a function of appraised worth using some economic model or rationale while price remains a function of negotiation. The only relationship between value and price is that value often becomes the reference point or threshhold from which price is negotiated.

Nevertheless, value and hence the price of a business primarily are affected by the following nine important factors.

Supply and Demand

This remains the first law of economics.The value of a business is greatly influenced by the number of buyers available compared to the number of businesses for sale. This shift between a "buyer's market" and "seller's market" may alter price by 40 percent or more. For instance, rapid price increases can be seen in periods of high unemployment when a large number of unemployed turn to small business ownership. "Values" are never created in a vacuum, but are always a function of competitive pressures.

Nature of the Business

Many industries are in decline, forcing a general decline in the number of interested buyers and hence in the obtainable price for any business within the industry. Business brokers report that fading industries such as independent clothing and hardware and drug stores continue to sell at very low prices relative to earnings, and in contrast independent convenience food stores have bounced back in their cycle and now sell at premium prices. Businesses that do not require specialized training and offer easy entry have historically sold for more than those with a more limited market. Similarly, "glamor" or prestige businesses attract many more buyers than do unglamorous enterprises which may sell at bargain prices in comparison.

Risk

Many buyers rightfully believe lack of risk or "downside" potential of the deal justifies a higher price. It's more than a reasonable viewpoint. When you have little to lose either in down payment or liability on financing, you can afford a more generous price to compensate for lack of risk. Consider, for example, the buyer who acquires the shares of a corporation for $15,000 with the balance of a $150,000 price represented by existing debts of $135,000 for which the buyer has no personal responsibility. This same buyer will resist the $150,000 price less than a buyer who must put the entire $150,000 at risk through down payment and/or personally guaranteed obligations. Risk and price are very much a function of each other.

Down Payment

Leverage has been mentioned earlier for purposes of calculating return on investment. However, as we stated earlier, down payment and the opportunity for a leveraged buyout often have the most dramatic influences on price. Buyers focus on down payment as much or more then they do price. Price resistance naturally goes down as down payment requirements decrease. As I say in the final chapter, many sellers have little difficulty selling their business at a premium price—often more than the original asking price—once creative financing is offered to cut the down payment. A reduced down payment, of course, expands the potential buyer market and offers lower risk, which justify a higher price than the same business available on conventional terms. Conversely, a seller demanding all cash may be forced to accept 30 to 40 percent less than if the business were sold with little cash requirement, or 20 to 25 percent less than if it were sold with an average down payment.

Financing Terms

Advantageous financing terms can also greatly influence price. Astute buyers always consider price in relation to financing costs, because the two together determine the actual total cost of the business.

High interest rates depress business values in the same way they reduce the prices for real estate, automobiles and other high-cost consumer items. Consider the economics of 15 percent interest on a 10 year, $100,000 loan versus the same loan at 10 percent. The interest varies by about $25,000, allowing a reciprocally higher price if the seller provides financing below market rates. Some buyers shrewdly take the position that if financing carries interest above the prime rate, the excess should be deducted from valuation. If the seller, however, offers financing at lower than bank rates, then interest saved should be added to valuation. It's a point worth remembering!

Interest is one important financing factor that effects value, but cash flow can be equally important. Long term payments can insure the surplus cash flow needed for expansion or modernization. A short pay-back period, in turn, can put an artificially low lid on the price as most buyers limit the price to what the business can comfortably afford to pay from cash flow, as they expect the loan to be self-liquidating.

Potential

Valuation must necessarily depend on the present profitability of the business, but price may still be influenced by the future potential of the firm. Yet, there is considerable difference between a seller who sells his enterprise with profits in place rather than one asking the buyer to achieve his own profits while demanding the same price.

Nevertheless, many sellers do try to sell marginal or losing ventures on the basis of the profit potential in the hands of the right buyer. While the buyer is essentially buying potential, the obvious question is why pay the seller for what the buyer will himself produce? The clear answer is that he shouldn't. At most, the seller of the marginal business may receive a nominal payment equal to one year's anticipated profit to reflect the potential factor, but nothing more is justified.

An opposite situation is when the business is for sale when it is at its peak earnings potential with no realistic opportunity to improve upon current performance. At best, the buyer can hope only to stabilize sales and profits at their present level. While the seller has the right to demand a price reflecting current income, the buyer should adapt a more conservative valuation because the business does lack potential for significant improvement.

Most experienced buyers agree that the best acquisition candidate is one that is operating at a small fraction of its true potential, can be acquired at a price consistent with its low present earnings, but can be rapidly energized into a money maker. These buyers typically pay something more than what the business seems to be worth based on present earnings and valuation standards; yet these same acquisitions often ultimately prove to be a bargain once their profit potential is reached.

Motivation

How anxious is the seller to sell? How anxious is the buyer to buy? Personal pressures ranging from illness and death to unemployment can have a dramatic effect on the price of a business. As personal factors influence each party's bargaining position, the price may vary by 50 percent from appraised value.

Personal Goals

As a seller may develop an emotional attachment to his or her business, a buyer may also expect the business to satisfy certain personal objectives. Many buyers are willing to pay a premium for the "right" business which offers enjoyment and self-satisfaction. These factors are far more important benefits of business ownership to many buyers than monetary rewards.

Cash Flow

The projected cash flow can be a decisive factor in the valuation of a business. Often companies are acquired at a premium because they generate substantial cash flow compared to businesses with equivalent "paper" profits or profits required to be reinvested in the company. The importance of cash flow is particularly important when the acquiring business wants the acquisition to help compensate for its own poor cash flow.

HOW TO VALUE SPECIAL BUSINESS SITUATIONS

In your search for a no cash down deal you will come across many different types of opportunities. As expected, the approaches to valuation can be as varied as the type of transactions. No one valuation method is suitable for every type acquisition, and special situations require their own unique approach. Discussed below are some special situations that you may encounter.

Valuing the Insolvent Company

As discussed in Chapter 8, more than a few insolvent businesses are acquired under bankruptcy, receivership or foreclosure proceedings. Rehabilitated and profitably operated, they indeed can make ideal leveraged buyout candidates.

Although the turnaround potential is the primary motivation for the acquisition, future profitability should not be the main criteria for determining value. Instead, approach valuation from the seller's perspective, which is to view a sale as an alternative to liquidating the assets at auction. Should other interested buyers bid for the business, the competition may influence the price upwards; however, each prospective buyer will use liquidation values as the basis for negotiating and will increase price only to the extent necessary to be the successful bidder.

Frequently, a buyer will cross paths with an insolvent business not yet under formal insolvency proceedings. In this situation the seller may arbitrarily set the price to match the proceeds needed to liquidate debt. A price designed only to bail-out creditors will, of course, bear no logical relationship to the actual value of the business. The proper approach in this situation is to encourage the seller to enter into formal insolvency proceedings, with the buyer acquiring the business at its liquidation value. As an incentive to the seller, the buyer may offer the seller some personal compensation in the form of a covenant-not-to-compete, a contingent pay-out as a percentage of future profits, or perhaps only the opportunity for employment.

Valuing the Service Business

Service businesses rely primarily on existing sales, accounts and customer lists as the primary assets on which to base their prices. The difficulty in establishing a value on a business such as a professional practice, a brokerage firm or a service trade, is that sales and good will are closely tied to the existing personal relationship between the seller and the customers. Once the business or practice is sold, many customers discontinue patronage.

Therefore, the safe approach when valuing the service business is to fix a price matched to a set percentage of future sales generated from the acquired customers. Tangible assets would, of course, be valued separately.

The percentage of sales on which such a price is based will depend on prevailing industry custom, generally between 15–35 percent of sales and the pay-out period will ordinarily extend from three to five years. Continued patronage beyond that time period is due primarily to the good will created by the buyer. There are, of course, instances where the buyer will acquire the account and customer lists for a set price. However, even in these situations, the price is ultimately determined by anticipated future sales measured over a reasonable time span.

Should the seller agree to a contingent pay-out, the seller's concern will, of course, be the buyer's ability to retain good will and build sales upon which the contingent price is based. Additional concerns include accounting safeguards to properly define earnings and contract terms to insure payment of the agreed price.

Valuing the Merged Business

When the acquired business is to be dismantled and functionally merged into the buyer's existing business, the buyer cannot reasonable base "value" on the profitability of the business as a separate or intact organization. The sound approach is for the buyer to translate the economic benefit of the merger profiled against his own income statement.

This exercise, in turn, requires a careful analysis of each of the operational changes resulting from the merger and an equally carefully reconstruction of the buyer's profit and loss statement so that the change in profits after the merger can be accurately pinpointed and used as a basis for setting price.

The functional merger may produce a synergy on profits where the combined profits will be greater than the profits of the two separate organizations. Less frequently, greater profits may be achieved by operating the two firms separately.

From the buyer's viewpoint, the functional or operational merger may justify a higher value than could be justified operating the acquired company as an independent unit; however, this subtle benefit to the buyer rarely enters into the negotiations.

Valuing the Business with Real Estate

Motels, hotels, nursing homes and similar businesses which feature real estate as their primary asset must still be considered and valued as business operations rather than passive real estate investments.

Frequently, a seller will offer commercial property together with the business for one package price. In this situation you must appraise the real estate and business separately. The fair rental value of the premises occupied by the business is used to determine the appraised value of the real estate. A licensed real estate appraiser can accurately set a value. The business can then be separately valued using procedures recommended in this chapter.

THE ROLE OF PROFESSIONAL APPRAISERS

Considering the complexity of business appraisal, buyers are increasingly turning to professional appraisers to help them establish a proper value for a business. A professional appraiser can bring to the valuation process not only well-honed appraisal skills but a degree of objectivity not always matched by the buyer. Moreover, the appraiser can often detect less visible but serious business problems a buyer easily may overlook.

Because business appraisal is a relatively new profession, there are still too few qualified appraisers to satisfy the demand for their services. It is important to find an appraiser with professional qualifications rather than settle for a business broker or consultant who may conduct appraisals but is without proven qualification.

The easiest way to find a qualified appraiser is to contact the Institute of Business Appraisers at Boynton Beach, Florida. The Institute both trains and certifies appraisers and can refer you to an appraiser appropriate for your type acquisition.

An appraisal can cost anywhere from $1,000 to $25,000, depending upon the size and nature of the business. It is an exceptionally wise investment, particularly when buying a larger business, as the appraiser may save many thousands of dollars on the price of the business.

KEY POINTS TO REMEMBER

1. Business valuation is not a precise science but a blend of many factors.

2. Don't base value on size and sales of the business alone, but focus instead on profit potential under your management.

3. Price and value may have little in common. There are many factors that can influence the price you pay for a business.

4. Pay the seller only for the profits *he* has generated, not the profits *you* will generate.

5. Consider a business appraiser for a more accurate valuation. A small investment in their service can pay big dividends.

6

Going Where the Money Is

Willie Sutton, the famous bank robber, when asked why he robbed banks, laughingly replied, "Because that's where the money is." In this chapter you'll see how you too can get money from banks and all those other lenders who have plenty of cash kicking around—and pocket it without a gun.

The "no cash down" approach may eliminate the need for a down payment, but you still have to find outside sources to finance most, if not all, of the purchase price. Perhaps you have figured out how to cover a $30,000 down payment on a $100,000 deal, but where will that other $70,000 come from? Conversely, $70,000 in financing may be in place; but now you have to scrounge around to find part or all of the $30,000 down payment. In either case your objective is to find lenders who will loan you what you need on whatever terms you need. You can achieve it if you understand loanmanship.

Loanmanship, much like robbery, does require its recipient to know where to look. Who has the money? On what terms will they lend? And what's the one best source for your deal? Those are the basics. But to really excel in literally having money thrust upon you takes only a few additional tricks. So let's start with the basics.

DEFINE YOUR FINANCING NEEDS

When determining your financing needs go beyond simply calculating the amount required to buy the business. You also must forecast the capital requirements to properly operate and build the acquired enterprise.

Many buyers mistakenly approach financing as a two step process. They exhaust their capital or borrowing power to fund the acquisition and later attempt to obtain financing to operate or build the business. These buyers are unsuccessful because the collateral has been previously pledged to buy the business and therefore is not available to accommodate additional financing. For this reason, the sound approach is to incorporate working capital requirements with the initial financing needs.

When projecting your total financing requirements, take into consideration capital you will need to:

1. Build inventory to levels required to generate the sales projected under your business forecast;

2. Renovate and modernize the physical plant;

3. Add or replace needed fixtures and equipment;

4. Finance accounts receivable;

5. Provide planned advertising or promotional launch programs; and

6. Maintain adequate working capital.

You will be guided closely by your own operational plans and financial forecasts for the business. It obviously makes little sense for a buyer to acquire the business on the premise of required changes without the matching resources to achieve it. Therefore, check each item that can affect cash flow and hence working capital needs.

For example, the balance sheet existing at the time of takeover must be carefully examined, for often you can redeploy assets or liabilities to release cash, thereby reducing financing needs. Inventory, for example, may be at excessive levels and may be partially liquidated. If you will not be assuming debts, the cash flow projections should reflect the cash equivalency of short term credit available to you. The purchase of the seller's receivables will certainly have significant impact on your financing needs. The purchase of receivables will generate an immediate income stream. Conversely starting by generating your own receivables will seriously dissipate cash flow during the early takeover stage. Also consider fixed assets that can be disposed of for cash. Each of these and many other factors should be considered by you and your accountant, not only for purposes of defining your total capitalization requirements, but also to plan the most favorable post acquisition cash flow and hence the opportunity to reduce needed investment.

WHY SELLER FINANCING BEATS THE BANKS

There is one best source of financing a business deal, and that source is the seller. Seller financing offers you numerous advantages over other financing sources. Therefore, never even consider other alternate sources of funds until the seller gives you his final "no." Consider the reasons for this advice:

Sellers Are Not "Interest-Hungry." As I write this book the prime lending rate charged by commercial banks to their best customers has climbed again to over 11 percent. As a small businessperson you can't qualify for the lower prime rate, but must instead pay anywhere from two to five percent above prime. Try the SBA and you will pay an additional one-half to two percent interest. Even benevolent friends and relatives may want to hit you up for 12 to 15 percent. Why not? They can often earn that amount allowing their money to sit in money market accounts featuring complete liquidity and safety. How then can you in good conscience ask them to lend to you at lower rates and risk losing money in the process?

But sellers are another breed. Their primary objective is to sell a business. They're not lending you money simply to earn interest. For sellers, financing the acquisition is often the only way in which the deal can come together. And here's a surprising fact—sellers frequently finance at rates that can cut your interest payments in half. And that can mean substantial savings to you!

In the majority of leveraged buyout deals most of the financing typically comes from sellers who hold the buyers' notes for the purchase price. Based on my own experience, seller-financed deals outnumber bank-funded deals by perhaps three to one. With sellers you can bargain for interest rates as low as ten percent. The average typical interest rate paid to sellers on my latest deals was, in fact, just under ten percent. Compare that to the rates charged by your friendly banker and you'll see how many dollars you can save.

Why will sellers accept such low rates? Why not? It compares favorably to what their money would earn at the bank. Further, you can raise that persuasive argument that with higher interest they would be earning a profit on their loan. After all, they should be satisfied just to sell the business.

Do a few percentage points on interest seem insignificant? Look at it in dollar terms. Borrow $100,000 from a bank for five years at 16 percent. You'll pay the bank over $40,000 in interest charges. The same loan from the seller at ten percent will cost you about

$25,000. That's a $15,000 savings. What could that $15,000 do to help your business grow? You get the idea. Every point on interest saved can put a pile of money in your pocket. And isn't that the best place for money to be?

Sellers Will Wait Longer for Their Money. Time is your best friend when financing a business. The longer the payback period, the smaller the payments and the easier the strain on your cash flow. This often can mean the difference between success and failure, or perhaps between growth and merely standing still. Banks are conservative. They may grant loans for up to five years, but seldom longer. Forget friends and their relatives. They may agree to a short term loan, but test their reaction when you stretch their loan to ten years.

So sellers win again as your best financing source. If the deal involves substantial money, sellers are customarily prepared to wait from five to ten years. On the average, seller notes extend for seven years, although there are many cases where seller financing extended for 15 to 20 years.

How would you like to buy a business and pay it off over 20 years? I've seen it done more than once. A seller may look upon it as an annuity. But from your perspective, those tiny payments can really make life easy.

Sellers Can Finance a Larger Part of the Price. For no cash down deals you'll need every dollar you can find, particularly if it's coming from someone other than yourself. A bank may finance 50 to 60 percent of the purchase price, while the SBA usually stops at 50 percent. And how much more can friends and relatives really afford to finance?

Sellers can be far more generous. Their money is already tied up in the business. Further, they need not be as cautious. They know what their business if worth. If you should fail they can easily step back in and take over the business again. Since banks and other lenders can only liquidate should you fail, a seller can afford to be more lenient.

Long term seller financing of 70 to 80 percent of the total purchase price should be your objective, but 100 percent is hardly uncommon if the deal has the right ingredients. Later in this chapter you'll see how to put those right ingredients together.

Everybody Wants Collateral. But sellers will often accept less collateral than "hard money" lenders. Banks and the SBA are collateral hungry. They'll gobble up everything you own, including your home, stocks, savings and even your pet German Shepherd if you allow it. If you have it they'll demand it. Banks can tie up $500,000 in solid collateral for a miserly $100,000 loan. But why shouldn't banks play it safe? They're not in business to lose money.

In contrast, sellers seldom have the nerve to demand excessive collateral. They undoubtedly will want a mortgage on the business you're acquiring and you can certainly expect to personally guarantee the note; however, anything beyond that is unreasonable. And if you should find a seller who feels insecure holding his own business as collateral, you have one hard-hitting argument to make—"Mr. Seller, if the business isn't adequate collateral for your $80,000 loan, it's not worth the $100,000 I'm paying for it." The logic is indeed overwhelming.

Sellers Can Be the Most Forgiving Lenders. Sellers can be such kind, forgiving and understanding folks, particularly when business is slow and you miss a payment or two. Now what do you think happens when you skip a few payments with your friendly bank? You guessed it. The loan officer catches heck from his branch manager. The manager in turn has to quickly come up with some answers about your "problem loan" to appease the bank President. Of course, the buck doesn't stop there. The president has some explaining to do to the board of directors and a host of regulatory agencies. Bureaucrats can be a humorless, ruthless and picky bunch. So to avoid this hassle and make their life easier they foreclose, wipe you out and make you just another statistic of a failed business.

A seller answers only to himself. You are more than a mere number to him. For starters, you probably have built a close personal relationship with the seller. Perhaps he even works for you. Besides, why should he impatiently foreclose? Sellers know about business problems and the meaning of cash flow troubles. The seller was probably in the same boat himself from time to time. And, now that he finally sold the business do you think he really wants it back?

HOW TO NEGOTIATE SELLER FINANCING

Here's a typical scenario. You find a terrific business for sale for $100,000. The usual haggling goes on, and finally you propose a $90,000 price, but the seller must finance $70,000 for seven years at 10 percent interest. The seller will have no part of it. He wants cash—"all cash!"

Such a noble idea. Selling a business for all cash is much more than that. It is typically wishful thinking. Your job is to convince him that it's the latter rather than the former. No, you're not going to let him off the hook on your demand that he finance you. No, you're not going to run to all those greedy banks that may lend you money on such disadvantageous terms. At least not yet. Not until you have tried every trick and negotiating ploy to convince the seller to finance the deal. You know why it's in your best interest, now show the seller why it's in his best interests as well.

Here are several strategies that can turn the most adamant seller into a willing lender:

Try the "Bluff." Bluffing is intrinsic to every deal. It's eventually a matter of who capitulates first. The seller will, of course, stick with his "no financing" posture as long as he thinks you'll run elsewhere to get him the money. That's where the bluff becomes essential. Let him know that bank financing is out. Either the seller finances you or there is no deal. Faced with that dismal alternative most sellers come around and, with some reluctance, extend financing.

Always Ask "Why." You won't always get the truth about why the seller refuses financing but you'll at least have an answer, and that's an important start. Does the seller need the money for other purposes? If that's the situation find out how much is needed. Few sellers have to completely "cash out." Perhaps they need some money at closing but not all.

Is the seller's concern the safety or security for the financing? If so, you may have an easier problem. Elaborate on the security you offer for the loan. Convince the seller why his downside risk is negligible. Your legal counsel can propose loan terms to sell even the most skeptical seller.

A seller's reason for refusing to finance can be turned in your favor if you have perseverance.

There are numerous reasons why sellers resist the concept of financing. As stated earlier, the seller may need the entire sale proceeds for personal use or a new business venture. Others can afford to self-finance but want a clean break with the business. Perhaps the most common reason is that self-financing poses a potential risk of loss. That risk is unacceptable to all sellers except those with a high degree of buyer confidence.

Despite a seller's predictable resistance to financing, there may be no alternative but to finance a sale. While sellers undoubtedly prefer cash buyers, the essential question is whether the seller can readily find the cash buyer and, in turn, whether the cash buyer would pay the same price.

Nevertheless, any proposed seller financing must be objectively analyzed by both buyer and seller from a strict risk/benefit viewpoint. The primary benefit to a seller offering attractive financing terms is the prospects for both a faster sale and a higher price. Buyers tend to place considerably more importance on the down payment requirements than they do price and when the two are negotiated together, a seller may find the higher price more than compensates for the secondary financing needed to reduce a down payment. Consider, for example, a business selling for $100,000. A buyer may be able to obtain $60,000 in bank financing, but only be able to raise $20,000 cash for the down payment. The final negotiations may lead the buyer to pay an increased price of $110,000 if the seller provides secondary financing for $30,000. From the seller's perspective the question becomes whether adding $10,000 to the price is a sufficient benefit to justify financing $20,000.

While the possible benefits can be accurately measured, whether in terms of a faster sale, higher price or other negotiable buyer concession, it is far more difficult to measure risk for it is difficult to determine the collectibility of the remaining balance should the buyer fail or default.

EXTERNAL SOURCES OF FINANCING

While finance books are replete with diverse small business financing sources, as a practical matter the small business buyer has few sources to choose from as lenders are generally asset based, relying primarily on tangible collateral to make the loan. The scarcity of loan sources within the small business field largely explains the popularity behind seller financing. It is not that seller financing is always desirable, but rather that it is all that may be obtainable.

And as many small business buyers frequently discover, aside from sellers, the only likely lenders may be relatives or friends.

If we are, for our purposes, to arbitrarily define a small business as one grossing under one or two million dollars annually or perhaps one requiring an acquisition loan under $200,000, then commercial banks and SBA guaranteed loans remain primary lending candidates. In fact, a study of over 500 small business acquisitions discloses that these two sources account for 85 percent of all external debt funding.

Nevertheless, other sources do exist and the buyer should understand the lending characteristics of each.

FOUR POINTS TO REMEMBER ABOUT BANKS

Even though you can find them on just about any street corner, banks still remain the most misunderstood and intimidating characters in the commercial world. Why all the mystery? It's a rare person who hasn't dealt with a bank. You have a checking account, and chances are you have a savings account or two. The fact is you may be one of the bank's favorite people and not realize it. Consider that they pay you seven percent for the use of your money and lend it to someone else for 13 percent. How did you think they paid for all those fancy buildings?

But then again maybe you were on the other side of the fence. A loan for a new car? A 20 year mortgage on your home? Sure, you borrowed money before. It wasn't hard. Walk in, fill out an application, wait a few days for a quick credit check and there's your check waiting for you. A business loan, however, is a brand new ball game. To be successful, far more is required than simply knowing how to complete an application.

Forget what you know or think you know about banks. If you're the average "hat in hand" borrower that continues to be intimidated by all those tall marble columns, you probably are operating on the myths used for years by banks to gain the upper hand. So let's explode a few myths about banks:

1. Banks are not in the business of lending money. Money is only their inventory. They are in the business of making money. Profitable loans are what they're after.

2. There's no such thing as a standard loan policy. Banks undertake to negotiate individual loan terms, depending on your persuasiveness.

3. You face stiff competition for the bank's dollars. Conversely, how many dollars a bank has to lend depends on immediate supply. But even in the best of times competition can be keen. For you to win financing you have to persuade the bank on the basis of profits and security.

4. Banks need you as much as you need them, if you have a deal that makes sense. As with any business deal attitude is essential. Remember, at 12 to 14 percent interest you are not exactly asking for favors. The bank will make plenty of money on you, so don't be shy.

KNOCK ON THE RIGHT DOORS

Knowing which banks to shop can be half the battle. No two banks are alike and neither are any two bankers. You have to find not only the bank best for you, but also how to spot and cultivate the banker within the bank who has both the authority and willingness to write your check. Start by selecting the right bank.

Walking into the wrong bank for your business loan will give you about as much success as walking into an Italian restaurant for a chicken salad sandwich. Banks, like most businesses, have their specialties or market niches. Narrow the field to put yourself on the right track.

Business loans are best obtained at commercial banks, while home mortgages and consumer loans are the domain of savings banks, cooperatives and credit unions.

If you're in the market for a loan under $100,000, concentrate primarily on small banks. Matching size of the bank to your loan is important. To a large metropolitan bank you are nothing more than a small fish in a big pond. How important can you be to the big banks when their customers frequently wheel and deal in $10 million transactions?

Stay close to home. Banks may have legal restrictions or internal policies against lending to businesses beyond a geographic area, and usually prefer to be close to their customers.

Banks may even foster ethnic preferences. Boston, for example, boasts two banks chartered primarily to make loans to Blacks and Hispanics, while another bank is controlled by those of Chinese origin. Interview a Jewish businessman and chances are he obtained his financing from one of three banks controlled by Jewish folks. Every ethnic group seems to have its favorite banking affiliations.

The industry has even advanced to "his" and "her's" banking. Several years ago a local woman's group chartered a bank exclusively for the purpose of lending to female entrepreneurs, and today they're reportedly doing a land slide business. Banks are more than brick and stone. They're operated by people, and people have likes and dislikes, prejudices and preferences. What one bank will turn down another may accept with unbridled enthusiasm.

However, all things being equal, the one best place to shop for a loan is the bank currently used by the business. The seller may have a working relationship with the bank and can probably arrange an introduction. Since the bank is familiar with the business and its financial history, it can help launch negotiations to a flying start.

SPOT THE CAPITALIST IN THE CROWD

Finding the right bank is only the beginning. It is as important to find the right banker within the bank.

It's positively amazing. People walk into a supermarket, assemble their weekly goodies, and with their shopping cart full, carefully analyze the situation to calculate which checkout line will get them out the door fastest. We've all done it. Nevertheless, we walk into a bank for a $50,000 business loan and never give a second thought as to who that right banker may be amidst a sea of mahogany desks. Choose the wrong desk, however, and you can forget that bank. Once some junior loan officer recommends "loan denied," you can bet her boss will support her decision to the hilt. Nor can you easily switch loan officers. That is why it's vitally important to position yourself in front of the right desk.

Based on my experiences there is only one "right" desk to be found in any bank, and that's the president's. You need be a little pushy to get there, but it's well worth the effort. Climbing straight to the top has its advantages as you avoid all the frustrating $15,000 a year junior loan officers with limited experience and even less authority who naturally avoid unconventional deals. It's all part of the process of refusing to be intimidated. And why shouldn't you be entitled to meet the president on a deal that will perhaps earn the bank $50,000 in interest payments?

I recall learning this lesson years ago, when I was one of a group of three partners seeking $25,000 in financing to start a local business. Our first stop was the desk of a young man with the title "assistant to the vice president—commercial loans." Apparently he was so low on the corporate totem pole that he was buried behind a steel desk alongside the teller's cage. After a few moments explaining our "deal" it was clear that our banker friend was in over his head and had no idea what questions to ask. After four weeks we still had no answer on our loan request. So we went right to the top man, and broke through the bureaucratic red tape. After one hour of comfortably chatting with the bank president we had our $25,000 loan. Never again did we settle for less than the president when negotiating a loan, or at the very least a vice-president with both the experience and authority to act decisively on our loans.

BANKS CAN SAY "YES"

Now the fun begins. Imagine yourself sitting across the bank president's oversized mahogany desk announcing you need only $66,000 to buy Joe's Restaurant. You ramble on about what a great deal it is, how much money you're going to make and how you intend to buy it on 100% terms when the banker politely shows you to the door—without the cash. Where did you go wrong? The answer is simple. You acted like an amateur, and banks rarely lend money to amateurs. If you happen to have a $3 million net worth they may conveniently overlook your eccentricities as they happily focus on your considerable assets. But not if you're a buyer going into business on nothing more than a wing and a prayer. That's when you have to think like a pro, act like a pro and sell your deal like a pro. And that, in turn, means knowing precisely what the bank will look for before they hand you the funds. I call them the three C's of loanmanship:

1. *Character*: Do you have a history of good credit, are you a deadbeat or like most people do you have a few blemishes on a spotty credit report?

2. *Cash Flow*: Does the business offer sufficient cash flow and profit after expenses to pay back the loan? Your best intentions mean little if you can't prove the numbers work.

3. *Collateral*: What does the bank risk if your loan goes into default? Will the bank have sufficient collateral to recover the balance owed?

Professionals know a bank views the loan application based largely on these three points, so they highlight them in a clear, logical and businesslike proposal. Follow this checklist and you can draft your own professional loan proposal:

I. Credit and Personal History (Character)

Name and address

Family status

Employment history

Experiences in related business

Education

Personal assets

Personal liabilities

Military status

Bank references

Credit references

II. Financial Information on the Business (Cash Flow)

Brief description of business

Brief history of business

Tax returns for two years

Projected cash flow statement for loan period

Summary of proposed business changes

Lease or proposed lease terms

III. Collateral

Business assets

Acquisition cost or replacement cost

Liquidation value of assets

IV. Proposed Loan

Amount required

Loan period

Interest terms

Identification of guarantors

Collateral to be pledged

A proposal addressing these points provides the banker every-thing he needs to thoroughly evaluate your loan. You made his job easier by anticipating his questions. More importantly, he knows he's dealing with a pro, which immediately adds to his confidence in both you and your deal. Have your accountant prepare the financial information, or have him join you in your negotiations at the bank. A banker may feel more comfortable if he knows an accountant is navigating your venture.

A final word of caution: be certain the numbers work. If your loan demands $2,000 monthly payments you're going to fail in your loan request if your cash flow statement shows only $1,000 per month shall be available. Be prepared to vigorously defend your proposal as your banker undoubtedly will ask probing questions. She may want answers or then again she may be simply testing to find out how much you actually know about the business.

WHEN THE BANK SAYS "NO"

Don't let failure discourage you. You may wander from bank to bank failing each and every time, but if you're wise you'll want to find out why. Once you detect the flaw in your proposal you can correct it.

Your first loan rejection should give you an important message. The banker sees a weakness you overlooked. If it was a significant enough problem for her to turn you down, then other bankers will likely spot the same problem and do likewise.

Don't foolishly think bankers are necessarily the world's best businessmen; nevertheless, they can often bring to your deal a certain objectivity that can put you on the right track and perhaps even save you from financial disaster. A retired school teacher wanted to borrow $200,000 to buy a nursery school. Bank after bank turned her down. One banker finally pointed out that the school never reached sufficient enrollment to generate income needed to pay the loan. Yet the teacher ignored the obvious warning signals, borrowed $200,000 from the SBA and predictably went bust 18 months later.

Sometimes banks say "no" when they really mean "yes," but to a somewhat different loan arrangement. Perhaps you have been rejected for a $100,000 loan, but prod further as the bank may be willing to loan $75,000. Perhaps your request for interest at 11 percent was below their current rate of 13 percent. It may be that more collateral would do the trick. Few deals are so fundamentally weak that they fail to qualify for any loan. Prod for a counteroffer which may still satisfy your needs. In any event don't take "no" for an answer. There's always more to the story than that.

Rejection can be beneficial. It can pinpoint a weakness in your loan proposal or a fatal flaw in your business idea.

Don't take a loan turndown and stroll on to the next bank until you find out why the loan was declined. Some banks hedge on a candid answer because they want to avoid offending or engaging in long conversation. But push for an honest answer. I can tell you about plenty of loan rejections that saved me a bundle on what turned out to be half-baked ideas. Sometimes it takes some fatherly advice from a banker to set you straight.

Don't look upon your banker as an adversary but an ally in evaluating the soundness of your plans. He may see weakness you overlooked or questions other lenders will raise. Listen closely. Pick his brain. If he raises some doubts in your own mind then move on and pick a few more brains. Still, you have to eventually follow your own entrepreneurial instincts. There are thousands of success stories thumbing their noses at bankers who said "no."

NEGOTIATE THE BEST LOAN TERMS

Once you receive the loan commitment, there's a right way and wrong way to structure the loan. Several rules of thumb can help save you money and make the difference between loanmanship success and failure:

1. *Do negotiate interest.* Like every other business deal, interest rates on loans are subject to hard bargaining. Banks often drop the interest rate by a point or two if they think your business plan is sufficiently strong.

2. *Do demand the longest loan period possible*—thus lowering monthly payments while conserving cash flow.

3. *Do pledge only the business assets as collateral*—protecting your personal assets in the event of default. Auction proceeds on business assets may satisfy the bank so it won't go after you personally if you signed a personal guarantee.

4. *Don't falsify your loan application.* Lies can cause you head-aches, including immediate foreclosure and non discharge of the bank debt should you declare bankruptcy.

5. *Don't grant additional collateral*—such as a house mortgage, without a fight. Banks may ask for it but that doesn't neces-sarily mean you must give it. Confine the collateral to the business (except for your personal guarantee, which will be required) and offer nothing more.

6. *Don't borrow personally.* Your corporation should borrow the money instead. If you personally borrow the money, the bank cannot take the proceeds of business assets in the event of default, and you will have to repay the loan personally. Your attorney can help structure the loan to provide you maximum personal protection.

7. *Don't settle for the first loan offer.* Remember, banks can be found on every corner. Shop around. You may land a better deal at the bank next door.

HOW TO BORROW A DOWN PAYMENT FROM A BANK

Borrowing a down payment from a bank requires a different strat-egy than you generally use to obtain a long term loan for the lion's share of the purchase price. There are several differences. A down payment loan represents a relatively small amount, typically ten to 20 percent of the purchase price; the down payment loan spans a short term, usually one year or less; and a bank won't consider business assets as collateral for a down payment loan if the assets are first mortgaged to the seller or other lender. If you are after a short term, unsecured (no collateral) loan available to borrowers with minimal personal assets or credit history, you must also learn the secrets of this type of loanmanship.

The most important thing to remember is never to disclose to the bank you need the loan to finance a down payment on a business. They'll turn you down every time. Why? Because banks are naturally conservative and believe a business buyer should invest 40 to 50 percent of their own funds toward the selling price. Of course, if every entrepreneur followed such cautious advice, many businesses, such as Monsanto which started with a paltry $5,000, would not be thriving industries today.

So how can you borrow your down payment from a bank? Remember that banks do understand these needs:

1. You need cash to remodel your house.

2. Your wife needs plastic surgery.

3. You're going back to school to get your master's degree in neoclassic literature.

That's right. Millions are available for "sensible" loans, but nary a dime for the daring entrepreneur hoping to bootstrap himself into business.

Should you need $10,000 to $20,000 for a down payment, you can nevertheless borrow it from a bank if you know how to maximize your personal borrowing power.

- Try the multiple loan and simultaneously borrow small amounts from several banks.

- Pledge some personal assets. Stocks, life insurance, automobiles and bank books can be money-raising collateral.

- If your credit doesn't allow a loan, have a friend or relative co-sign. It's easier to persuade friends or relatives to guarantee a loan than to make the loan.

Be careful. If you borrow $10,000 to $20,000 for a down payment, loan it to your business. Repay yourself and pay off the bank as quickly as possible. Once the business repays your loan you will have achieved a no cash down deal. Once you recouped your investment you have also eliminated investment risk, released whatever collateral was pledged and improved your credit rating through accelerated payment on your loan.

Short term 30 day down payment loans are a form of "bridge financing." Watch how Charlie Samuels effectively used it. Charlie wanted to buy a profitable Nashville auto parts store for $60,000, with $15,000 down. Try as he might, Charlie couldn't coax the seller to reduce his down payment demands. However, Charlie knew three ways the business could generate $15,000. So Charlie persuaded his father to co-sign a bank note, borrowed $15,000, bought the business and went to work.

First, he sold excess auto parts to quickly raise $6,000. He then channelled $7,000 from daily sales and deferred his own salary for the final $2,000, fully paying the bank within a month. For good measure he raised a few additional dollars to send his father to Hawaii as gratitude for the loan guarantee.

Charlie's story reminds me that when I studied for my MBA degree, my finance professor would continuously remark, "To finance a small business you need to know only one number . . . that of a wealthy relative's telephone." You may not have that rich uncle, but other no cash down techniques can work as well.

HOW TO BORROW 100% OR MORE OF THE PURCHASE PRICE FROM A BANK

Although a bank usually won't lend more than 50 to 60 percent of the purchase price of a business, the true value of a business may, in fact, be substantially more than you agreed to pay for it. Every business has a subjective value. How then does one determine the true value of a bakery, restaurant or flower shop? Unlike real estate, which lends itself to accurate appraisals, a small business has no quickly determinable value.

You can therefore increase the contract price of the business for the purpose of obtaining a higher loan, and subsequently reduce the actual price to equal the amount borrowed.

Suppose you want to buy Acme Supply and agree on a $60,000 price. In addition the seller wants $40,000 over five years for an agreement not to compete with you. If you approached a bank, it would probably lend you $36,000 or 60 percent of the $60,000 price. What if you instead word the contract so the price is increased to $100,000 and the noncompete agreement from the seller is valued at $1. Armed with the contract disclosing the $100,000 price, the bank might loan $60,000. Once you obtain the $60,000 loan, you may simply amend the agreement to its original terms with the seller receiving $60,000 for the business and $40,000 for the noncompete agreement payable over five years. This does not suggest you should ever deliberately mislead a lender and you certainly should have your attorney guide you so you avoid wrongful conduct.

THE INSIDE STORY ON SBA LOANS

Many entrepreneurs erroneously believe the shortest path to small business financing is to casually stroll into the nearest Small Business Administration office. The SBA can give you the details, but you must understand the big picture before you rely on the SBA. What you see may have you running, not walking, in the opposite direction.

Here's why SBA loans (and most other types of government handouts) are low on my money raising list.

- The SBA will consider you for a loan only if you are refused a loan from a bank. Think for a moment. If your deal is sound and logical you'd obtain a bank loan and wouldn't need the SBA. Through the process of elimination the SBA involves itself and specializes in nonsense deals and weak loans. In fact, the SBA has helped more people into bankruptcy than into business. This is the end result of financing deals that had little possibility of making the grade in the first place. When the SBA loses, they lose only a few tax dollars, but you lose everything.

- No matter what the SBA says to the contrary, SBA loans strongly favor minority groups. Unless you're in a minority group you'll have an uphill fight to get your loan approved.

- The SBA is even more collateral hungry than banks. If you own a home, be prepared to have an SBA mortgage encumber it. With banks you have a fighting chance of avoiding a pledge of personal assets, but not so with the SBA.

- The SBA invented red tape. It can easily take six months to process an SBA loan. Will your seller sit still while your loan application is buried on some bureaucrat's desk?

- The SBA will want you to match revenues. Therefore you'll need to put up 50 percent of the purchase price yourself. Unlike banks, the SBA frowns on secondary sources of financing.

Despite these serious financing shortcomings the SBA does offer several positive points:

- SBA loans can extend over ten years (and in some cases up to 20 years), compared with a bank's maximum five to seven year loan, and thus help cash flow.

- The SBA will lend to businesses in distressed areas whereas banks may not.

- The SBA does not demand a strong credit rating, because the SBA is committed to start where the banks stop.

The SBA offers two major types of loan arrangements, direct loans and participating loans through a bank. Under the bank participation arrangement, the bank actually lends you the money, but the SBA guarantees to the bank 90 percent of the loan. If you were to borrow $100,000 and immediately default, the bank would absorb a $10,000 loss and the SBA $90,000.

The Federal government has more than 1,000 loan programs, many of which are designed to finance small businesses. Inquire at the SBA office. If they can't help you, they may tell you other governmental programs that may.

SHOE LEATHER AND PERSEVERANCE

Old Casey Stengal was a perennial optimist. When his New York Yankees once returned from a disastrous road trip he simply announced, "You can't win them all."

That message should ring loud and clear in this chapter. You may not find the cash you need on your first try and you may need to beat the pavement and finally accept terms that will make life somewhat more difficult. But regardless of how and from whom you borrow, someday the loan will be paid and you'll own the business free and clear. It's a great feeling when you look back on how it all started with shoe leather and perseverance.

KEY POINTS TO REMEMBER

1. Seller financing beats bank financing. Don't even think "bank" until you get the final "no" from the seller.

2. Banks are like snowflakes, with no two quite alike. Match your deal to the right bank.

3. Know what the bank will look for. Remember the three C's—credit, cash flow and collateral.

4. There's a right way and wrong way to borrow. Negotiate and structure the loan for your benefit.

5. You can borrow 100 percent of the purchase price if you know how to structure your deal.

6. You're worth more than you think. Your signature alone may land you the down payment.

7

Partners for Profit: Your Brains, Their Cash

Yes, Virginia, there are investors out there—cash-bearing partners anxious to lend an ear to a proposition to earn them more money. You'll find them in all shapes and sizes. Some want to be "silent" partners watching their money work while others want to roll up their sleeves and work beside you. Some look for existing businesses on their way to the next plateau, others like nothing better than to take a flyer on an exciting idea. Some can offer you only a few scrimped dollars, and others offer an endless river of gold. Some will work with you to create wealth, and some will work against you and create ulcers and headaches. So, Virginia, whatever you find, you'll find partnership an interesting relationship. It's either paradise or purgatory. Seldom is it in between.

Say you've lined up your dream no cash down deal but need $50,000 to invest in additional inventory and new fixtures to make the business profitable. Your cash flow projections verify that the business will make you wealthy if only you can get your hands on the necessary $50,000.

Should you sell a piece of the action to an investor, who then becomes a silent or not-so-silent partner? Surely lots of investors would cheerfully spend $50,000 for a piece of the pie. But will your partnership become paradise or purgatory?

DO YOU REALLY WANT A PARTNER?

By legal definition a partner is anyone who invests money in a business and shares in its profits or losses. An expanded definition would include stockholders in a corporation or beneficiaries of a business or real estate trust. Partners come in all sizes and shapes; they can be Moe and Joe, each putting up $5,000 to buy a corner fruit stand, or a sophisticated venture capital firm investing heavily in a business and taking a passive management role. Other "partners" are the hundreds of corporate stockholders scattered throughout the country who rarely meet company managers.

Regardless of the number of partners or the amount invested, all partners have one thing in common. Once they are aboard, you're accountable to them. You no longer work just for yourself. Everything you do or want to do can be heavily influenced by your partners. Say goodbye to being a loner or a rugged individualist.

Examine yourself. Are you the type who wants to share responsibility and decision making or would you prefer total control?

Three classic situations can make partnership an attractive alternative to sole ownership:

1. You need money to buy or capitalize the business, and you can't raise it any other way.
2. You need management skills to complement your own.
3. You lack confidence and are simply afraid to go into business on your own. A working partner can provide psychological as well as financial or managerial support.

Take the case of a young man who lacked the self-confidence to go it alone. He became friendly with an equally timid soul with the same business interests, and together they did what neither could do alone. Today they own 17 thriving appliance stores in upstate New York. One of the partners has since branched out and owns several other successful businesses. Without having a partner to lean on, our two prosperous businessmen might still be clinging to their self doubts, continuing to work for others.

But if you need partners for money only, move more cautiously. A partner's small investment today could return to them many times that amount over the years. Partnership money can be the most expensive money you'll ever buy. So move slowly. Beg or borrow the money from any source you can, but consider partnership funds your last resort for raising capital.

Here's a mathematical example that underscores the point. If you take in a partner for a $25,000 investment, giving her 50 percent of the company in exchange, she will receive 50 percent of all future growth, equity buildup and profits. Grow the venture to a business worth $1 million and your partner will be worth $500,000. Instead, borrow the $25,000. Once it's paid, you're forever through with the lender. Once a partner gives you her cash, she's with you all the way.

PUT YOUR PARTNERS TO THE ACID TEST

Act in haste, repent in leisure! Choose a partner without really testing him and you'll learn this lesson the hard way.

I have a client who operates a wholesale bakery business. Over the past two years our baker friend has entered three bakery deals with a different partner each time. Unfortunately he never bothered to carefully investigate and select his partners. All he demanded from each partner was $15,000 to $20,000 and a willingness to spend all day at a baking oven. In short order his first partner physically ousted him from the premises and the litigation is still dragging on. His second partner walked away with $18,000 to pay gambling debts and was last seen heading west. Partner number three spends his days drinking bourbon and his nights at Alcoholics Anonymous meetings.

Think about it. It wouldn't have taken our baker long to assess his first partner's personality, or the gambling or drinking problems of partners two and three. A prudent businessman would have run a more thorough check when hiring a stock clerk. A partnership is indeed a marriage and you have to know your "mate."

What about personal friends? They seem to be a logical choice. What could be more fun than going into business with your bowling buddy or your college sorority sister? Unfortunately, what you prize in a friend is not necessarily what you need in a partner. Friends must satisfy social needs; partners must satisfy business needs. Don't confuse the needs of each relationship.

This is probably the most common error when selecting partners. In my younger days I ventured into a partnership with a close friend. We would spend our social hours planning and conniving. It was a lot of fun, and my partner was a great guy. He just didn't have the business talent to pull his own weight. But my management talent also left something to be desired—after all I picked my friend as my teammate. Luckily we're still good friends. He's successful at what he does and fortunately I found other fields for myself. It is a bitter lesson to learn your best friend is your worst partner.

If your working partner offers full time management support, you must be sure you can get along with him, because you'll spend more time with him than with your spouse. Personal compatability is essential.

Look for partners whose strengths offset your weaknesses. You may be a super salesman but be bored with production. Perhaps you're good at production but abhor accounting. Effective management requires a combination of many varied talents. Match your partner's skills with your own to cover as many important business areas as possible.

The right partner can create instant synergy, the sum total of the two of you becoming far greater than your individual abilities. On the other hand, the wrong partner can neutralize your skills, cause tremendous emotional strain and eventually destroy all chance for business success.

So how can you distinguish the "swans" from the "ugly ducklings?" Evaluate your potential partner's work history. Does he have a solid record of work experiences? Is he a "doer" or a "drifter?" Does he display the management skills you need? Does he command your confidence? Look for stability.

What about his personal history? Poor health can pose major problems. What do you know about personal weaknesses, such as gambling or drinking? Check out his criminal record. You'll be surprised at the skeletons that lurk in some closets.

Has your prospective partner been involved in other business deals? How did they work out? What do prior partners say about him?

How about his or her personal lifestyle? You may prefer to live conservatively and plow profits back into the business, while your partner may be a high roller living only for today. Such a clash in basic goals can cause huge partnership woes.

What do you know about your partner's spouse? Most wives and husbands wield great influence on their mates. You may find the perfect partner and still end up broke because of interference from a spouse that meddles in the relationship or the business.

Does your partner possess the required financial resources? He may initially be able to match your down payment but can he help you expand a year later? If the business needs another $30,000 you certainly don't want to mortgage your house while your penniless partner whistles Dixie. By the same token, it may not be a good idea to select a partner considerably wealthier than yourself because you may eventually find yourself on the short end of a squeeze out.

Matching financial resources is most important. You may be the brains behind the business but money always wins out. I can give you countless examples of financial backers asserting financial muscle to take over when their financially weaker partners run out of money. For example, I recently represented one partner in a food processing plant. Each partner owned 50 percent of the company, but they suddenly found that the firm needed an additional $100,000 for working capital. My client had already borrowed against all he owned to buy into the business. The other partner went into his power play and eventually bought my client out for very few dollars. Partnerships can be like a poker game. Make certain your chips match your opponents.

Most importantly, consider whether your partners business ideas are compatible with yours. Does he agree with you on important issues such as growth, operations, responsibility and financial philosophy? Does he share your view of what the business should be and how to get it there? That blending of ideas is the key to every successful partnership.

"HAVE I GOT A DEAL FOR YOU!"

Let's return to where we started this chapter. You lined up a pizza parlor and only need $50,000 for additional inventory and new fixtures. Since you can't swing any more loans, you typically approach your old school chum who made it big in plastics, saying, "Have I got a deal for you!" For a mere $50,000 investment, what does your buddy get? A percentage of the business? But what is fair? Twenty percent? Thirty percent? Possibly he'll ask for 50 percent based on his money and your labor or "sweat equity." Maybe your well heeled college pal will decide that for his $50,000 he should have a controlling interest or 51 percent of the company.

A clever partner might invest $10,000 for 30 percent of the company and loan the company the other $40,000 at 18 percent interest over five years, demanding the right to convert outstanding debt for additional shares in the firm. If the company succeeds he can cancel the remaining debt and pick up a large percentage of the business. But is that a fair deal? Your pal might even offer to divide his $40,000 "loan" into a $20,000 secured note and a subordinated $20,000 debenture coupled with a warrant for an additional 10 percent share. As "Plasticman" mixes his next martini he casually adds his lawyers will insist on simultaneous registration of stock so he can sell if you go public.

Of course, by now your head is spinning. All you wanted was your friend's $50,000 so you could buy "Happy Harry's Pizza Emporium." You knew you'd have to sacrifice a piece of the action, but you're confused by all this financial mumble-jumble.

Leave the financial rhetoric to your accountant and lawyer to decipher for you. The question remains: Is the deal fair?

There's no easy answer. The "fair" partnership deal is the best deal you can get from potential partners. No magic formula exists. No computer can spill out the right numbers or what the right deal will look like. Your potential partner will simply fight for as much of the business as he can get, while you will struggle to give up as little as you can.

Undoubtedly, you have nothing but unbridled enthusiasm for Happy Harry's Pizza Shop, envisioning enormous profits and an ultimate coast to coast chain. If you're right why shouldn't your potential partner accept a smattering of shares for such a ground floor opportunity?

However, your college friend undoubtedly has other thoughts. What do I risk? How soon can I cash out? How does my investment evolve over time? What are the chances for a public stock issue and substantial capital gains? What tax writeoffs apply if the deal goes sour? How can I increase my benefit and reduce my risk? What will you really give up? Whom else can you turn to?

Your perceptions of a "fair deal" may be far different from your prospective partners. There are so many variables that all you can do is shop around to negotiate the best deal you can.

If you encounter problems with your prospective partner's offer ask yourself, "What am I really selling?" Many bootstrap entrepreneurs offer an exciting concept but ignore the many rocks on the road to success when trying to attract partnership capital.

One leading capital source firm reports that only one or two out of a hundred entrepreneurs develop a business proposal that makes sense to the financial community. The other 98 percent spin their wheels with nonsensical ideas, poor packaging of their plans or bad timing.

What will excite an investor about Happy Harry's Pizza Emporium? If the investor gets 50 percent of the company for $50,000 but the business only generates a $10,000 profit, the investor obviously earns only 10 percent on his investment. His money would earn more and be safer in the bank.

So how can you sweeten that deal? Show the investor that Happy Harry's Pizza Emporium's product is superior and holds a clear competitive advantage over existing pizza parlors. Have him visualize perhaps another Pizza Hut chain. Since investors logically want their money to grow into a fast fortune, you somehow have to demonstrate how that's both possible and probable not just for them, but for yourself as well.

Is Happy Harry out of luck in attracting partners if his Pizza Emporium cannot mushroom into a national chain? No. All Harry has to do is restructure his deal so it makes sense based on reality rather than on a dream. In that case an investor might give Harry the $50,000, but not for a mere equity or small ownership interest. If someone loaned the business $40,000 (secured by assets) to be repaid over five years with 16 percent interest, and also received 50 percent ownership for the other $10,000, the deal might still be attractive. The $40,000 is secure and earning interest. The $10,000 equity investment will earn the projected $5,000 profit, creating a 50 percent return. And who knows? Maybe Happy Harry's will end up a national chain.

PACKAGE YOUR PROPOSAL TO SELL

Everything to be sold must be packaged to sell. You must make it attractive to the buyer. That's why showroom cars are buffed daily to a shining gleam and why my publisher, hopefully, will spend a small fortune to design an appealing jacket for this book. It's no different when it comes to selling a piece of your business. You want the most for the least and you therefore must package it properly. So put on a prospective investor's eyeglasses and look at your idea the way he would.

Sell Your Business Concept

Make it come alive. Paint the picture so the investor can visualize it. Why will it be successful? That's the key question. Explain the market, the competition and precisely how your business plan will turn projections into profits. Show how you plan to operate the business in as much detail as possible, backing it up with costs, financial projections and plans.

It doesn't have to be an exotic business idea to be a winner. Common everyday businesses often show exciting profits and have no difficulty finding investors because the basic business premise is sound. In one of my first retail ventures I quickly sold a 20% interest in the venture for $30,000 to an industrialist. Now there's nothing particularly interesting about a small general merchandise discount store. America needed it like it needed another recession. But the town I had my sights on needed it and I could prove the business would gross nearly $1 million annually and generate a $50,000 profit. A three-inch-thick file packed with facts and figures backed it up. We weren't far wrong.

Investors buy projected profits. Your job is to prove that the profits will be there.

Sell Yourself

It's more realistic to say investors buy a piece of management rather than a piece of a business. That's you. So you primarily have to sell yourself. Once you've convinced investors you know what you're talking about they'll then gain the confidence to buy whatever business idea you're selling. Watch a shrewd investor in action. In his test of management he'll ask plenty of questions and try to punch holes in every answer. He will if he's a shrewd investor, and frankly I've come across very few with that unusual combination of stupidity and money.

Don't be afraid to blow your own horn. Play up your education, special skills, experience and your track record. Your first deal will be the toughest sell and because you're unproven you'll probably end up on the short end of the deal. Once you have a success or two behind you, start mixing your own martinis. You'll have a pack of investors at your door crooning, "Have I got a deal for you!"

Sell the Deal

This is the tricky part. Don't suggest the proposed deal. Let that come from the investor. Your job is simply to provide the basic information needed for your prospective partner to frame an investment offer. What will he want to know?

- The amount of capital needed.
- How it will be used.
- The other sources of capital.
- If and when additional funds will be needed.
- How profits will be utilized.

Your investor must be able to put all relevant considerations together in his mind to make an opening offer, glancing over his shoulder at potential gain versus possible risk. It may be a far more generous offer than you imagined. It will be, if you packaged your proposal to sell.

Package your proposal to sell, tell investors about:

Background of the Company: Present its history, organization, financial statements to date and legal structure.

Management: Identify management people, their backgrounds and accomplishments. Show that the company has or will obtain an effective management team. Remember, to investors good management is most important.

Competitive Advantages: Outline why your company, product or service is unique. What advantages would convince an investor that the company might grow beyond projections?

Competition: Analyze your competitors. How do their products compare with yours? How might they respond to you?

Marketing: Describe advertising, promotion and sales costs. Detail distribution channels. Identify your market segment. How large is the market? Can it be reached? Will they buy?

Financial Information: Project financial statements for several years. Justify your numbers and involve your accountant who must be prepared to support the figures.

Investment: Show how you will use the money you seek. Will additional funds be needed? From what source? How will you raise money for expansion?

The Deal: Sell the investment plan in terms of safety, return on investment and growth potential.

Review your proposal. Can you back it up with hard data? In an effort to discover how much you know about your business, investors will try to pick apart your plan. And they'll never open their wallets unless convinced you have an intelligent approach to using their money.

WHERE THE MONEY LURKS

A good business plan naturally attracts potential investors like bears to honey. Why? More people are looking for good investments than there are good investment opportunities. However, you still must learn where to look for investment capital.

If you require less than $100,000, approach private investors, prosperous relatives, well-to-do acquaintances, your physician, your lawyer or an executive neighbor. Those earning $50,000 or more a year are your best bet, because they can spare funds for investment, want a hedge against inflation and seek opportunity for gains more conventional investments do not offer. Moreover, if the deal collapses, they can deduct losses to reduce income so that the IRS will share their losses. If your deal involves real estate or equipment that can be depreciated, these investors may be stimulated by its tax shelter aspects. Oftentimes tax implications will sell the deal. A sharp accountant can show would-be investors how your proposition and the tax code can work in their interests; however, the new tax code has made "passive investments" less attractive for many investors.

Here are a few tips for capital seekers:

Put your accountant, banker and lawyer to work. They undoubtedly have clients who may be likely investment candidates.

Advertise. Place a simple ad in the classified section of your local paper, describing your deal and the amount of cash needed. The New York Times prints an entire column of "Capital Needed" listings. So will your local newspaper.

Promote your deal. Mention it to your barber and you may end up with his brother-in-law for a partner. Many partnership marriages come about only through word of mouth.

Beware of "little old ladies in tennis shoes." They may be delightful at tea, but they can spoil business deals. Your "darling" company may excite them more than clipping AT&T dividend coupons, but rarely do their investment objectives or expectations match those of an entrepreneur.

Avoid close relatives. Business is business. It's hard for relatives to say no, and they seldom bring objectivity to the deal. Lose $100,000 for a stranger, and you lose an investor. Lose it for your mother, and you become the black sheep of the family. Don't risk family relationships over money. The same goes for close personal friends and anyone else whose relationship means more to you than dollars. Money is a most peculiar commodity. I have seen it turn brother against brother and transform parent and child into vicious litigants. I have one acquaintance who tells a sad but common story. He wanted to buy a carpet showroom for $75,000. For the down payment his mother mortgaged her house on the promises that she would receive 40 percent of the company and the company would pay back her loan. Within six months the carpet store failed. Without the business paying the house mortgage, that personal loan fell into arrears and the house was soon foreclosed on. Today our young entrepreneur is too ashamed to visit his mother and remains ostracized by his brothers and sisters. Remember, family money is the most costly money you can find.

Run away from cry-babies. Unless your business becomes another Xerox, they'll nip at your heels every step of the way. Lose a few dollars for them and they'll mutiny. Accept partners who can afford to risk their capital, are practical about what their investment can accomplish and conversely understand the risks.

Hunt retirees who have succeeded in your type business. They are fastest to invest because they know your business, have more confidence in it and often enjoy "re-living" their careers through your venture.

Don't overlook people who can also benefit from doing business with the company. Suppliers come under this category as I explain in Chapter 9, and so do distributors or potential customers.

BIG MONEY FOR SMALL BUSINESSES

Once your capital needs exceed $100,000, you cross the threshhold to venture capital and Small Business Investment Companies (SBICs).

Venture capital groups take partnership positions in businesses with vast potential. Historically they go for high technology companies and other "glamour" situations, like bio-engineering, computers and other fast-growth enterprises; but in recent years they have diversified into more traditional operations.

SBICs are like venture capital groups. They are private organizations (often bank-sponsored) who obtain loans from the Small Business Administration. SBICs then take this borrowed capital and invest in equity positions in young start-up or acquired companies. Whereas the SBA and banks can only loan money, SBICS can provide capital on a partnership basis.

Money-finders or capital search firms can put you in touch with appropriate venture or SBIC groups, help you professionally package your proposal, disseminate it to appropriate sources and negotiate the most favorable deal. In turn they'll probably want a nonrefundable retainer and a percentage of the capital proceeds you receive. But move cautiously. Deal only with capital search firms with respected reputations. Many live off advance nonrefundable retainers and rarely find the promised capital.

Massachusetts with its north to south artery called Route 128, is a mecca for venture capital deals. The only scenery along it is hundreds of budding "hi-tech" industries, most of which were started with nothing more than a bright idea, venture capital funds and some luck and pluck. Many of the founders are now worth millions, and they started with no money of their own.

Here's how a typical venture capital or SBIC deal may work. Once sold on your idea for a venture, the money men advance you $300,000—$100,000 for 40 percent of the company and $200,000 as a loan. The venture capitalists may demand the option to convert the loan into additional shares and may bargain for an option to buy further shares at a nominal price. If the company issues 100,000 shares, the owner holds 60,000 and the venture capitalists 40,000.

At $100,000 they have paid $2.50 per share for their 40,000 shares. The company succeeds. Sales skyrocket to $20 million a year with consistent 15 percent profits. You decide to go public, so the company issues and sells another 100,000 shares at $20 per share. You quickly raise an additional $2 million to help finance future growth, while your venture capital people find that their 40,000 shares are now worth $800,000. An 800 percent gain in a few years is not a bad return! Yet that is exactly the potential return venture capitalists expect.

Venture capitalists look for a company that eventually can go public. Their money starts it and finances it until it does, at which point the shares they purchased for a few dollars become worth considerably more and can be readily sold to the public.

To secure venture capital funds an idea alone may suffice, in which case I call it adventure capital. If you think your business has the potential for venture capital funds, develop a detailed proposal and shop around. A few years from now you may be another Polaroid or Apple Computer, both of which started with venture capital funds.

The first step is to find an appropriate venture capital firm. This would depend upon the firm's investment criteria, its interest in the entrepreneur's type of business, its stage of development and the amount of funds required.

Information supplied to the venture capital firm should include the history and type of business you seek to buy, description of the product and market size, amount of funds needed and its use, and financial projections for up to five years.

If the venture capital firm is satisfied with the information submitted in the initial proposal, then a complete business plan will be required. A complete business plan should be very thorough. It should include data from trade magazine publishers, trade associations, suppliers and customers to verify information and statistics provided.

Positive elements a venture capitalist looks for from the applicant are:

- The company should have a marketable product or service with a long term need.

- The management team should be professional and have solid business backgrounds.

- The entrepreneur should be willing to invest some of his own assets in the venture.

- The business plan should be realistic and should show both the strengths and weaknesses of the company.

Venture capital firms usually are in a strong position to dictate terms. The percentage of equity a venture capital firm may want to control will depend upon several factors, including the maturity of the applicant company, the risk factors at stake, its growth prospects and its profit potential. If a venture capital firm is investing practically all the funds, their control may reach as high as 90%. Some may prefer to control their investment with a majority stock position. Sometimes, the venture capitalist gives the entrepreneur a buy-back option—a chance to buy out the venture equity several years later at a preset price.

The structure of financing agreements varies with the aim and type of business seeking the venture capital equity. Many take the fairly standard approach of buying private stock in a leveraged buyout and waiting for a big capital gain when the company goes public or is sold to another concern. For a company with big growth potential, venture capital may be the best way to raise the down payment.

WHATEVER HAPPENED TO GOING PUBLIC?

Should you take your idea to buy a great business public and offer people stock? Will that bring you a barrel of money? Probably not.

Since the late 1960s investors have been wary of offerings to finance bootstrap acquisitions. The concept worked beautifully in the 1920s before the great depression and again in the 1960s, but when the dust settled many investors found that "too good to be true" deals were just that. In those bull-market eras all you needed was a catchy name, a crazy idea and a desk for the investing public to come running. An all too typical example was that of Heimberg Zippers, Inc. In 1967, Heimberg and his two sons eked out a living making zippers for clothing manufacturers. Occupying 600 square feet of loft space, their modest enterprise generated sales of $200,000 a year. Wild about going public, they went to the underwriters who suggested sprucing up the company's image prior to the public stock issue. Since Heimberg's Zippers, Inc. didn't stimulate the imagination, they changed the name to "Great American Techtronics." A bevy of business theorists sporting degrees from Harvard and Wharton joined old man Heimberg and his two sons on the board of directors. By reading the prospectus, no one would guess they were buying into a zipper factory, especially when it proclaimed the company "engages in innovative and advanced technology in protective hardware and fabrications." But the public bought it and shelled out $500,000 for 40 percent of Great American Techtronics. They got old man Heimberg and his two sons making pant zippers in a walk-up loft. Heimberg could succeed at it in the '60s but you won't in the bearish '80s.

Today, going public to raise capital to buy a business can work if you have a market of buyers for your shares each with a self-serving reason to help you finance your takeover.

Let's assume you have an idea for a business, perhaps a laundry service for nursing homes in your area. Obviously, nursing homes will benefit from one centralized laundry specializing in their needs. From your viewpoint, even at lower prices you will benefit from having committed customers. After some quick calculations you find you need $200,000 to buy the business. Let's assume that 50 nursing homes are each interested in capitalizing the company, each investing $4,000 for a percentage of its ownership.

First you may set up the corporation with 2,000 shares of stock, 1,000 shares for you, and another 1,000 shares for the 50 nursing home stockholders who will collectively pay $200,000. Since they can benefit from your new business, they may be the ideal stockholders to finance you.

MORE IS NOT ALWAYS BETTER

If you must go into business with partners or investors, keep the number as low as possible. Finding two people who think alike and get along is no easy feat, and problems increase proportionally with the number of partners actively involved in business affairs.

Susan Herbert renovates old homes in St. Louis and sells them for fabulous profits. Early in her career she contracted to buy ten houses with ten partners, each investing $20,000 to capitalize the business with $200,000. Susan contributed "sweat equity" for 50 percent and the partners divided 50 percent ownership for their $200,000. A fair deal? Sure, but two months after the business started it disbanded and the partners predictably are suing each other. What went wrong? One partner constantly interfered with development and renovation work. Another criticized "overspending." A third and fourth partner joined forces to scare off two other partners so they could buy them out cheaply. Two more partners wanted the first five houses sold before the second five were started, squabbling with two others who wanted all ten renovated simultaneously. Everyone wanted to call the shots then tried "shooting" the others. Meanwhile, Susan spent all her time soothing ruffled feathers instead of developing the properties.

Susan learned her lesson. She set up her next project differently. For each house she accepted only one partner. If she had ten houses under renovation, she had ten separate partnerships, one for each house. She can easily handle one-on-one partnership situations and now follows the axiom that "the best things come in small packages."

GUARD YOUR FLANKS

Strive for the best but prepare for the worst. If "divorce fever" sets in, it may be too late. You must set up the no cash down deal so you control it at all times and can always maintain the upper hand. Otherwise you may quickly find yourself on the outside looking in as your partner walks away with the business. Following are a few tricks you can use to protect yourself.

Don't overestimate potential profits. If you sell an investor on a projected $50,000 profit, you will face a lot of explaining when profits come in at $6,000. Always underestimate profits and overestimate costs to look like a genius.

Emphasize every significant risk associated with the venture. If you fail to disclose substantial problems you may incur personal liability.

Don't rely on standard corporate books and by-laws to document your deal. Have a written agreement on all major points, including salaries, bonuses, expenses and division of responsibility.

Watch out for secret deals or conflict of interest situations. If you have a side deal or hidden profit from the business, bring it out into the open. Be honest.

Don't let minor feuds mushroom into major battles. Discuss areas of disagreement the moment they pop up.

Create a formula for buying out your partner in the event of a disagreement. Make this buyout provision an important part of your overall business agreement.

Demand at least 51 percent ownership. This at least gives you voting control. If your partner insists on a 50-50 split, try to obtain majority voting control by having your partner assign proxy rights to you for the percentage of his shares which will give you voting control. Remember, minority interests are for dreamers!

Kevin had such a problem and now agrees with this advice. Several years ago he bought a small chain of fabric stores in the Chicago suburbs. Since he had no money of his own, Kevin formed a partnership with two financial backers who advanced $100,000 toward the purchase price of $300,000. The partners carved a deal whereby Kevin received one-third of the shares of the corporation and the investors received two-thirds. Kevin was to provide the management or "sweat equity" in return for his one-third interest. And Kevin certainly did sweat. For two years he averaged 70 hours a week and through his skillful management doubled the size of the chain, generating substantial profits in the process. Everything looked rosy until Kevin proposed to his partners that his salary be raised. They refused, and a big argument broke out. One word led to another and before Kevin knew what happened, he was suddenly without a job.

Since his partners controlled two-thirds of the corporation, they voted Kevin out as president of the firm and hired a new man at an appreciably lower salary. Kevin fell victim to the "squeeze play." Any partner owning less than 50 percent ownership is vulnerable. Of course, Kevin still held a piece of paper showing that he owned a one-third stock interest, but what would that do for him? Sure, Kevin would be entitled to one-third of the dividends due stockholders, but dividends in a small corporation are rare. Kevin would also be entitled to one-third of the proceeds of the business if it were sold or liquidated, but that might not occur within his lifetime. Kevin will always be outnumbered on any vote affecting the company, and he cannot even collect a paycheck. The fact that Kevin was a minority stockholder secures no employment rights. If in doubt, buy a few shares of General Motors stock, then show up at their employment office demanding a job.

So don't delude yourself. Unless you own at least 50 percent of a company you have little more than a job. But you don't want a job, you want a business of your own. Pass up any deal unless you are a full partner.

Does all this sound like paranoid pessimism on partnerships? Hopefully not. I do believe that partnerships are a major source of business troubles and I do believe that if your only motive for bringing in partners is their money, then it should be your last resort. But if you must go the partnership route you must know the pitfalls as well as the opportunities it presents.

KEY POINTS TO REMEMBER

1. Partnerships are not for everyone. Do you really want to be accountable to others?

2. Put your partners to the acid test: Does your partner have what it takes to help the business succeed?

3. Be realistic about your deal and the money it can make.

4. A "fair" partnership deal is the best deal you can drive. Forget magic formulas; they don't exist.

5. Package your proposal so it makes sense. No one will invest if he can't see the benefits of your deal.

6. Structure the deal to protect yourself. Guard your flanks and never accept less than 50 percent.

7. A partnership is another form of "marriage." It can work if you know what you're bargaining for.

8

How to Turn a Seller's Nightmare Into a Dream Business

Nothing can make money for you like a bankrupt business. Sound farfetched? Believe me, it's not. Particularly if you have what it takes to turn it into your own perpetual money machine. And here's the best part—there are thousands of troubled businesses that you can grab without investing a dime of your own.

Someone else's problems can work for you. I don't care what size or type of business you want or whether it's in Boston or Los Angeles. The techniques for buying and making money with troubled companies always follow the same principles.

Look around. There are plenty of examples:

- A grocery superette now doing $400,000 a year, purchased for its liabilities only. The new owner earns $40,000 a year income. All with absolutely no cash down.

- A nursing home bought from the bankruptcy court earns its owners $60,000 and again was purchased with no cash down.

- A glass installation company picked up from a foreclosing bank by an imaginative buyer now produces $50,000 profit a year. As with the others, it was acquired with no cash down.

The startling fact is, companies in trouble can present fabulous opportunities for no-cash takeovers. Some of the very best deals I have seen involve companies just one short step from the auctioneer's hammer. Imaginatively exploited, these companies have created more than one millionaire.

THERE'S NO SUCH THING AS A "BAD" BUSINESS

So who wants a "bad" business, you ask? Father Flanagan of Boys Town was fond of saying "There's no such thing as a bad boy." The same applies to businesses. Every business, like every boy, has redeemable virtues. If you're smart, patient and willing to work, you can extract something good from virtually any troubled company. Frequently, what you can extract is a small fortune!

It may be that the business "as it is" is a loser, but the company's insolvency is typically due to nothing more than the sad reality it lost money year after year. But isn't this a blotch against its management rather than against the business? In reality a "bad" business is a victim, the product of incompetent management unable to properly utilize assets, capture customers, expand markets or control costs. In other words, present management may be incapable of properly making the thousands of decisions necessary to shape that business into a winner but you may bring to the business precisely the skills it needs to become enormously profitable.

In my legal practice I handle quite a few business bankruptcies. Most of these bankrupt businesses easily could have become profitable when placed in the right hands, although major surgery in some instances was required. Chrysler's Lee Iacocca proved an effective management team can do wonders for even the most insolvent and desperate company. Read five books on this subject and you still will not cover all the business failures that were nothing more than management failures.

Our firm recently liquidated a printing plant. Why did it fail? The problem involved three partners who wasted their time and energy fighting each other. The firm's valuable equipment in the hands of an aggressive and success-oriented printer would have the company churning plenty of profits overnight.

Only two weeks earlier we auctioned a supermarket blessed with a great location. Unfortunately, its owner was too busy as the neighborhood playboy to tend to business, spending at best only 20 hours a week on the job. Acquired by a strong, no-nonsense supermarket chain, annual sales increased from $1 million to $3 million and today this same supermarket enjoys phenomenal profits.

Still another story involves a men's clothing store owned by a hard-working and knowledgeable haberdasher who made one fatal mistake. The business languished in the town's most deteriorating neighborhood. This same business, acquired for pennies on the dollar and relocated to a high-traffic suburban mall, now flourishes under new management.

The list of "turnaround" opportunities goes on and on. Managers often don't deserve their title. Management may fall apart due to illness, marital problems or any human weakness. Management is people. Businesses fail because the people who run them fail. The toothpaste on a druggist's shelf doesn't fail. The Campbell's soup on the grocer's shelf certainly doesn't fail, nor does the haberdasher's neckties. These are the tangible assets of the business. They only do for a business what good managers make them do.

That's how you must think about a troubled company. Separate in your mind its problems from its assets. What could you do with such a business? What changes could and would you make to rescue the company? How could these very same assets in your hands be transformed into your personal moneymaker? What opportunities do you see?

Now I'm going to reveal a painful but essential truth. If you cannot effectively diagnose and turn around a troubled company in your particular industry, you probably shouldn't be in that business. The management skills necessary to keep a deeply indebted company afloat are much the same skills required to keep a highly leveraged buyout successful. The only difference is that with an unprofitable company you must first change the direction of the company and make it profitable.

Here's a second important fact: Management skill must come from you. Nobody is going to tell you how to do it. You'll be very much on your own.

Forget about your accountant and your lawyer. Your accountant may provide basic financial navigation and keep a log of your voyage in the form of financial statements, but she can't sail your ship for you. Your lawyer might help you buy the business, organize your corporation, negotiate the lease and deal with creditors. After that he's on to his next case. Employees? There may be a few good ones in the pack, but nevertheless they'll expect you to call the shots. If they can run the business better than you they will soon have their own businesses to run.

So where do you turn? At best, management books and courses can only give you broad "turnaround" concepts. Unfortunately, 99 percent of all business texts are written by Ph.D.s who have never stepped outside the warm cocoon of academia, or met a payroll. Although fine theoreticians, they won't or can't tell you how many shrimp make a profitable shrimp cocktail or whether Prestone antifreeze will sell at $4.75. Yet it's those practical secrets that make a business successful.

So it all comes back to you. Remove bad management and plug in sound leadership. Given the metamorphosis of good management, any business can become a good business.

But a word of advice. Know thyself. I encourage you to ask yourself hard questions about the type business you are best suited for. Now, before we move on to the nitty-gritty of taking over problem businesses, I pose one more question: Can you provide skilled management to make your troubled business fly? The current mania for "how-to-do-it" business and real estate books creates the impression that any idiot can buy an apartment house (or business), and will tomorrow be enshrined in the millionaire's Hall of Fame! Though I'm all in favor of liberal optimism and motivating those who truly have what it takes to become successful, I long ago abandoned looking up the chimney for Santa Claus or under my pillow for the tooth fairy's quarter. Take all those evangelical books and success stories with a big grain of salt. Know your limitations. Move on a sure footing. Have realistic confidence in yourself, but emphasize *"realistic."*

SPOTTING THE PROBLEM BUSINESS

Every business has some problems, even the most successful companies. It comes with the territory. In this chapter, however, we'll look at businesses that are more than just a bit sickly, but businesses that are in fact terminally ill and teetering on the brink of bankruptcy.

On Sunday mornings while semiconsciously dining on my usual toast and eggs, I scan the auction pages of my local newspaper.

Where the casual reader sees restaurants, motels, stores and manufacturing plants scheduled for auction, I see more than that, much more. Each of those failed businesses represents a failed dream and a discouraged owner who must start over again from scratch. Each story spells lost savings and personal disaster. I visualize the many thousands of dollars owed to creditors. A dismal vision indeed. Only the obituaries rival the auction pages for misery. Unfortunately, people cannot come back to life, but businesses can and often do. And they often do when taken over by shrewd buyers without one cent of cash invested.

Since the auction pages are a final farewell, they frequently don't give us ample time to move in and leisurely structure a no cash down takeover deal. So you want to spot the problem business at an early stage, to be first in line with time to negotiate just the deal you want.

There are three proven ways to detect a company in trouble:

1. Visible signals.
2. Financial statements.
3. External information.

Visible signals can loudly announce problems within a company, particularly if it is a retail business where its operations can be readily observed. Stroll down main street in any town and with fair accuracy you can predict who's in trouble, and by how much. Examine inventory, for example. If you see low inventory it signals one of two facts. Either the owner is operating hand to mouth without credit to adequately stock the store, or he is poorly merchandising and sales and profits are therefore suffering. Distinguishing one situation from the other can be easy. A merchant who allows a $50,000 inventory level to steadily drop to $25,000 is likely draining inventory to cover cash flow and operating losses. Sometimes you spot a "dummied" inventory: the twelve across but one deep assortment of soup or one gondola devoted to $12 worth of Kleenex. Such stories remind me of the bald man who tries to cover up his hair loss by a strategic arrangement of his three remaining hairs. Try as he might, he can't fool even the most casual observer.

The physical plant can confirm the story. Poor lighting, damaged fixtures, peeling paint, unkempt premises or defunct equipment, all represent visible signals of trouble.

Once negotiating for a business you may rely on financial statements to disclose serious problems. Financial statements can lie, but never quite enough to hide serious trouble. If you lack financial expertise, study an accounting text so you can intelligently read financial statements. Keep your accountant at your side while you dissect the balance sheet. How much debt is owed? How old are payables? Can the business make all its note payments? To what extent are creditors closing in? Next examine the profit and loss statement. How much did the company lose, and for how long? How much is the owner taking out of the business according to the books? What do you think he's taking out "off the books"? Within ten minutes you should pinpoint two important items:

- Precisely how much trouble the business is in, and consequently, how desperate the seller is.

- How to best structure the takeover, using liabilities as a major financing building block.

That brings us to using external sources to help locate good leads. It sometimes takes a good detective to uncover a potential deal. Perhaps you can find leads from business suppliers. Talk to bankruptcy lawyers and turnaround consultants. Want to check on a particular business? Interview the company's landlady to see if she is owed back rent. Sometimes the firm's employees are the best source of such information. Has anyone's payroll check ever bounced? Are there public records of tax liens or judgements?

What does their credit report disclose? No one can hide a problem business. They're as subtle as crackers in bed.

"WHAT—ME IN TROUBLE?"

Owners of the troubled firm always seem to say it. Predictably, they then gulp hard and foolishly argue they've got the best thing going since the hula hoop. Finally they assure you the only reason they would think of selling is because the wife must relocate to Yuma, Wyoming, to cure her impetigo. Sometimes sellers half-heartedly believe their own tall-tales.

Sellers, like the rest of us, hate to admit failure. Why should they? To do so would bruise their fragile egos, and would certainly do little to strengthen their bargaining position.

So the first negotiating rule is to never back the seller into a corner and thus force him to confess he's on a first-name basis with the process server. Instead, figure out what face saving strategies you can use to coax the seller to hand you the keys to his troubled business. Develop an understanding of human nature. Lift the seller's head higher and higher, increasing his self-esteem with well-timed flattery and you'll soon have him eating out of your hand. Downplay the problems. Don't forget the seller's position. He probably confronted a dozen potential buyers who slammed his business, and then attempted to brass knuckle the business away from him. Such a heavy handed strategy creates resentment and sellers seldom cooperate with buyers they resent.

One client successfully acquired seven businesses for no cash down in a single ten month period. And each was in serious trouble. To win seller cooperation, he wisely used the flattery approach. First, he told the seller, "I've fully analyzed your company. Since I'll have to put a lot of money into it to develop its full potential, I can offer you very little for it. However, you are its most important asset. I'm only interested in it if you stay on. I can provide the money the business needs but your continued involvement is essential for this business to succeed."

Imagine sellers waiting for my client to tell them they are behind the "eight ball," ready to thank heaven for anything short of bankruptcy, when all of a sudden they hear praise for their management genius. It's easy after that.

Of course, some sellers say, "I'm glad you want me to stay on, but I'm committed to another job after two weeks." With that, my client replies with hidden relief, "Too bad! I really need your know-how, but perhaps you can teach me some of what you know in two weeks."

So much for the psychology of the seller of the problem business. Later we'll discuss how you can put money into their pockets if they insist, but first let's discuss how you can capitalize on the seller's mistakes to finance your takeover.

HOW A SELLER'S DEBTS CAN WORK FOR YOU

Let's try an elementary lesson in finance. If a company has $100,000 in assets but also has corresponding liabilities, what should you pay the seller? The answer is obvious—nothing. You may pay her $1 for her interest in the company and then assume the assets together with the liabilities. Now you own the business with nothing invested. That formula explains why troubled companies offer such interesting takeover targets: they offer built-in financing in the form of existing debts.

Let's explore liability takeovers further. First, you find that perfect business, then you analyze it from every angle until you're convinced you can make it successful. It's in obvious trouble. The seller's asking $75,000, but the books show the business owes trade creditors $60,000. At best the seller can only clear $15,000 should you pay the asking price. Once the seller admits this dismal fact you have locked in $60,000 worth of financing. Now you have only a $15,000 problem to contend with. Other chapters in this book will show you how to raise those additional monies without dipping into your own cash.

Look at another successful takeover. Harry wanted to own his own bakery after having worked for a large commercial bakery for many years. Finally he discovered a bakery that was in serious trouble. After some homework Harry found that the bakery had liabilities of $40,000. Armed with that information he began negotiations. The seller wanted $50,000. Since Harry valued the business at $30,000, he asked, "How do you arrive at a price of $50,000?" The seller exclaimed, "I have bills of $40,000 and want $10,000 for myself." The seller was, of course, unrealistic. If his bills were $90,000, would he expect a buyer to pay $100,000?

Harry nevertheless nursed the deal along. Finally, after months of negotiation, the outstanding bills mounted to $48,000, which remained far in excess of the value of the business, but to Harry this was only a temporary statistic. The seller, finding himself ever deeper in the hole, finally agreed to sell for the takeover of debts and a job for himself.

The formula for liability takeovers is simple:

1. *Calculate outstanding debts.* This may involve notes, taxes, accounts payable or expenses payable. The nature of the obligations is not as important as the total amount of indebtedness the seller must pay creditors should he find an all cash buyer.

2. *Agree to accept the debt for all or part of the purchase price.* Thus structured, the deal may require little or no other down payment.

While it's generally not a difficult process, your lawyer can, of course, handle the legal complexities, which in some isolated instances can pose serious problems. If the seller's business is incorporated the problems are minimal. All the seller need do is transfer his shares of stock in the corporation to you. If his business is operated as a sole proprietorship, the seller must sell the assets. In that case, the seller must first notify creditors of his intentions to sell, unless the buyer agrees to assume the debt. Further, a creditor who holds a security interest or mortgage against the assets must grant permission before a transfer of assets can take place.

Some sellers are rightfully reluctant to transfer liabilities they are personally accountable for. Should you fail to pay, creditors can go after the seller who originally incurred the debt. For example, a seller may have guaranteed a bank note for $50,000 which you agree to assume. If the company subsequently fails, yielding the bank only $10,000, the seller would remain liable to the bank for the $40,000 balance. The seller may, in turn, have the right to sue you, but that still doesn't relieve him of his responsibility to the bank, nor does it assure him he will in turn be repaid.

Personal liability obligations, if they exist, are a common stumbling block to liability takeovers. However, you can successfully overcome that obstacle in one of two ways. Convince the seller that if he doesn't sell, the business will not survive and he will face personal liability. With you at the helm, however, the business may have a much better chance of paying the debt. Often it's a matter of alternatives. Or, consider a personal agreement to pay the debt, providing the seller legal recourse against you should you not pay. Limit your guarantees to an amount consistent with the value of the deal. If you believe the business can have a value of only $15,000 to you, then the guarantee should be limited to $15,000 or less. Always make certain risk is proportional to benefit!

PUT CASH IN THE SELLER'S POCKET

Stubborn sellers abound. No matter how burdensome their debts, they refuse to part with the keys without cash in their pockets. For such sellers no amount of flattery will replace cash.

It's understandable. No matter how bleak the financial picture, a seller hates to walk away from a business without something. If he does not care about being absolved on personal liabilities, or doesn't worry about saving face in the community by announcing "I sold the business," rather than "I filed for bankruptcy yesterday," you may have to enrich the seller with some "walk-away" money. Usually it won't take too much and you can often establish an easy payment schedule. The trick is to give the seller something more than he would gain by throwing the company into bankruptcy. After all, why should a seller otherwise go through the hassle of selling when he could turn the business over to his creditors to liquidate?

But you can convince any seller that a sale is better than bankruptcy. Offer the seller employment. Many sellers will gladly turn over their business in exchange for a good job. A steady paycheck, free from the headaches of running the business, may be just what the seller wants. Knowing where his next paycheck is coming from can often be quite an inducement. A word of caution—don't sign long term employment contracts. If the seller is a good employee he won't need a contract. If not, don't burden the business with an unproductive employee. You'll have your hands full straightening out the business as it is. Also, you might offer the seller a small percentage of future profits. If he's convinced you can save the company, he'll envision a lucrative payoff later as sufficient inducement to sell.

Scores of entrepreneurs have become rich because they know how to motivate sellers of troubled businesses. For example, a few years ago I noticed an ad in the Wall Street Journal that caught my eye:

"Wanted: Insolvent Companies. We pay cash direct to the sellers." Intrigued, I wondered who in their right mind would give a seller anything in exchange for taking over debts far in excess of assets. I called and scheduled an appointment during my next trip to New York. Upon arriving I was ushered into an enormous office decorated in Early American Rich. Immediately the "big man" and his cadre of lieutenants surrounded me at his mahogany conference table. Conveniently, I had at the time a client with a troubled toy distributorship who faced almost certain bankruptcy, and was therefore a likely candidate. Sensing a possible deal, I enthusiastically pulled out my client's financial statement showing assets of $500,000 offset by liabilities of $800,000.

After my brief presentation of the sorry facts and a few superficial questions on their part, they retired to deliberate their interest in my client's company. Upon returning to the smoke-filled room, they offered to take over the company "as is". The seller would simply transfer his shares and receive a contract entitling him to 20 percent of the earned profits over the next three years.

I raised all the usual objections. After all, profits are no more tangible than the smoke in the room. But the buyers had a better argument. What did my client have now? A failing company heading for bankruptcy? The possibility of something, they reminded me, was better than the certainty of nothing. Their argument was indeed compelling!

We didn't go along with the deal because I had other plans for my client's business, but that's not the point. Many other sellers in similar circumstances did. These same buyers since acquired fifteen companies with combined sales of over $22 million a year and achieved it all without one cent of their own invested. Today they boast a net worth of over $6 million. Watch the Wall Street Journal. Many companies such as theirs are still advertising—and are anxious to take over troubled businesses that can make them even wealthier. Here's how they do it.

CREATING INSTANT EQUITY

Thousands of people have made their fortunes taking over problem companies which provide not only no cash down financing opportunities but also instant equity. Should you find a business with $100,000 in assets and $150,000 in liabilities, you may say, "Who needs it? The debt exceeds its value." Although you are mathematically correct, you must go one step further to see the magic of instant equity at work.

Assume you could take over that same business for nothing and reduce the debt from $150,000 to $30,000. Wouldn't you indeed enjoy that instant equity of $70,000? (The $100,000 assets minus the $30,000 liabilities.) You might then sell the business for $100,000, pay off the $30,000 in debts, and pocket $70,000 for yourself. Perhaps you would prefer to borrow $60,000 against the business. After paying creditors their $30,000 you would have $30,000 for yourself and still own the business with $40,000 equity. On the other hand, you may want to build the business so it can give you a fat paycheck each week. You win, no matter how you exploit the situation.

Knowledgeable entrepreneurs make phenomenal fortunes taking over sick companies, quickly reducing their debt, then cashing in their equity through a quick sale. It happens every day.

Suppose your objectives are different. You're reading this book because you want a business of your own; a business not to resell but to own and operate. The mechanics are nevertheless the same. You first take over the company and then clean up the debt, generating instant equity along with creating a healthy solvent business. Once achieved, you can concentrate on your second important objective: making a profit.

Never forget "profit." Avoid becoming involved in any business unless you know you can make it your perpetual money machine.

Creating a solvent business is only the prelude for shaping the business for long term profitability. Unless you want to be a wheeler-dealer, quickly selling your business for a profit, concentrate on making it that profitable and enjoyable business of your own.

THREE QUICK WAYS TO A HEALTHY BUSINESS

Does it all sound too simple to you? How hard is it to reduce liabilities and cancel all those nasty debts you're now saddled with? How do you do it?

It is far less difficult than you may think. Every day, hundreds of companies strike deals with creditors willing to walk away with as little as two cents on the dollar. Understand a creditor's alternatives and the concept of debt reduction becomes easy to understand. Creditors will accept any amount beyond what they would receive if the business were liquidated. It does not matter how much the business owes them. For example, $10,000 or $50,000 might be owed a creditor, but all that's relevant is what it would pocket should the business be auctioned. Offer just a bit more. If the creditor accepts, the rest of the debt is discharged and cancelled. Watch how this worked for one street-smart entrepreneur who mastered the strategies.

A good-sized hardware store was recently for sale in a Boston suburb. Since Donald had worked for a competitor in the next town, he was hardly surprised when he heard this store was for sale. For several months the owner had been ill, and the business was rapidly going downhill. The financial statements disclosed liabilities of $200,000 and assets worth only $70,000. Although the company's debts nearly tripled its assets, that didn't discourage Donald. He knew he could make the business successful. Several weeks later Donald acquired the shares of stock in the troubled hardware store for a nominal payment; then he went to work on the creditors who were still bombarding the business with lawsuits demanding payment.

First, Donald's lawyer hired an experienced auctioneer who handled many liquidations for the bankruptcy court, instructing him to appraise the assets and determine what they would bring if the store were auctioned. The answer was $20,000. That's right—$70,000 in hardware inventory, fixtures and equipment would net only $20,000 under the hammer.

Armed with this information, Donald convened a creditor's meeting and presented the financial facts of life. The business owed creditors $200,000. If the business under-went bankruptcy and liquidation the creditors would split only $20,000, giving each creditor less than a dime on the dollar after court costs and auction expenses. Donald instead offered creditors 20 cents on the dollar, payable over two years, or twice as much as they could hope to get under bankruptcy. But they must, of course, accept it in full settlement. Oh sure, the creditors grumbled and mumbled. They always do. Nobody wants to forfeit 80 percent of what is rightfully due them. But what choice did creditors realistically have? Logic prevailed and $200,000 in debt quickly shrank to $40,000. Donald had his instant equity of $30,000 and easily paid the creditors their $40,000 out of future profits from a thriving hardware business that today grosses over $3 million.

Is Donald's story unusual? Nope. Here are a few high-lights from some "instant equity deals" that have recently crossed my own desk.

- A gift shop with a $50,000 inventory. Debts of $60,000 was slashed to $15,000, producing $35,000 instant equity.

- A garment manufacturer with inventory and material worth $400,000 and equipment valued at another $100,000. A debt of over $2 million was negotiated down to $150,000 while the new owners picked up $350,000 instant equity.

- A shoe store with inventory of $100,000 and debts of $90,000 generated instant equity of $70,000 after creditors agreed to cancel $60,000 in claims.

One of my favorites involved a pet shop featuring puppies for sale, that was also burdened with $300,000 in liabilities. How much can you auction a cocker spaniel for? Creditors didn't want to find out, so they agreed to walk away for a paltry sum of $6,000, leaving the buyer with a highly profitable business.

Lawyers commonly use three surefire methods to reduce debt and create a healthy company. Composition agreements offer a quick and informal out of court settlement. As in Donald's case, the insolvent company convenes its creditors, reviews the fiscal alternatives and negotiates a compromise which is usually a percentage on the dollar payable from profits over time. However, normally nearly all the creditors must consent to the composition agreement for it to be useful, and thus this strategy does not always achieve the desired results.

Chapter 11 of the Bankruptcy Code is a more common method used to rehabilitate an ailing company. Under bankruptcy court protection a company is fully shielded from creditor action while the debtor obtains time to negotiate a "plan of arrangement," which in reality is a composition agreement under the auspices of the bankruptcy court. Once a majority of creditors accepts the plan, it binds all creditors. Chapter 11 worked for the giant Penn Central Railroad, and it can work just as well for your small business.

Thirdly there is the "Dump Buy-Back" method. No, I didn't invent the idea, but I take credit for perfecting it. Suppose you offer creditors a fair ten cents on the dollar but they won't listen to reason. They want all that is owed, or at least far more than you are willing to pay. As a counter-strategy, why not let the company go to auction and borrow enough from the bank to buy back the assets at auction, which invariably allows you to pick up the assets for a small fraction of their true worth? The creditors of the original company would disappear and you would now own a business of your own at a bargain basement price.

Whatever your approach, hire an experienced bankruptcy lawyer to guide you through this phase of the deal. While it's helpful to know the basics, leave the creditors for your attorney to handle. Your job is to make the business profitable.

Remember the story about the toy dealer who had assets of $500,000 and liabilities of $800,000? The New York buyers knew precisely how to capitalize on my client's problems. If the deal went through, they would have thrown the company into a Chapter 11 reorganization. They figured they could reduce the debt from $800,000 to $200,000, producing for themselves an instant equity of $300,000. Their management team projected an $80,000 a year profit under their ownership. Not a bad return on a no cash investment with no risk. A seller's nightmare can indeed be your dream come true!

At my no cash down seminars the question invariably pops up, "If it's so damn easy and profitable, why doesn't the seller do it himself?" That's a legitimate question. Many owners of troubled businesses do not sell out. Their owners stay with the business and fight to save it, struggling to reduce their debt and effect a turnaround just as a new owner would. Still, many others grow tired and become mentally beaten, while others realize they have neither the skills nor resources to turn the business profitable. Believe it or not, many business people hastily throw in the sponge because nobody, not even their lawyers, show them the many possible ways to save a business. So forget those who won't turn their problems over to you. There are still plenty of others waiting out there anxious to deliver their disasters into your more capable hands.

BARGAINS FROM THE BANKRUPTCY COURT

The best time to take over a troubled business is when it's still in the seller's hands. The sooner you locate it the better, because terminal insolvency cases are harder to handle. Perhaps you didn't realize the flower shop around the corner was in trouble until you heard they filed bankruptcy. If you had only known! Your green thumb could have done wonders with it.

But contrary to popular belief it's really never too late. Some great no cash down deals have been plucked right out of the bankruptcy court. When I say bankruptcy court, I literally mean any type of insolvency liquidation, which may include a receiver appointed by the local court, or an assignee under an assignment for creditors. The IRS may have seized the business for nonpayment of taxes, or a bank may be foreclosing. It doesn't matter. The objective is always the same: sell assets to pay creditors.

Regardless how the business is to be liquidated, offer substantially more than the assets would bring at auction because you want the seller to finance you. Creditors offered a choice of receiving $20,000 now or $20,000 over three years, will obviously go for the immediate money. However, should you instead offer $25,000 payable over two years at 18 percent interest they may listen. If the offer is sufficiently attractive, they'll not only sell to you for pennies on the dollar but finance you as well. Even bankruptcy courts anxious to close out cases will entertain time payment deals that benefit creditors more than would a quick cash sale.

Our law firm, for instance, recently was involved in the liquidation of a stereo shop to satisfy creditor claims. Our auctioneer advised that he expected assets to bring about $40,000 at auction. Suddenly a prospective buyer offered $50,000, payable over three years with 15 percent interest, and all adequately secured. It made sense so we agreed. The buyer soon expanded into video cassettes and his business is now booming! Former creditors are selling to him on

C.O.D. terms and making a profit. Had we auctioned the business, creditors would have one less customer today. Remember, there is no eleventh commandment that says "Creditors shall auction thy goods." Offer a better deal and everyone can come out ahead.

REFINANCE AND PUT MONEY IN YOUR OWN POCKET

Once you have generated instant equity by eliminating debt, why not consider refinancing? You will have cash on hand to develop the business or expand into other businesses, and remember, refinancing proceeds are not taxable.

One of Philadelphia's largest food wholesalers built its business this way. The owners would search for small wholesale food distributors in trouble. Next they would negotiate a no cash down takeover, followed by a quick composition agreement or Chapter 11 to reduce debt. The firm would then refinance with a bank that would loan them 70 percent of asset values. Last year they completed their most impressive acquisition—a company grossing over $3 million a year selling exotic foods, such as venison and bear meat, to gourmet restaurants. Its major assets were refrigeration and food processing equipment. To replace the equipment easily would cost over $400,000, yet the auctioneer would be lucky to get $80,000 under the hammer. Inventory was negligible since porpoise livers have a very short shelf life. Liabilities, in turn, amounted to over $750,000. The owner was happy to sell because the buyer offered him a challenging position in another division of the buyer's company. After haggling, creditors wound up with $70,000. Borrowing $300,000 against the assets, the buyers paid the creditors and pocketed $210,000 for themselves. Was it a good deal? You bet. The major asset was not the equipment but the seller's customers and the good will of the business, which had no value at auction but enormous value to the buyer. Today the gourmet distributor grosses $5 million and reaps over $500,000 in profits. The successful buyers are now negotiating to take over a fish processor doing $8 million a year, parlaying the $210,000 obtained on refinancing to swing the deal. Such is the magic of leverage!

KEY POINTS TO REMEMBER

1. A business never fails. Only management fails. Good management can turn around even the worst situation.

2. Make sure you have what it takes to turn a loser into a winner.

3. Be on the lookout for companies in trouble; they're easy to find if you know how to spot them.

4. Flatter the troubled seller. Help him save face while you save money.

5. Let the debt be 100 percent or more of the asking price.

6. When you reduce the debt you have instant equity, even if it's only on paper.

7. Don't let creditors intimidate you. They'll accept a fraction on the dollar to settle their claims.

8. Refinance your instant equity for easy money in your pocket.

9. Put yourself in a no-risk position—what can you lose?

9

Supplier Financing: Yours for the Asking

Your business should be that proverbial money tree. Not only will it put money into your pocket year after year, it will also put money into the pockets of your many suppliers, those kind folks who will benefit immensely from selling you merchandise for your money-making venture. In fact, no matter how much money the business will earn for you, it will earn far more for your suppliers.

This brings us to a simple proposition. If your suppliers stand to profit so handsomely from doing business with you, why not call upon them to advance those few dollars that can put you into business? You have plenty of persuasive arguments. Once suppliers see the profit potential your business represents, more than a few will quickly advance the cash needed to help with the down payment.

Imagine negotiating to buy a $1 million-a-year food market. Suppose the seller wants $200,000 but will finance only $120,000, leaving you to find the $80,000 down payment. With a little re-search you discover that this supermarket buys about 60 percent of its merchandise from one grocery wholesaler. Assuming the supermarket has a gross profit on sales of 25 percent, its total annual purchases will be about $750,000. This translates into $450,000 of sales for the grocery wholesaler year after year. Stick a price tag on that $450,000. What is it worth to your supplier? A bit more research reveals that grocery wholesalers earn about 10 percent gross profit. The knowledge that the wholesaler stands to make $45,000 a year from your one account gives you a powerful bargaining chip.

Why not walk into the supplier and lay your bargaining chip on the table? You want your supplier to loan you perhaps $30,000 in return for your continued business. Your wholesaler not only gets the $30,000 back, but will reap $45,000 in profits each and every year you're in business. Think about it. That comes out a whopping 150 percent annual return on the original loan, enough to motivate even the most greedy among us.

Supplier financing is very high on my list of money-raising sources. Intelligently engineered it can work with any type of business that purchases products for inventory; particularly firms that rely on primary suppliers.

My first experience with supplier financing was many years ago when one of my more entrepreneurial clients called to say he had found "his perfect second liquor store." Bill already owned one thriving liquor store, but, since he purchased it only two years earlier, the store was heavily mortgaged. Bill could squeeze barely a dime out of it to help finance the purchase of his second store. Bill confided that the seller of the second store wanted $200,000, but demanded all cash. Bill had already lined up a bank to loan $120,000 and the cooperative business broker agreed to help fi-nance the deal by contributing his commission of $20,000, to be repaid with interest over two years. Additionally, the seller would allow Bill to assume about $20,000 in outstanding liabilities. The problem was the $40,000 remaining to cover the balance of the down payment.

Bill asked me to come along on a visit to his major liquor wholesaler in the event some legal questions arose. Bill glowed with confidence as we walked through the liquor wholesaler's door and met the president of the company. After the usual pleasantries, Bill immediately swapped his air of confidence for a look of despair. It was a convincing act. Turning to the wholesaler he said, "I've got a problem and want to go over it with you. As you know I'm presently buying about $600,000 a year from you. I came across a second store I want to buy, but the current owner buys all its merchandise from your competitor, Company X. I understand he spends about $500,000 a year buying from this wholesaler. Well, when Company X heard I was interested in buying the store they were, of course, afraid they'd lose the account to you. So they made me an interesting proposition. Company X will lend me $50,000 to help finance the purchase of the second store if I continue to buy from them, and further, they will allow me an additional two percent discount if I give them the business from both stores." While the liquor wholesaler mopped his brow and looked for the nearest window from which to jump, Bill smoothly continued the scenario. "I couldn't understand their offering me an interest-free loan of $50,000 or an additional profit of over $20,000 a year (two percent of combined purchases of $1,100,000) until they explained what a high volume customer like myself would be worth to them." With that, Bill confidently glided into his finale. "I knew I had to come to you with the problem, because all things being equal, I owe you the opportunity to match their deal. I want to continue my business with you if at all possible." With that, Bill looked despairingly at the floor, pretending to be the victim rather than the victimizer. After a few grunts, groans and half-hearted attempts to extol the virtues of his company over Company X, the president asked us to wait a few moments while he conferred with his general manager. Upon his rapid return he sheepishly announced that he would help Bill with the same $50,000 interest free loan, grant the same two percent additional discount and would do even one better! The supplier would increase Bill's current credit line by $20,000 and his merchandising team would help spruce up Bill's store displays.

Bill looked up and happily blurted, "That's great! I couldn't sleep all night with the thought I might lose one of my best friends as a supplier. But, just one more thing—Company X mentioned something about giving me as a dealer's bonus a free trip to San Francisco to attend the liquor dealer's convention. I assume that will be your policy too?" Even that final straw didn't break the camel's back, for the president good-naturedly surrendered as we exited amidst another flurry of pleasantries.

Walking to the parking lot I asked Bill why he didn't tell me about Company X's offer. He laughed and said. "There was no such offer. I never once spoke with Company X. But my friend the president would never know that. Since he is a bitter competitor of Company X, they certainly won't compare notes. Besides, I bet I could have bargained that deal from Company X. Even if my friend had turned me down for the $50,000, I knew he would have to come up with some counter-offer, and I could have saved face by simply accepting whatever he offered out of longstanding friendship and loyalty." Then Bill delivered his clincher, "You know I only needed $40,000 to close the deal, but I figured why not go for $50,000. If I received it I'd have another $10,000 for working capital."

Bill played the game perfectly, using a well-woven blend of psychology, logic and the business reality that little white lies are sometimes necessary. Bill, of course, had his supplier in a bind. The supplier knew that Bill's account was worth the $50,000 loan and that the extra two percent discount was a small concession to win the combined volume of the two stores. The outcome was inevitable. Shortly thereafter Bill owned his second store without plunking down one dime of his own. And in his pocket was $10,000 to spare!

Targeting a supplier for a business acquisition loan is not a flim-flam but good business. Suppliers may be the most logical source of your down payment, considering the benefits they will derive from your new business.

Nor is supplier financing a new concept. Entire industries have been built through supplier financing; businesses which increase the volume of the supplier's own products. Supermarket chains, for instance, now set up convenience store franchises with practi-cally 100 percent financing. It's not altruism. The supermarket chain serves as supplier and thus earns its profit as wholesaler to its convenience store chain. Do you want a car dealership, boat deal-ership or even a sewing machine dealership? Nearly 100 percent financing is available to you. Suppliers of these products face little risk from such generous financing. Should you fail, they can easily reclaim their goods. But should you succeed, they now have a flourishing money tree as you continue to push their products and keep their factories humming. Although franchisor financing can be an attractive way to get started, this chapter will primarily focus on how to deal with suppliers who are not in the franchising business, as everyday suppliers can, and often do, offer even more attractive financing possibilities.

HOW TO STRUCTURE THE SUPPLIER LOAN

As in life, everything in business operates on a "value for value" system. Each party to a deal must realize sufficient benefit if the arrangement is to work, otherwise either it won't happen or the relationship will soon fall apart.

How can you structure a mutually profitable deal with a supplier? First determine who your primary supplier is. Most businesses purchase the lion's share of their inventory from a handful of suppliers, and the balance from a scattered number of secondary suppliers. Approach your primary suppliers since your account means more to them. Concentrate on family-owned companies as large national firms may lack the flexibility to accommodate you.

Calculate the approximate amount of annual business your supplier can expect to receive from you. Determine your supplier's percentage gross profit on sales to you. Don't concern yourself with operating expenses since his expenses are basically fixed. Your supplier will usually value your business in terms of the gross profit he will earn. If you have experience in an industry you will know the profit margins at various levels of distribution. If not, you can easily find the answer by asking industry veterans or checking the trade journals or reference guides that publish comparative financial statements for specific industries. Multiply the profit percentage by the annual volume. This discloses the supplier's annual profit to be earned from your account or what we call your "supplier's profit." For example, if a paint supplier sells you $300,000 in paint products annually and his gross profit is 20 percent, your supplier's profit is $60,000.

Once you have calculated your supplier profit, you should start the negotiating process. Induce your supplier to lend you money in exchange for giving him your profitable business. How high a loan can you justifiably request? A reasonable loan is about six months' of projected profit, although supplier loans equal to one year's or even two years' profit are not unusual in highly competitive industries.

Consider other terms of the supplier loan. For example, what's the payback period? Your supplier will want repayment as quickly as possible, while you want extended loan terms. As with other loans, never undertake a supplier loan that cannot be safely repaid from future cash flow.

How about security? Like any other lender, your supplier will be concerned about the safety of his loan. Be prepared to offer a mortgage on business assets, and, if necessary, a personal guarantee. Your attorney should negotiate these terms.

Your buying commitment is essential. Your supplier isn't loaning money without good business reason. He's doing it because he wants your business and the profits it will earn him. Therefore, your supplier will expect a buying commitment or a guarantee you'll buy a minimum quantity of merchandise over a specified period of time. Should you fail to satisfy your buying commitment, your supplier may reserve the right to demand immediate payment on the unpaid balance. This is a key bargaining point. Play it straight. Don't accept a supplier's money and then switch suppliers. Not only will such tactics stimulate quick legal action but it could serve to blackball you within the industry as well.

After all is said and done, how good a loan you negotiate depends on many variables, most of which you cannot control. The competitiveness of the industry is one major factor. Competitiveness is determined not only by the nature of the industry but by geographic considerations. For example, the wholesale drug business in the Boston area is exceptionally competitive. No fewer than six major drug wholesalers compete for the rapidly dwindling number of drugstore accounts. New discounts, bonuses, giveaways, more lenient credit terms and other creative forms of buyer inducements are everyday concessions. You could likely land a supplier loan on attractive terms from any one of these suppliers. On the other hand, Wyoming has just one such wholesaler. Without question you would approach this lone supplier with far less confidence. Later in this chapter I'll show you how you can get suppliers to bid for your business, provided there are sufficient suppliers to whom you can "auction" your business.

Nevertheless, success in obtaining supplier financing primarily depends on your bargaining power, or your future value as an account. A large volume account obviously justifies a far larger loan than a small volume customer who represents only marginal profits to the supplier. What can you do to enhance your clout? If you plan to expand, let your supplier know. Let him visualize how he will benefit from your expanding business. If you're in a position to feature lines that are particularly profitable to your supplier, sell that important point. For example, tobacco jobbers earn the highest profits on sundry merchandise such as household items, film and school supplies. Liquor wholesalers generate the greatest profits on private label or house brand liquors and wines. Don't "cherry pick" the lean items. Show the supplier that your account can be worth more in terms of more profitable lines. How much money a supplier ultimately loans is proportional to how much profit your account will likely generate. Expect your supplier to think in selfish terms, just as you will. Your job is to convince the supplier his loan will yield exceptional dividends.

There's one final ingredient—you. Suppliers think no differently than other prospective lenders. After all is said, the nod of the head will come only if your supplier has full confidence and trust in you. Underscore your prior experience, your plans for the business and any other positive points to convince the supplier you have both the know-how and desire to make your business succeed.

Perhaps the best way to instill confidence is to offer the endorsement of one of the supplier's more prized customers. Should you be friendly with one of his better customers, have him arrange the initial meeting. You probably know people within the industry and chances are they already deal with this supplier. The introduction serves as an endorsement, and the supplier may treat you more favorably to maintain the good will of your mutual friend. Essentially you're trading on your friend's influence but it's a proven way to turn prospective suppliers into new friends.

Suppliers usually enjoy solid and long-lasting business relationships with their customers. So they'll also want to know about your planned or potential growth. For example, a year ago Bill had one liquor store. Today he has two. Perhaps five years from now Bill will own five thriving stores. Today's chains and conglomerates are yesterday's "mom and pop" operations. As you grow so will your supplier's sales and profits. If expansion is in your plans use it as a dynamic sales tool!

KEEP THE UPPER HAND

Supplier loans present some dangers. Insist upon a "value for value" deal, and that means refusing to pay an outrageous price for the loan.

Several years ago I heard a common but sorrowful story at a management seminar for nursing home operators. As business people generally do, the administrators compared notes on the subject of food costs. One participant volunteered the fact he received an eight percent rebate from his food supplier. Another countered that his supplier gave him ten percent. Around the table it proceeded, obvious to all but one unaware participant who was amazed to discover food suppliers customarily grant eight to 11 percent discounts to nursing home operators. Our bewildered friend, Mildred, an owner of one of the larger local nursing homes, sat back, looked around and confessed she had been in business for two years and never once received a discount from her food supplier. She was equally shocked to learn that such discounts commonly existed within the industry. Her anger accelerated when she heard two other participants claim substantial discounts from one of her own suppliers. Eventually, Mildred admitted her food supplier had loaned her $30,000 for a down payment on her nursing home, which had long been repaid. When she confronted her supplier the following week, he reminded her of his generous loan as justification for her "missing" discounts.

Mildred was the victim of what I call "supplier lock-in. " Mildred felt so obligated to her supplier for the $30,000 loan that she allowed herself to forfeit many thousands of dollars in earned discounts. What did the supplier loan cost Mildred? To start with, she paid the money back within the first year together with interest. Over two years of doing business with this supplier she purchased nearly $300,000 in food, thus forfeiting approximately $30,000 in discounts, and she stood to lose another $15,000 in lost discounts each year she blindly allowed it to continue. Mildred unwittingly paid over 110 percent interest for her loan.

Suppliers, of course, are not and should not be a charity. But steer clear of any supplier loan that carries a price tag of lost discounts or waiver of any other valuable trade terms or concession. Losing important discounts erodes your profits and makes the true cost of the loan outrageous. Make this clear when first negotiating the loan. Offer only your steady business and a fair interest rate in return for the loan. That's all you owe the supplier.

Incidentally, Mildred's story had a happy ending. Her attorney notified the wholesaler that since Mildred did not agree to forfeit the same discounts her competitors received, his actions constituted price discrimination violating the Robinson-Patman antitrust laws. Accordingly, Mildred would be entitled to damages equal to three times her lost discounts, or about $90,000. Within ten days Mildred had a settlement check for $45,000. It was precisely the amount Mildred needed as a down payment on her second nursing home. As Mildred discovered, there's more than one way to extract a down payment from a supplier.

HAVE THEM BIDDING FOR THE ACTION

You shop several car dealers before you buy a new auto. You may even comparison shop for your weekly groceries to make sure you're getting the best deal. If such minor acquisitions justify shopping several sources, a deal that may eventually involve millions of dollars deserves no less consideration.

You need the very best deal you can get from a supplier, whether it's loan terms or trade concessions. Therefore you must play one supplier against the other and have each bidding against others for the action.

Let me guide you through the bidding process by telling you about the no cash down techniques of an acquaintance, who found himself in the movie theatre business using remarkably little money coupled with lots of imagination.

A theatre was available with full financing, if only my friend could raise the $60,000 down payment. With a creative stroke, the buyer convinced the seller to sell gift certificates for future admissions at a 25 percent discount with the proceeds paid to the seller and deducted from the down payment. The exceptionally successful promotion generated $42,000.

Where should the buyer turn for the remaining $18,000? Movie theatres have but two primary suppliers—film distributors and candy jobbers. Since film distributors adhere to a strict cash and carry policy and are as generous as Attila the Hun, the buyer opted to tackle the candy jobbers. A quick trip on the adding machine revealed the theatre sold more than $100,000 in candy each year. Since candy jobbers enjoy a gross profit of about 20 percent, the successful bidder for the candy business could anticipate a profit of about $20,000 annually.

Scanning the telephone directory, the buyer found no less than 15 candy suppliers anxious for theatre sales. Approaching each supplier, the buyer obtained bids that ranged from "Sorry, not interested" to a $15,000 interest-free loan not due for repayment until the theatre stopped doing business with that supplier. Of course it was a great deal for both parties. The new movie mogul got his loan and the supplier insured himself a profitable lifetime customer.

USE THE "CAPTIVE SUPPLIER" THEORY

Some business people are blessed. They furnish their supplier so much business that the supplier would go broke if the account switched suppliers. This, in turn, creates a further possibility for a highly advantageous supplier loan useful for expansion.

A printing plant, for example, expanded from a small print shop doing $150,000 a year to a mini-conglomerate engaged in sophisticated printing services and a profitable volume well in excess of $3 million. The owner accomplished this phenomenal growth through strategically negotiated supplier financing alone.

As it happened, the printer initially gave a local typesetting shop about $200,000 a year in subcontract work. This $200,000 represented most of the typesetter's business, without which the typesetter would be forced to close up shop. When the printer came upon an opportunity to buy a graphic design shop for $25,000 down, he tapped the logical source for the money—the typesetter who could hardly afford to say "no" and chance losing his one major account.

As the printer expanded and diversified, the typesetter enjoyed parallel growth and prosperity. The following year the printer expanded again with the acquisition of a retail stationery supply firm. Again, the typesetter was called upon to finance the down payment with another $30,000 loan. Today, this same printer owns twelve successful corporations within his mini-conglomerate, each financed with money advanced from this one typesetter who just couldn't afford to say "no."

At first glance it might appear that the "captive supplier" theory works only if you're already in business with an existing supplier totally dependent upon your business. However, that's not quite true. There are many possible "supplier-customer" relationships to which the same principles apply.

For example, a small local awning company with annual sales of $400,000 became a financer. Its owner, Anthony, was a manufacturing man who abhorred sales, installation or service. Jim, a born salesman, talked Anthony into financing Jim's sales in return for which Jim would exclusively represent Anthony's awning company and handle all installation and service calls. Anthony could forget sales problems and concentrate on what he did best—manufacturing. Within one year Anthony's sales approached $1 million due primarily to Jim's strong sales skills. In turn, Jim quickly repaid his startup loan. Because Anthony was protected by an exclusive contract with Jim, both became "captive suppliers" of each other, but the symbiotic relationship made sense for both men.

Look around. How many companies would welcome the opportunity to sell and finance an operation you could better handle? Can you foresee a plan whereby such a company finances your business expecting to benefit from better service, a higher quality product, lower production costs or other means for improved performance? Opportunities for merging your capabilities with the money of existing or prospective suppliers are indeed countless.

A FINAL WORD ON SUPPLIER FINANCING

Did you ever hear the story of the insurance saleswoman trying to sell a policy to a well-heeled acquaintance? Every Sunday the saleswoman played racquetball with the prospect in hopes of selling a policy. After a year of competition the insurance woman unhappily learned her playing partner had bought a large policy from a competitor. Exasperated, she blurted out, "I've been playing racquetball with you every Sunday for a year. You know I'm in the insurance business. Why didn't you buy from me?" The prospect softly replied, "You didn't ask."

Don't fail because you never asked. Suppliers won't offer to loan you a down payment on a business, but it can indeed be yours—if you ask.

KEY POINTS TO REMEMBER

1. Consider supplier financing for the down payment.

2. Sell the supplier in terms of "supplier profit" and what your account can mean to him.

3. Negotiate a supplier loan that represents a fair deal for both sides.

4. Avoid supplier "lock-in." Pay back the loan but don't give away your profits.

5. Shop around and have suppliers bidding for the action.

6. Use leverage with a supplier dependent upon your continued business.

7. Look for opportunities for potential suppliers to set you up in your own business.

10

A Little Cash Flow Can Go a Long Way

Let's talk about what you're most interested in—money, money, money! Before you start making it, however, you need to find enough of it to land your own business.

Now here's one interesting statistic that will show you just where that money can come from. Do you realize the average business rings up in its cash registers in just two or three weeks sufficient sales to cover the down payment? Think of it. Imaginatively handled, the money the business accumulates in only a matter of days can be yours to satisfy the seller's down payment demands. Since no rule states you can not "borrow" some of those dollars piling up in the register, study this chapter carefully to find out how you can turn those dollars into your own down payment.

TAPPING CASH FLOW FOR YOUR DOWN PAYMENT

It can be amazingly easy to use cash flow accumulated *after* you buy the business to buy you the business. This approach requires two steps. Although there are variations, the basic strategy always remains the same. Determine the net cash flow generated by the business over the first several weeks by calculating the difference between cash receipts and what must be paid out. Then structure the deal so the seller receives his down payment out of the cash flow available once you acquire the business.

Follow how it worked for one enterprising young lady. Sandra was anxious to buy a prosperous Cape Cod restaurant with annual sales of $850,000, for which the seller asked $200,000 with $80,000 down. The seller readily agreed to liberally finance the $120,000 balance over ten years with 10 percent interest. Sandra's problem, of course, was raising the $80,000 down payment. Fortunately the broker agreed to loan her $10,000 from his $20,000 commission, and two friends loaned her $30,000, bringing the cash she needed down to only $40,000.

Sandra's accountant quickly went to work and prepared a cash flow statement for the first month of operation. Projected cash sales were $60,000, while anticipated disbursements for that month were $2,000 for rent, $6,000 for salaries and about $15,000 for miscellaneous costs. The business would therefore generate a tidy $40,000 surplus cash flow within the first month. Sandra's suppliers would not demand payment for the first month as she was starting clean without bills, and she rightfully figured they would extend her at least one month's credit.

With the cash-flow analysis completed, Sandra confidently believed she could draw the $40,000 down payment from the business within the first several weeks. Step two in her plan loomed the bigger problem: How could Sandra persuade the seller to wait 30 days for his $40,000? The seller understandably expected a certified check at closing.

Sandra found a way out of her problem. She shrewdly promised to pay the seller $10,000 a week during the first month. For security the seller held his bill of sale and other closing documents in escrow until he received every penny of his $40,000. If Sandra missed a payment by even one day, the seller could immediately step in and take back ownership of the business.

How could the seller lose? What did he risk? Those questions helped wear down his resistance. Sandra then suggested the seller work for her in the restaurant for the first month at top salary. Not only could the seller help acquaint Sandra with the business, he could also make certain everything went according to plan and that he was punctually paid. That was the clincher. Sandra honored her every word and today her restaurant grosses $1.2 million and nets over $100,000 a year.

Recruit a good accountant who can professionally guide you over the magic cash flow numbers quickly and accurately. It's not difficult to calculate what you can extract from the business. Be conservative in your projections. If you over estimate income, your financial plan will be in immediate jeopardy. And be equally careful when estimating the money you must pay out within that same time period. Be cautiously pessimistic so you build into your projections a comfortable margin of error. Operating expenses such as rent, payroll and utilities must, of course, be paid when due. The major questions are when suppliers must be paid and how long you can stall. The answers, of course, depend on many factors, including the credit rating of the business, industry custom and your own ability to persuade creditors you deserve credit if they are to deserve your business.

Subtract your anticipated expenditures from your income, to calculate the surplus case you should have on hand at any given time to apply to your down payment.

Sometimes you need only parlay cash flow accumulated over a weekend. Jane Roland successfully negotiated the takeover of her colorful Atlanta cheese shop precisely this way and is a master at the game. After considerable haggling, Jane finally worked the seller down from a requested $30,000 down payment to $15,000. The transfer of ownership was set for a Wednesday at one o'clock, but Jane nervously called me the preceding Monday to insist the closing be delayed until Friday at three o'clock. Though it was not a convenient time for me or the seller's attorney, we nevertheless assented. Friday arrived. Working late into the afternoon we were in the midst of signing the documents when Jane suddenly excused herself to make an urgent phone call from a nearby office. After waiting 20 minutes for her return, I proceeded to retrieve her when Jane anxiously pulled me aside and asked that I stall the closing until five o'clock. Bewildered, I revisited the conference room and desperately manufactured half a dozen small legal obstacles needing further resolution. The seller and his attorney understandably grew edgy and impatient. At precisely five o'clock Jane dashed back in the room, completed signing the papers and casually handed the seller her check for $15,000. Amidst farewells and best wishes for the upcoming three-day weekend the deal was completed. Turning to Jane I asked, "What was that all about?" With a wry smile Jane confessed, "My $15,000 check has no funds behind it. But bright and early Monday morning I'll cover it with the weekend receipts from the business. Had we closed the deal before five o'clock, the seller just might have called my bank to see if the check was any good and, of course, it would have been goodbye deal!"

I don't recommend passing worthless checks to buy a business, although it happened to work beautifully for Jane and probably for many others as well. But visualize all the businesses that produce such tremendous cash flow that two or three days' receipts could easily cover a conventional down payment. Fantasize over the hundreds of supermarkets, discount stores and other cash rich ventures one could take over, if only the seller would patiently hold a personal check for several days. It can indeed be a tempting way to take over such a business.

MAXIMIZE THE INCOME STREAM

Unfortunately, sellers will grow inpatient to get their hands on the down payment you hope will appear from cash flow. As with most endeavors, timing can be everything. For example, the seller may willingly wait a few weeks for his money, yet the business may not generate sufficient cash within such a short time span. Should you meet an impatient seller flip instead to another strategy and increase cash flow to raise the necessary money within the time period imposed by the seller.

Picture yourself in this common situation. Perhaps you find a men's clothing store for sale. The seller agrees to accept a $20,000 down payment in two monthly installments of $10,000. Based on projected income, the business can generate only $10,000 in surplus cash flow over a two month period. Since most expenses are fixed and can't be decreased, increasing income may be your only answer. But how can you rapidly build sales? If you answered, "Run a sale and increase the next two months' receipts by at least $10,000," award yourself a masters degree. When you successfully achieve it you have earned your Ph.D.

A cash-raising promotion can often double or even triple business income. This may be the perfect answer, particularly if the business has excess inventory it can quickly turn into instant cash.

I once observed with fascination a retail hardware company expand into a formidable chain using just that method. Targeting prospective takeovers loaded with inventory, the buyer would negotiate the smallest possible down payment payable over several months. Once a store was acquired, the company would call in its own promotional staff to orchestrate a sales campaign. Stores routinely grossing $20,000 a week suddenly enjoyed sales of $50,000 or $60,000. Once inventories decreased to their appropriate level the sale was discontinued. Cash proceeds from the sale, however, typically satisfied the down payment requirements and the company was poised for its next leveraged acquisition.

THE ESCROW METHOD

Let's return to the conference table for a moment. After hours of strenuous negotiations the seller shows no sign of backing down. He's adamant, "$50,000 down or no deal!" He rejects your crazy ideas about paying from cash flow after he hands you the keys to his business. He wants your check at the closing.

It's time for another strategy. Confronted with this impasse, try the escrow method. Before I explain how it works, let me provide a strong word of caution. Properly handled, the escrow method requires consummate legal skill. Confide in your attorney so she can properly word the agreements and safely guide you in your "sleight of hand."

The essence of the escrow strategy is that you insist your down payment not be deposited in an escrow account until certain post-closing conditions are satisfied. If and when all conditions are satisfied, the deposit will go straight to the seller. Here's the trick. The escrow check is only to be held, not cashed, during the escrow period. That, of course, buys you the necessary time to accumulate cash flow from the business to cover your check.

A local car wash recently changed hands by clever use of the escrow method. The buyer promised a down payment of $20,000; however, his attorney argued that the deal should be conditional upon the buyer's obtaining a transfer of the car wash franchise, which would take about two months. Naturally, the buyer's attorney wouldn't hand the seller $20,000 as he might have to fight to get it back should the franchise transfer be denied. Therefore, the agreement provided that "the buyer's down payment check of $20,000 shall be held intact by buyer's attorney pending transfer of the franchise, and in the event the franchise transfer is not approved, the escrow check shall be returned to buyer upon rescission of the sale by buyer." Notice the key words: the payment check *"shall be held intact,"* and *"the check shall be returned to buyer."* This language insures that the check will not be deposited into an escrow account where it would bounce. Here, the escrow agent simply holds the check without suspecting there are insufficient funds to honor it.

Most transactions can easily justify the escrow method. You may need permits for the business, perhaps the seller must repair some equipment or contingent claims may arise against the business. An astute seller may agree to an escrow arrangement but demand a certified check, or require that the money go into an interest-bearing account to earn interest until released. Such demands are not a matter of right or wrong but of your matching wits with the seller. The trophy goes to the smartest player.

A similar method can also work successfully. Hand the seller a series of postdated checks for the down payment. Legally, this provides the seller no more protection than a short term promissory note calling for periodic payments. However, a check creates an important psychological advantage. Though people are wary whether you'll pay on a promissory note, they are more likely to respect your personal check. Unlike a promissory note, a seller need not worry about your mailing payments on the due date, for they already have your payment in hand in the form of a postdated check.

MORE POINTERS ON CASH FLOW MANIPULATIONS

Everybody juggles cash flow. Who at one time or another hasn't delayed paying certain bills to have enough to buy groceries? It's the great American game. It's also a game you must successfully play with your new acquisition if you expect to quickly raise money for your down payment. But manipulating cash flow to accomplish that objective need not be too difficult. Follow these steps.

Defer every possible expense. Your cash flow projections will include a weekly payroll. Consider the dramatic increase in short term cash flow if you can coax high priced employees to defer salaries for several weeks. Such requests are possible when dealing with employees at the executive level. This short story proves it. An elderly couple I knew wanted to sell their employment agency for $30,000. They would accept a long term note for the $15,000 balance if they received a $15,000 down payment. The buyer was aware that three high priced employees each earned $500 per week. However, the buyer first convinced the seller to drop the down payment to $10,000 and increase the note to $20,000. The buyer next approached the three employees, asking each to defer salary for one month. The buyer would pay the back salary within three months with interest together with a generous year-end performance bonus. Fortunately each of the employees agreed. Armed with their commitment, the buyer approached the seller and said, "I'll give you a check at the closing for $4,000 plus four postdated checks for $1,500, each due one week apart," and thus cemented the deal. By deferring salaries these employees helped their new boss buy the business. Incidentally, the $4,000 down payment didn't originate from the buyer's pocket, as the buyer previously lined up a new client who advanced the buyer a $4,000 retainer to have his agency locate several employees for his new plant.

Dramatically reduce the amount of money needed for incoming merchandise by simultaneously returning to suppliers excess or unsaleable goods. Every business with inventory is saddled with dead or excess stock returnable to suppliers for credit. Any business that can defer payments to merchandise suppliers can instead put this cash into the seller's pocket and that may be just what is needed to put together a deal.

Aggressively negotiate credit terms with your suppliers. Every dollar in credit is another dollar you can offer the seller toward the down payment. The credit game is not recommended for the timid buyer. Yet, some of the biggest and most prestigious companies in the country have mastered the techniques of optimizing cash flow by holding creditors at bay, oftentimes expanding with this cash. Even the federal government builds cash reserves today in exchange for a debt to be repaid in the future. Look at our social security system.

Have you ever fended off a bill collector with a "Your check is in the mail" story? Show me a business that buys $50,000 worth of goods a month, regardless of its credit rating, and I'll show you how an experienced, forceful and imaginative buyer can haggle at least one month's credit. $50,000 can indeed go a long way on your no cash down deal.

ADVANCE CASH FLOW CAN SOLIDIFY ANY DEAL

Let's return to the seller who stubbornly says "I want my cash up front! " No, they don't want to hear about short term notes, escrow of deposits or any other fancy talk that allows you to plunder cash flow to buy their business.

Faced with such a recalcitrant seller, alternatively you may suggest the seller take his down payment from "advance cash flow." In this instance it's the seller who does the plundering before he turns the business over to you. This does have its advantages. The seller has his cash before the closing and doesn't have to worry about your scraping up the money afterwards. Also, if the seller enjoys a strong credit rating, he may convince suppliers to extend necessary trade credit more easily. Since nearly ten percent of all no cash down deals rely upon the advance cash flow method, it's a strategy worth exploring.

A record store in downtown Boston changed ownership a year ago and serves as a perfect example of how advance cash flow can satisfy a seller's down payment needs. The seller wanted $75,000 for the business with the buyer assuming an existing $35,000 bank loan. To help finance the acquisition, the seller would accept a $20,000 note and the buyer would add a $20,000 down payment. Though the seller claimed substantial buyer interest, apparently no buyer could handle the $20,000 down payment.

The successful buyer successfully employed the advance cash flow strategy. "You want to walk away with $20,000 cash and a $20,000 note in your pocket," he reminded the seller. "Within the next month the business can generate a surplus net cash flow of $20,000. If you withhold payment to your suppliers during that month, your trade debt will increase by $20,000. Rather than pay creditors, take the cash, and I'll assume the $20,000 in trade payables as part of the purchase price." A month later the seller had pocketed $20,000 and the buyer owned his own business with no money down, assuming the seller's liabilities instead.

This strategy underscores an important point made earlier. While a seller wants cash from the deal, a seller doesn't necessarily care where his money comes from. You can borrow it from a bank, your Aunt Matilda or his creditors. Your job is to show the seller how he can raise the money he wants for his business, even if the cash is to come from his own business.

Does all this seem too slick? Who was cheated on that record shop deal? Nobody. The creditors will eventually get their money, even if it takes a bit longer. The seller received exactly the $20,000 he demanded. The big winner? The no cash down buyer, of course.

Journey back to the compelling statistic I shared with you at the beginning of this chapter. The typical business generates enough cash in the two or three weeks before or after the sale to equal the down payment necessary to buy that business. Your down payment can be as close as the cash register if you're smart enough to know how it can help you ring up that one big sale!

KEY POINTS TO REMEMBER

1. Use cash flow to buy your business. The average business generates enough cash in a two or three week period to cover its down payment.

2. Offer the seller a short term note instead of a cash down payment, then pay it from the cash flow of the business.

3. Calculate the cash flow potential carefully. The success of your deal depends on it.

4. Increase cash flow by increasing sales. It can shorten the period the seller must wait for his money and thus reduce seller resistance.

5. Let the seller take his down payment from the business. It's far better than taking it from you!

11

Twelve More No Cash Down Techniques

Your down payment may be staring you right in the face and yet you may have trouble spotting it. It doesn't look like money, but it can be just as good if you have the imagination and know-how to make it work for you.

In this chapter you'll see how you can transform "hidden assets" into immediate cash to finance your down payment. Every business has hidden assets, but the trick is to spot those with cash conversion potential. They can be turned into instant money to finance your down payment.

You may see "cash-raising" possibilities never considered by the seller. After all, sellers can be short-sighted. They have been so close to their businesses for so long that they may not realize the potential gold mine locked up in their hidden assets.

Let them sit on their assets. Sellers may not need instant cash, but you do. And that is precisely why you should always consider the hidden assets of any business deal as a creative way of raising the down payment.

Perhaps "hidden" is a misnomer. The asset may be in plain view. Perhaps it's excess inventory, which is certainly visible. Possibly it's a large machine collecting dust in a far corner. That too is hard to miss. When I use the word "hidden" I give it a different meaning. I define a hidden asset as any asset, whether tangible or intangible, that can somehow be turned into a cash generator.

The ability to convert hidden assets into a down payment has always fascinated me, particularly considering that the list of potential "cash conversion" assets seems endless. Just when you think all the possibilities have been exhausted, another imaginative buyer finds another clever way to create cash.

AN "INSTANT MONEY" CHECKLIST

What assets do sharp buyers look for? Use this convenient checklist the next time you scout a business.

- Excess inventory
- Disposable fixtures and equipment
- Concession space possibilities
- Customer lists
- Trademarks and patent rights
- Distributor territories
- Advertising and display space available to rent
- Real estate and leases that can be sold or assigned
- Parking areas to sublet

- Subsidiary spinoffs
- Prepaid subscriptions or enrollments and other customer financing
- Excess motor vehicles
- Credit rating to borrow or raise cash
- Supplier credits due

Consult this list as you engineer your takeover. Let's review how these items can be turned into cash and your down payment.

EXCESS INVENTORY

Look for excess inventory first. It's the most common hidden asset you can tap for a down payment. Observe how one shrewd buyer turned excess inventory into a $20,000 down payment for a prosperous gift shop grossing $300,000 a year. The seller demanded a total price of $100,000 based on a $70,000 inventory. The seller would finance $80,000 with a $20,000 down payment. Barry knew that the inventory could be reduced to $50,000 without hurting sales, so he proposed a simple but effective proposition to the seller, asking the seller to run a sale and reduce inventory by $20,000. The $20,000 cash thus generated by the sale would go to the seller in place of the down payment, and the price reduced accordingly. Using this inventory reduction gambit the buyer walked in without investing a dime of his own.

Turning inventory into cash represents a common method of exploiting excess inventory as a hidden asset. However, a "simultaneous sell-off" can be an equally effective technique. With it you locate a buyer in a similar business who agrees to buy excess inventory from you at the time of sale. All you do is exchange checks. Unfortunately, with the "sell-off" method you often must sell below your wholesale cost. With a gradual inventory work-down you can usually obtain a far better price.

One of the most imaginative no cash down deals involved a furniture store with stock jampacked from basement to rafters. The seller posted a $1 million price based on an estimated $800,000 inventory, and wanted $150,000 down with the balance paid over five years. Along came two promotional-minded young men without a dime in their pockets but a plan that could satisfy the seller's and their own objectives. They informed the seller that they would pay him not $150,000 down but $250,000, if the seller would accept a deal where this amount would be paid in five monthly installments of $50,000 following the closing. To protect the seller, all sales receipts would be deposited in an escrow account requiring the seller's signature for withdrawal.

Once the seller consented, the buyers ran a spectacular inventory clearance sale. Within the following five months the new partners sold over $350,000 in excess inventory, paid the seller his $250,000 and had another $100,000 to cover expenses and provide working capital.

The steps for converting inventory into a down payment are easy. First determine the amount of excess inventory, and then either you or the seller work off the excess inventory in place of a down payment, with proceeds going to the seller. Alternatively, you line up a buyer to take over excess inventory at the time of closing.

Whenever you consider excess inventory as a way to your down payment, you have some interesting statistics on your side. A study conducted by Northeastern University discloses that 45 percent of all retail stores studied have an inventory at least 20 percent in excess of that needed to maintain sales. Wholesale and distributor firms averaged just slightly lower. Think of it. Almost one out of every two businesses may have your down payment sitting idle on the shelf.

MAKE CAPITAL ASSETS WORK FOR YOU

Now that you see the possibilities with excess inventory, you can see how you can tap equipment and real estate in much the same way for a down payment. The "sale-leaseback" is one of the most common techniques. For example, a small family owned landscaping company recently sold for $75,000. Its assets consisted of three trucks, assorted gardening equipment with an approximate value of $25,000 and the good will of 100 accounts providing a seasonal volume of $125,000. The seller asked $75,000 for the business with $25,000 down. At the time of closing the buyer sold the trucks to a physician friend in a high tax bracket for $25,000. The physician, in turn, leased the trucks back to the buyer for a monthly rental of $500. The $25,000 down payment and a $50,000 note for the balance was handed to the seller. Since the seller gave up some loan security by agreeing to the truck sale (the trucks would have been additional collateral for the note), the buyer gave the seller a second mortgage on his home. The score? The seller had his $25,000 down payment and a fully secured note for the balance. The physician had a tax break from the depreciation on the trucks, and the buyer had his landscaping company with no cash down.

The sale-leaseback is common with any type equipment and real estate, but it works particularly well with computers, high technology items, material-handling equipment and motor vehicles.

Time sharing on essential but underutilized high-cost equipment presents another way to raise a down payment. Whether it be a computer or a printing press that remains idle 50 percent of the time, why not rent it when it's not working for you? If you have a $50,000 piece of equipment with capacity to handle three times the work you demand from it, you may be able to charge others as much as $25,000 to $30,000 a year in rental fees.

Time sharing can get you up-front money for your down payment if you know how to get your time sharing customers to prepay the rental fee. Here's how it works. Assume that the business has a piece of equipment that can be time shared with another company. It is agreed that the annual rental or time sharing cost would be $24,000 for the year. Now ordinarily that would be paid at the rate of $2,000 a month. That routine won't finance your down payment, although it is a smart move to increase profits once you own the business. So say to the customer, "Pay the first year's rent in advance and I'll discount the rent by 20 percent." The customer saves $4,800 and you immediately have your hands on $19,200 to hand over to the seller.

TURN INTANGIBLE ASSETS INTO TANGIBLE CASH

More than one enterprising fellow financed the total purchase price of a business through imaginative exploitation of intangible assets. Here's a classic story that shows the potential cash generating powers of those intangible assets. Ralph's story goes back to 1975, when he came upon a company that manufactured artificial brick used for interior walls and household decoration. The business produced over $3 million a year in sales. It distributed its product through lumber yards and major hardware chains. Since the buyer could assume existing bank loans for $400,000, all he needed was a $150,000 down payment on the purchase price of $550,000.

The $150,000 down payment was a big stumbling block for Ralph, who didn't have enough money to buy a new car. But that didn't discourage him. He discovered instant cash that closed the deal in hidden intangible assets. Here's how he performed his miracle. First, Ralph learned that the company held international patent rights to the artificial brick-making process. Armed with this information he lined up a Japanese company to license the patent rights for Japan for an advance payment of $100,000 plus a royalty of 5 percent of all Japanese sales. Ralph next turned the mailing lists into cash. Over the prior five years, the company had accumulated more than 600,000 names of customers inquiring about the bricks. Who could benefit from these lists? Ralph rightfully reasoned that they could be valuable to companies selling related items to homeowners and handymen. He duplicated 50 lists and sold each for $3,000 plus duplication costs, netting $150,000.

When Ralph learned that no product of similar quality was competitively priced in Canada, Ralph negotiated for a Canadian distributor to pay $75,000 for Canadian distribution rights. Flushed with victory over the Canadian deal, Ralph next focused attention on Mexico, where he arranged a similar agreement with a Mexican concern for $50,000 up front. Now Ralph had $375,000 in income committed, more than enough to finance the $150,000 down payment.

But there's more to the story. The brick company also held exclusive rights to distribute a special cement filler within the United States. After Ralph analyzed shipping costs to markets west of the Mississippi, he proved such sales incurred a loss to the company. Undaunted, he found a west coast company anxious to penetrate this market and willing to pay $150,000 and a percentage of sales for subdistribution rights.

Ralph had converted intangible assets into a colossal $525,000, yet that's still not the end of the story. Ralph imagined all the "do-it-yourselfers" who would gladly pay to learn how to install artificial brick in their own homes and avoid expensive labor costs, so he announced seminars at local high schools. More than 3,000 homeowners flocked to the courses for the small admission price of $10 each. This $30,000 income less modest expenses boosted Ralph to $550,000 or the full purchase price of his new business. And you'll note Ralph didn't give away anything essential to his future success. In fact, each transaction not only put money in Ralph's pocket, it also potentially improved the future sales or profitability of the company.

Certainly Ralph worked like a madman, and he was blessed with loads of imagination. And luckily the seller gave him the leeway to negotiate the deals he needed before the closing.

Today the young brick manufacturer grosses $9 million a year with profits of $1 million. Invisible assets can be pure gold for those smart enough to strike the right mine.

A GOOD LEASE CAN BE A BANKABLE ITEM

Look carefully at your target business. What is its major asset? No, it may not be the thousands of dollars in overstock merchandise, nor those modern and glistening fixtures, but its location. Without location, business assets might as well be auctioned for a dime on the dollar. The right location can turn most businesses into a thriving moneymaker. A lease gives you the location, and a lease, believe it or not, can help you raise the down payment for your business.

Portland Maine's Long sisters developed a successful approach while negotiating to add to their existing seven store chain, a large suburban supermarket located in a small nearby town. Actually, the store was not a typical supermarket but a modern "general store," selling everything from jogging shoes to antifreeze. The store listed for $325,000 with $125,000 down. Either the seller or a local bank would finance the $200,000 balance. Although the Long sisters had already made a small fortune and could easily raise the down payment, they enjoyed the challenge of another no cash down deal.

The supermarket's fine location provided that opportunity. After visiting several local banks, the Long's persuaded one bank to rent space within the supermarket for a bank concession at $35,000 a year for five years. The Longs would drop the rent to $25,000 if the bank paid the entire rent in advance. With the advance rent in hand, the Longs acquired their eighth supermarket without spending a cent of their own. And over the years the bank concession substantially increased store traffic, thus greatly enhancing profits for the supermarket.

It's an easy concept to follow. Enter into an advance agreement to sublease part of your rented space, collecting the rent in advance (at a discount if necessary) and apply it towards the down payment. It can work for countless businesses. A pharmacy near a major hospital concessions space to a florist, a discount store leases space to a luncheonette and a luggage shop rents space to a travel agency. Only your imagination limits the possibilities.

Sometimes outside space can produce even greater opportunity. An outdoor billboard helped raised the down payment on a car dealership for sale for $150,000 with $50,000 down. The buyer, Paul, searched fruitlessly for the necessary cash. Day in and day out he beat the bushes, but could find no one to invest, lend or advance the $50,000 down payment. Gazing out the window of the car dealership Paul noticed thousands of cars speeding by on the elevated expressway overhead. A thought struck him. Who would pay for a billboard on the roof of the dealership? The advertiser would enjoy 100 percent visibility from this high traffic highway. Without revealing his intentions to the seller, the buyer negotiated from him a lease for the rights to the roof and air space above and the seller agreed to a delay in rental payment for three months on the lease. Paul quickly turned around and negotiated a five year lease with a major billboard company bargaining an advance payment of $50,000. Paul now has his dealership. He was smart, but perhaps not smart enough. A year later the billboard company erected an ad for a competing car agency.

Even an idle parking lot can be turned into immediate cash. A semi-retired couple literally turned a parking lot into a thriving restaurant with a volume of $500,000. Their story started when they came across a restaurant for sale for $150,000 and $30,000 down. The restaurant, right on one of the busiest beaches near Portsmouth, New Hampshire, offered fabulous potential. The buyer lined up a young married couple interested in leasing the parking lot each day during the summer months. At 5 p.m. the space would revert to the new restaurant owners, who opened for business at that time. The couple agreed to lease the space for $15,000 for each of two summer seasons. With the lease in hand, our client pledged it to a bank who loaned them $15,000. With an additional $15,000 raised from other no cash down sources, the industrious restauranteurs are now busy in their second career.

MORE HIDDEN ASSETS TO LOOK FOR

Accounts receivable can also help finance your down payment in many different ways. Let's take a typical business with ordinary receivables and see how it might work. Suppose the seller wants $100,000 for the business, $50,000 for inventory, $10,000 for fixtures, $10,000 for receivables and $30,000 for good will. The seller demands a $20,000 down payment. How can the receivables replace half the down payment?

One solution is to give the seller the accounts receivable and thus shave $10,000 from the price and down payment. The receivables will turn into cash for the seller within 30 to 60 days, and you will not have the chore of collecting them yourself.

Alternatively, you can "factor" the accounts receivable. Through factoring you sell the receivables to a factor who will immediately pay about 90 percent of their face value depending on how they are sold. If sold on a "recourse" basis, the seller guarantees their collectability, while on a "non-recourse" basis the factor takes all the risk. Even in the latter case the receivables would generate about $9,000 cash for the seller, and thus justify a corresponding decrease in down payment.

DON'T OVERLOOK MOTOR VEHICLES

Another hidden asset to investigate is motor vehicles. Does the company own cars or trucks? Are there any loans against them? If unencumbered you have an easy job. Determine how much you can borrow against them, obtain a loan commitment and use the proceeds toward your down payment.

Vehicle financing helped one young entrepreneur take over a laundry company. The seller asked $70,000 for the company with $30,000 down. The buyer simply arranged to borrow against the four delivery trucks to fund his no cash down deal.

If motor vehicles comprise a substantial part of your business assets you may have just the opportunity you need. Do a quick analysis. Does the company really need all the trucks it owns? Can you refinance the vehicles? Most businesses do not pledge vehicles as collateral for general business loans and therefore even if the business has a mortgage against other assets its vehicles are probably unpledged. Under this situation you can borrow against vehicles.

Vehicles are also prime for sale-leaseback arrangements. Look for a buyer in a high tax bracket, sell him the trucks for immediate cash and then lease the trucks from him.

LET YOUR CUSTOMERS BUY YOUR BUSINESS FOR YOU

Are you considering buying or opening a business that serves a particular market or group of customers? Does your target business offer a product or service that's greatly needed or unique? If you answer yes to either of these questions, you may take advantage of customer financing.

Several years ago I was involved in a classic example of customer financing. Throughout the country drug cooperatives were organized to buy promotional merchandise and coordinate the promotional programs for participating drugstores. Although the stores were individually owned, each advertised under the group name and logo. Collectively the stores could command better prices for merchandise and the concentrated advertising effort of a group of stores beat the small uncoordinated ads of individual pharmacies in drawing power. An idea whose time had come, thirty such co-ops soon prospered throughout the country.

Then we developed the idea for a "super co-op," or a "co-op of co-ops," that would buy for all member groups. After all, if a local co-op representing 100 stores worked better than any one member store, it only stood to reason that the super co-op representing many co-ops could do even better.

The "super co-op" founders obtained capital by charging each of the participating co-ops a $20,000 entry fee and in addition a percentage of purchases thereafter. Finding money for this business was no problem, and today the business grosses many millions of dollars.

You can apply the same concept to less grandiose schemes. For example, a canteen service was entirely financed by customers scattered along its route. This canteen service was the only one serving a large industrial park located in a desolate area far outside the city. Since the average American worker cannot survive the day without a coffee break, a young promoter decided to corner the market but needed $40,000 for the truck, equipment and supplies. He next convinced each industrial plant in the park to provide him an outright $500 grant plus a non-interest loan, based on their number of employees. The companies benefited from happier employees while the young promoter had his no cash down business.

There are hundreds of examples of how customers, as the major hidden asset of a business, helped finance the startup or acquisition. Here are a few more examples that can illuminate your path:

- Advance orders on a stock market newsletter allowed its publisher to obtain the funds needed to print and mail his first three issues.

- A flea market promoter rented "stalls" collecting advance rents, and generated sufficient cash to lease a drive-in movie for weekend flea market promotions. He now clears $40,000 each summer.

- A company boasting a new veterinary formula for curing a common livestock disease was quickly capitalized by advance orders from thousands of ranchers.

Having customers "front-load" your startup or acquisition costs has enormous potential. Take a lesson from American Express. They have millions of card holders, and each pays a hefty membership fee to belong. Multiple this fee by the number of card holders and you get some idea what advance payments from customers can do to raise cash. And it can do the same for you. Just ask yourself that one question. What customers would pay you in advance?

So far in this chapter we have been talking about converting assets into cash for your down payment. But how can you control an asset you do not yet own, and turn it into cash at the precise moment of closing? The mechanics depend largely on the nature of the transaction.

It's usually best to let the seller in on your plans. Be candid because you may require the seller's assistance. Discussions with others about assets you have yet to purchase can filter back to the seller, who may logically resent your wheeling and dealing with her property.

TURN A BROKER'S COMMISSION
INTO A DOWN PAYMENT

A broker's commission can be the answer to at least half your problem. Here's why. The typical seller usually expects less than 30 percent of the sales price as a down payment. But bear in mind that's only an expectation. If you study completed deals, you'll find the average down payment to be less than 20 percent as a result of negotiation. The buyer conventionally raises the other 80 percent from a bank or seller financing. Your job is to somehow reduce the 20 percent to zero.

Surprisingly, the source of that 20 percent may be sitting right there at the negotiating table with you. Look around. You see the seller to your left, but overlook him for a minute. Next to him sits his lawyer. Don't look for his help. But turn to your right. The person with the big smile on her face is the business broker. She wants to put together a deal as badly as you do, so she can walk away with a 10 percent commission check in her pocket. Think about that for a moment. If you are after a $100,000 business for which you need $20,000 down, the seller will simultaneously fork over to the broker $10,000, or 50 percent of your down payment.

Why be afraid to ask the broker to help finance your down payment with her commission, thereby cutting your cash needs in half? Why should the broker lend you her commission? One good reason is that if she doesn't the deal might collapse, leaving her with nothing for a commission. Most brokers would rather "loan" their commission than lose it altogether.

I've seen broker financing help close hundreds of deals, but, as with everything else, timing and approach are crucial. Broker financing will not work if the broker thinks you can raise the down payment from other sources. She'll rightfully insist she's not in the finance business. But once you convince her there is no other way the deal can go through, she'll probably agree to cooperate.

Play fair with the broker. She must make a living too. Agree to pay her back within a reasonably short time with fair interest. Secure her "loan" with whatever collateral the business can provide. Since brokers handle two-thirds of all businesses sold, opportunities for broker financing are likely.

You can use this concept even without a broker if you play "let's pretend" with the seller. One veteran of the game, Sam, has plenty of money but fancies himself a top-notch negotiator. In fact, he's one of the best. Sam had previously taken over two restaurants, in each instance obtaining broker financing. On his third deal, a $200,000 restaurant, Sam discovered he couldn't use broker financing since no broker was involved. Since Sam could not turn to the broker to assist with the down payment, Sam's attention turned instead to the seller, an equally sharp and crusty wheeler-dealer. After three testy hours of intense negotiation Sam reduced the price to $175,000 with $20,000 down. Then Sam played "let's pretend." Turning to the seller he said, "If a broker were involved in this deal you would have to pay a $17,500 commission, right? Of my $20,000 down payment you'd receive only $2,500. Let's pretend a broker is involved. Reduce the price by $17,500 and the down payment to $2,500 and I'll sign the papers this afternoon." "Are you nuts?" blurted the seller. "I agreed to $175,000 with $20,000 down because no broker is involved."

Sam sat back and smiled. "True, but a sharp seller like you would have squeezed the broker to lower his commission. Even so you would have agreed to sell for a price that would have netted you, after commission, something less than $175,000 or $20,000 down. Who knows what you'd end up with after a three-way negotiation. Why don't we compromise? Make it $170,000 with $10,000 down." When the seller finally caved in, Sam had his third restaurant. And Sam did not pay the $10,000. He instead persuaded the cigarette vending company, anxious to place a high volume machine at the restaurant, to advance the necessary cash.

Sam's strategy was simple. He reduced the price and down payment by showing the seller how much less he may have settled for had a broker been involved. Why shouldn't the buyer share the benefit of not using a broker? Don't forget that a broker can be your partner in the down payment.

PYRAMID YOUR CREDIT INTO A DOWN PAYMENT

Everyone has some borrowing power, but the "multiple-loan" game can legally and easily increase your borrowing power five to ten times, so let's see how a multiple-loan game works. Suppose you find a business you want, but after exploring every source of financing, you find you still need $10,000. Though you have limited personal assets, you are confident you can obtain a $2,000 bank loan. If one bank will lend you $2,000 on the strength of your signature, five banks should collectively loan you $10,000.

However, there's a trick to it. If you already had a loan, you would have to disclose that liability to other banks, who would believe you had exhausted your borrowing power and deny your loan. But if you instead apply to the five banks simultaneously, you can truthfully state you have no other outstanding loan, and effectively increase your borrowing power five-fold.

A word of caution. Always review loan applications with your lawyer. Answer all questions honestly, for false statements can get you into big trouble. However, until banks redesign their applications to include the question "Loans applied for" you might turn a "shoestring" into a shoe store.

Name the type of business you want. How much cash would you need for a down payment? How much of that could you borrow from a bank on your signature alone? If you need $15,000 but your present borrowing power is only $3,000, you might benefit from the pyramid strategy. Within three months your signature alone might help you raise $15,000 once you know how to pyramid your credit rating. Follow these five easy steps:

- Apply for a $3,000 loan payable in 30 days at a local bank.

- Take the loan proceeds and place it in a high-interest account at another bank.

- In 25 days withdraw the $3,000 and pay off your loan at your first bank.

- Now you're ready to start pyramiding. Two weeks later return to the first bank and apply for a $6,000 loan. You'll probably obtain it because you have proven credit reliability. Now invest the $6,000 and pay back the loan in 25 days.

- In the third month repeat the entire process with a $10,000 loan. Once you pay it ahead of schedule the bank will be delighted to lend you $15,000. Each loan fortifies your credit rating and your borrowing power grows.

What will it cost you to increase your borrowing power five fold? In terms of effort, all it costs is several trips to the nearest bank. You'll pay a few dollars difference between interest earned on the savings and interest charged on the loans. In the above example, the actual cost of interest would be less than $200, but that could be the wisest $200 investment you can make, for it will give you the borrowing power you need, when you need it, to land a business that over the years may increase your earnings by hundreds of thousands of dollars.

Unfortunately, many people have poor borrowing power only because they haven't developed a strong credit history. Yet, the majority of unsecured loans are not turned down because the borrower isn't creditworthy, but because he hasn't proven himself creditworthy. No credit history, like a bad credit history, means no loan.

THE GRADUAL TAKEOVER

Key employees often take over their employer's business with no cash down through a gradual takeover. This approach works beautifully with a seller approaching retirement age who wants to gradually relinquish ownership and responsibility, as so many owners do.

Ben, a loyal manager, used this technique to buy his prosperous Los Angeles furniture store. Working for ten years as a stock clerk, Ben advanced over the years to sales manager. When the owner turned 62, he decided it was time to cut down his working hours and enjoy more leisure time. Although the owner wanted $200,000 for the business, he was flexible on the down payment as he did not need immediate funds.

Ben wisely proposed the gradual takeover. Under his plan, Ben offered to buy 5 percent of the shares of stock in the company each year for ten years. Ben would be able to pay the annual $10,000 price partially out of his own earnings, and the balance from his share of accrued profits. At the end of ten years, Ben would pay the owner the $100,000 balance, and Ben would then own 100 percent of the company. Since the furniture store owned twice the assets necessary to collateralize a $100,000 loan, Ben would have sufficient equity to borrow the needed money. The deal satisfied both parties objectives because:

- The owner retained control of the business for the first ten years. When he reached 72 he could completely retire and collect Social Security.

- The owner would receive $10,000 a year toward the purchase price, while still drawing a salary and other owner benefits.

- The business was presold. The owner needn't worry about finding a buyer when he finally wanted to retire.

- Over the first ten years, the seller could confidently relinquish management control because Ben's own financial success rested his on skillful management of the store.

- Ben would wind up with his own business with no down payment.

If you're an employee who wants to own the business you now work in, keep these benefits in mind. Every year thousands of small businesses go up for sale for retirement reasons. Few successful business owners want to go directly from full time work to full time leisure. Most prefer to gradually slow down. In these instances, the gradual takeover may be the perfect solution for both you and the seller.

LIFE INSURANCE CAN FINANCE YOUR BUSINESS

Few people realize life insurance finances almost as many business acquisitions as bank loans. No, I'm not talking about cashing in your policy or knocking on Prudential's door. I am talking about a little known but highly advantageous technique called "partnership buy-out insurance."

This is how it works. Jill and Joan own a business with a net worth of $50,000. Jill takes out a life insurance policy on her life for $25,000 and names Joan as beneficiary. The women agree that upon Jill's death, Joan will purchase her partner's interest and pay Jill's estate the $25,000 she receives from the insurance. Joan will make the same arrangement with Jill. Best of all, both partners pay the premiums from the business, producing a nice tax deductible expense.

This same approach works equally well between employee and employer. Consider Harry, who purchased a prosperous auto body shop from Angelo, who was getting along in years and wanted $75,000 for his shop. Harry worked for Angelo seven years, so the two men had developed a strong friendship. Angelo agreed to sell to his friend Harry if the sale could occur upon Angelo's death. Angelo then bought a $75,000 life insurance policy, naming Harry as beneficiary. Since Harry would benefit from the policy, Harry agreed to pay the premiums. Three years later Angelo died. When Harry received the $75,000 insurance proceeds he paid the money to Angelo's estate in return for ownership of the business. With this strategy Angelo's heirs didn't have to worry about selling his business as they immediately received $75,000 for it under the existing agreement, and in turn, Harry acquired the shop for the price of three years' insurance premiums.

Perhaps you can combine the gradual buy-out with a life insurance plan. For example, Ben could have instead negotiated a life insurance plan to finance the immediate acquisition of the furniture store upon the seller's death. If you are that employee with a strong desire to take over your boss' business, contact a life insurance specialist, who may be able to put together a no cash down deal the seller can't refuse.

LEASE A BUSINESS—A NEW TAKE-OVER TREND

Ownership isn't everything. You can often reap the same benefits from leasing a business as from buying it. And you may receive one added advantage: Leasing can eliminate your down payment problem. People lease cars, apartments and equipment with no cash down, so why not a business?

Many businesses lend themselves to leasing or purchasing on lease terms. Broadly speaking they are service businesses whose limited assets are fixtures and equipment, such as gas stations, printing plants, car washes, auto part stores, laundries and vending machine routes. These businesses can be easily leased because the seller doesn't have to worry about turning over inventory to you. Whether you turn the company into a smashing success or not, the owner has the security of knowing his assets won't depreciate in value and can be easily reclaimed.

How might such a strategy work? Follow this example. Jack wanted to buy a small vending business consisting of six computer games at various retail locations. The seller wanted $25,000 with $15,000 down with the seller financing the $10,000 balance at 15 percent over three years. A $15,000 loan existed against the machines and the seller would use the down payment to pay it off. Jack did not have $15,000, so he offered instead to assume the seller's $15,000 loan. Although that seemed sensible, the seller rejected the idea as he had personally guaranteed the note and would remain liable if Jack defaulted. Jack then approached the lending bank and asked them to rewrite the note in Jack's name. Since Jack's credit was poor, the bank refused. The deal was on the verge of collapsing when Jack hit upon an alternative: leasing with an option to buy. Jack proposed to lease the machines for three years in such a way that the rent would equal the monthly payments due the bank plus the $10,000 due the seller. At any time during the three year period Jack could exercise an option to purchase the machines for the balance of the note due the bank plus the balance of the seller's $10,000. Mathematically it added up the same way as under the original terms, but Jack's plan allowed the seller to retain title to the equipment until Jack had either fully paid for it or exercised the purchase option. If Jack missed a payment, the seller could immediately cancel the lease.

Jack eventually bought the computer games and went on to expand to 15 machines that now gross $250,000 a year. Without the lease-option alternative, Jack would still be a salaried employee.

Does leasing seem to be an indirect way to pick up a business? It may, but in some situations it's the only alternative. If equipment is heavily mortgaged, a seller cannot sell it without the consent of the mortgage holder, but he can lease it. If the buyer can't pay off or assume the mortgage, he has no choice but to lease, and in effect the buyer leased himself a business.

DO YOU THINK MONEY GROWS ON TREES?

I do. At one of my seminars I met an ingenious chap who put together the weirdest amalgamation of no cash down techniques I have seen and ended up with ownership of a franchised donut shop grossing $480,000 a year. Here's how he did it.

Last winter a six acre piece of land located on a major highway came up for sale. Henry spotted it and knew it would be the perfect location for his donut shop. The only problem was the $160,000 price. Since it was raw land, financing 100 percent would be impossible. Nevertheless, Henry gave the seller $1,000 to hold the land for 60 days. Next he found a firewood company to buy all the timber on the land for $20,000, with the timber to be removed once Henry took title. Henry then found a buyer who agreed to pay $80,000 for two acres of the land, leaving Henry four other acres. Henry was hardly through. The donut franchisor agreed to buy his four acres for $120,000 then lease it back to him, complete with a turnkey donut shop to be constructed by the franchisor, all for an annual rent of $22,000. Now Henry had commitments for $220,000 on land that would cost him only $160,000. Henry knew just how to wheel and deal with property he didn't own. With $220,000 in hand he easily paid the $160,000 price, pocketing $60,000 as profit, and was soon in business with a thriving franchised donut shop. Where others saw trees, Henry saw money. Sometimes money does grow on trees!

All the Henrys in this book share a common trait. They don't sit back and wait for somebody to come by and drop a bundle of cash at their feet. Wishing is for dreamers. Those who really want their own business never let lack of money stand in their way. They always have what it takes to grab the initiative and find ways to make it happen. And as any one of these now successful people would say—"there's a way into every deal, and every deal has its way."

KEY POINTS TO REMEMBER

1. Brokers end up with a big slice of every down payment. Why not ask them to loan you some of it?

2. You can increase your borrowing power by playing the multiple-loan game.

3. Talk to your boss about selling. He may just be willing to give up gradual ownership.

4. If you can't buy, consider leasing. It works for many types of businesses.

5. Lock up the lease. It's better than a down payment.

6. Prepaid deposits can give you all you need to buy or start a solid business.

7. There's a way into every deal—and every deal has its way.

8. Don't overlook hidden assets. They can often be turned into the cash you need to buy the business.

12

Negotiating to Win

Wouldn't it be great to possess the sophistication of Henry Kissinger, the wit of Will Rogers, the financial genius of J. Paul Getty and the persuasive power of Dale Carnegie? Even if you did, you wouldn't necessarily negotiate more effectively because you must necessarily bring to the bargaining table your own unique personality and skills. No matter how many books on the subject you read, negotiation ultimately boils down to one objective: winning what you want from someone else while convincing him he's getting what he wants. You can best accomplish that objective through your own unique style.

Successfully negotiating a no cash down deal is no different than negotiating any other deal. First you must discover what the seller wants, then you must determine how to best satisfy his needs while achieving your own goal of not investing your money. To succeed you must first understand the seller's point of view and bargain with his position in mind.

This lesson is underscored with the dramatic tale of a small Manhattan tailor shop. One day a developer bought the building housing the tiny shop and announced his intention to demolish the building and construct in its place a high-rise condominium complex. The aged building housed numerous small shops as tenants, and most had three to five year leases yet to expire. To empty the building and prepare it for demolition, the developer generously offered each tenant $3,000 plus full moving expenses in exchange for their lease cancellation. All but one quickly accepted. Max, the shrewd tailor, wanted no part of the deal. Frustrated, the developer raised his offer to $5,000 and one year's free rent in any other building of his choice. Still Max the tailor said, "Not interested!" Despite increasing offers that eventually topped $25,000, the tailor remained adamant. Finally, the exasperated developer asked, "Max, what do you want?" Quietly the tailor replied, "$500,000." The developer choked. "How dare you demand $500,000 to vacate this crummy little shop? You pay only $175 a month rent." "Why not?" countered the tailor. "I hold a lease, so you can't evict me for five years. Unless I agree to move, you can't demolish your building and build your high-rise. I figure it will cost you at least $1 million in lost income over the next five years should I decide to stay. But I'm not greedy. I only want half of what I'll save you by giving up the lease." The tailor soon had his $500,000.

The moral of the story? While other tenants thought only in terms of what was important to them, our friend Max focused on the developer's position. What does he want? What's in it for him? How can I parlay his needs into a better deal for me? Max shrewdly bargained from the seller's position.

Successfully negotiating no cash down deals requires careful preparation so you fully know the seller's position. You must investigate every fact necessary to exploit that position. Then you must design tactics that will strengthen your own bargaining position. You may call it a game, but always remember the stakes. It's a game that you can't afford to lose if you need no cash down terms.

But before you can successfully jump into your first no cash down deal, you must first know how to play the basic game of buying a business. You can then sharpen your skills to concentrate on no cash down terms.

If the process of buying a business mystifies you, don't despair; you have plenty of company. Few people buy more than one business in their lifetime. By the same token, few people sell more than one business in their lifetime. So if you need to match wits with a seller, chances are he won't know any more about selling than you do about buying. Most business deals involve two rookie players, one wanting to sell and one wanting to buy, while the ever-present coaches—the accountants and lawyers—yell advice from the sidelines. Perhaps a business broker plays referee and keeps the game in motion until he walks away with a hefty commission check.

Who will win? Of course each side declares himself the winner when the papers are signed, but only time will tell who really won or lost. When the seller hands you the bill of sale he acknowledges his satisfaction with the deal. If he bargained to sell for $100,000 he can declare himself the winner when the $100,000 is paid, unless the business perhaps increases in value overnight to $200,000. Then the seller is back in the loser's corner.

But your final score depends less on the deal you initially carve than on what success you achieve with the business. Tens of thousands of buyers have fumbled when negotiating to buy the business, but nevertheless won far larger stakes by making a great deal of money from the very day they received the keys. Still, you'll come out far ahead if you can strike the best deal possible when negotiating to buy the business.

TACKLING SELLERS AS THEY PULL THEIR PREDICTABLE PLAYS

Sellers come in all shapes and sizes, and most, in one fashion or another, play the same silly games. Why not? They want your money or as much of it as they can possibly squeeze out of you. So study this lineup of characteristic seller plays and negotiating postures.

The "I Don't Want to Sell" Tactic

This common play is almost a religious ritual preceding every sale. You spot an interesting business in the paper and pay the seller a visit. There he sits with his hands folded behind his head as he mumbles, "I don't really want to sell, but as long as you're here I'll listen to what you have to say."

This negotiating play is designed to intimidate you and immediately put you on the defensive. There he is, the rich, successful seller as he languishes in his money tree listening to you grovel for his business. No matter how many months he spent beating each bush for a buyer, he shrewdly attempts to keep the upper hand.

I first fell victim to the "I don't want to" seller nearly twenty years ago when I was a young rookie player. My prey was a large gift shop that I was anxious to buy with two equally "rookie" partners. What a sorry sight we were. The seller, a real veteran of the playing field, immediately had us fall victim to his never ending protestations about not wanting to sell. His wife was another "don't want to" type. Between them we became convinced they must have a real money maker as they were holding on to their business so tightly. For weeks we chased to buy the business. We did everything but beg, although from time to time I could hear whimpers from one or two of my partners. Tripping over ourselves to buy the business, the ante kept going up and up. Playing hard to get paid big dividends for this savvy seller. In retrospect we probably paid twice as much for the business than was necessary had we been smart enough to see through his posturing.

This lesson was learned the hard way—with hard cash. But I never forgot this important lesson. Now when I come against this type seller I know how to handle it. I listen and then quietly inform the seller that I too wasn't seriously interested in buying, but "if you are willing to sell in a hurry, I might be interested in picking up a business such as this at the right price." It's the only way to bring the "don't wanna" seller tumbling down from his high perch.

The "I've Lots of Interested Buyers" Play

This master intimidator also enjoys playing hard to get and will get you bidding against yourself every time. Of course, the other "interested buyers" are merely wishful thinking, but what you don't know can't hurt him. And it can indeed look like the real thing as he arranges phony telephone calls from his secretary, engaging in a one-sided conversation with yet another "anxious buyer." Be patient, if you play a few rounds of the game you're bound to come across this type.

My advice? Never worry about other "interested buyers" and never concern yourself with who may "outbid" you. Let the seller know that you can't worry about other buyers. Besides, two can play the same game. There's more than one business to buy. Use one-upsmanship. Hand the seller your business card and tell him to call you when things quiet down, and expect a call no later than the next morning.

The "Just Testing" Gambit

Unfair as it is, some sellers play "let's pretend." They pretend their business is for sale and waste your time and money. They may go down to the wire with you but never quite sign. Why? There are several possible reasons. They may want assurances their business is saleable at a given price. Others honestly think they want to sell, but suffer from their own emotional roadblocks when it comes time to pack up and leave it all behind. Still others simply enjoy the game of "selling" but never intend to relinquish the ball. Finally, we come to the seller who plays "let's pretend" and offers his business for sale at an exorbitant price. Should he find a sucker, he'll indeed sell, but not for a penny less.

The "tester" is a most dangerous player. He can drive you absolutely crazy; and it's almost impossible to spot him for what he is until it's too late.

I have found only one method to successfully ferret out the true sellers from the tester. The tester never spends money to play the game. The solution: Should you suspect you're up against a tester, ask him to have his attorney draw up a contract for you to review. That, of course, means money out of his pocket. This is when the tester knows it's time to quit the game.

Are there other fiendish players on the field with still other games to play? Sure, but with a little experience you'll be able to handle anything they can throw at you. And after all the posturing and side-stepping is through you'll have an honest to goodness seller ready to honestly deal with you.

CLOAK AND DAGGER STORIES

Even with sincere and honest sellers you'll have your share of frustration. If you want to see real cloak an dagger stories, turn off your TV and skip the movies. They're child's play compared with what you'll experience as you try to put your deal together.

Here are several more hurdles you'll have to jump before you get to the goal line. First we come to secretive sellers. They won't show you the books and financial statements until you give a deposit. But how can you give a deposit before you check out the business? It's a vicious "no-win" cycle. But there are solutions. Put your cards on the table. Tell the seller more about yourself and your interest in the business, and he'll be more likely to open up to you. But go slowly. Sellers don't want "lookers" tipping off employees and customers that their business is for sale. Let the seller know you're a "buyer" and not just another "looker." Respect confidentiality. If the seller thinks you'll spread stories around town he'll rightfully stay as closed as a clam.

Nor should you get discouraged if negotiations bog down; because it's par for the course. Keep your anxiety level under control. Seldom do buyers and sellers move at the same speed. Some sellers make decisions at a snail's pace, while others want the deal closed "yesterday." But beware of the hard sell. If the seller is too pushy, step back and take whatever time you need to objectively evaluate matters. You may find the seller has something to be "pushy" about.

"Red tape" can also give you gray hairs, and every deal has its share. It's inevitable because the typical deal involves more than just you and the seller. For a deal to come together other interests need be satisfied—a landlord holds out for a higher rent, the deal can't close without approval from some licensing agency, a squabble develops amongst partners on the seller's side over how to share the sales proceeds. There's no end to what can delay a deal.

Patiently tackle the problems one at a time. Buying a business is a tedious process, not a sudden event.

EGOMANIA AND THE EAGER BEAVER SYNDROME

Dangerous diseases do run rampant among rookie buyers. Buyers with strong egos aren't necessarily foolish; they just do foolish things. They let their ego and emotions guide them while their intellect takes a short vacation. Successful deals depend on hard, cold and calculating objectivity.

Most first time buyers are far too anxious. Why shouldn't it be a big fantasy land? They never once met a payroll. And raw eagerness can be particularly dangerous with no cash deals, when you aren't restrained by the sobering influence of drawing your life's savings from the bank. Protect yourself from emotion and ego. Emotion is for lovers. Objectivity is for successful business people.

Egomania is easy to spot. Those who are afflicted ignore reality and can't be bothered with numbers or hard facts. Show the problems and pitfalls to such a buyer and your advice goes in one ear and out the other. Forget the aesthetics, the excitement and the glamour. You want a business for one reason—to make money. Everything else is secondary.

Related to egomania is what I call the "eager beaver" syndrome. The two diseases often strike simultaneously. Those stricken by the eager beaver syndrome not only must have their fantasy business, but they must have it today. Is there a cure? Sure, bankruptcy. But that's one cure more painful than the disease. Bankruptcy, however, does tend to help develop an immunity for the next time around.

Diagnose yourself:

- How many businesses did you consider before you decided to buy?
- What is there about the business that interests you?
- Have your advisers given the deal the green light?

You get the idea. Sit back and take that long, hard look at the deal. Buy it for all the right reasons, not the wrong ones.

With your team in place and your level-headed objectivity operating at full capacity, you're ready for the playing field and hand to hand combat against any seller.

TESTING THE WATER

Before you romp in the entrepreneurial battlefield, you'll have to resort to just about anything legal to drive the very best deal you can and neutralize the hundreds of sellers' tricks. The "Man From the East" is one of the best. You may recognize it as the "Straw Man," "Front Man" or "Pathfinder," but regardless of the title, each tests and probes the seller's position to establish a threshold from which to negotiate.

Consider the "Man From the East" your personal pathfinder as he pretends to be an interested buyer. He can offer ridiculous terms without worry he'll offend the seller and kill the deal. Should he succeed in getting the seller to concede major points, this information is now available to you. Once the "Man From the East" finishes pushing the deal as far as he can, you, as that "new interested buyer," can step right in where he left off. The water has been tested with an expendable toe. The following example demonstrates the value of the "Man From the East" far better than any textbook definition.

What is a small lounge grossing $400,000 a year worth? There's no right answer, because it ultimately depends on what willing buyers will pay. Let's say our seller places his small lounge on the market for $150,000, and you are willing to pay it. However, your willingness doesn't mean you will pay that price. Rather, you want to play the negotiating game. To psychologically position the seller, you recruit three close friends to act as "Men From the East." The first approaches the seller, feigns interest and offers a top price of $70,000. The second arrives and offers $80,000, while the third, being less charitable, spends three hours explaining why he wouldn't pay a dime over $60,000. All this confuses the now shaky seller who suddenly contracts a bad case of "owner doubt." Is the lounge worth $150,000? Perhaps its value is grossly overestimated. If the best he can get from three prospective buyers is $80,000, maybe he should grab it and run. The stage is set and all is ready for you to move in.

With an offer of $90,000, the seller's ears perk up. Perhaps he counters with $100,000 with $5,000 down, considering it far better than $80,000. Finally, after much negotiation, he agrees to $112,000 with nothing down.

Had you hit the seller before your "Men From the East" softened him up, you wouldn't have succeeded with such a low offer because the seller would still have believed his asking price was fair and attainable. Everything in life is relative. Compared to prior offers, yours looked good. What did it cost you to save thousands of dollars? A few hours of friends' time.

The "Man From the East" routine can help land no cash down deals. You can prod and probe to see just how far a seller will retreat and explore every negotiating angle. When he's through, you can step in. Entering negotiations without knowing how far a seller is willing to go is a disadvantage you can ill afford.

A "Man From the East" may also uncover why the business is for sale and the pressure a seller may be under to sell. "Seller pressure" can dictate how advantageous a deal you may structure. How badly does the seller want out? The greater the "seller pressure," the better the deal is likely to be. Most sellers, of course, protest they can't bear to forfeit their goldmine, but poor health, a brother in Los Angeles who won the Irish Sweepstakes or a sick wife might be making it time to get out. Be skeptical. I accept the seller's tale at face value only when he's 85 or older and negotiates with a nurse at his side.

OVERCOMING "SELLER'S BLOCK"

A psychological problem I call "seller's block" prevents many sellers from understanding or accepting no cash down deals. Although only a temporary mental state, seller's block can nevertheless present as formidable an obstacle as a 300 pound All-American tackle looming between you and the goal line. You can't easily go around it, so you must somehow overcome it.

Here's how seller's block works. Sitting at the negotiating table, you slowly but surely chip away at the financing until you have accounted for 100 percent of the purchase price without one solitary nickel coming from your own pocket. Suddenly the seller freezes. The strange fact you're about to take over his beloved business with everybody's money but your own rings loud and clear. Suddenly he begins to resist the deal.

Don't be surprised when you encounter seller's block. No matter how logical or fair a deal may be from the seller's perspective, a seller forgets to think about his own position at this point and instead looks at you as if you're another John Dillinger and he's your next heist. He may not admit it, but deep down he believes you're up to no good.

I know the feeling well. By the time I had completed my third no cash down deal, I was fully familiar with seller's block. I had seen it in operation three times, the last of which serves as a classic example of how irrational it can make a seller. This particular seller wanted to dispose of her small tobacco and wholesale business. Grace's business was on the market for over a year. At long last her buyer John arrived, willing to pay $200,000 for the business as they hassled over other terms.

John had his financing in sight. The seller had previously agreed to finance $150,000 over seven years with 15 percent interest, leaving only a $50,000 balance for a down payment. John proposed assuming $20,000 in business liabilities as part of the price, while the broker agreed to loan $10,000 from his commission, which reduced the "key money" to $20,000. John proposed the seller finance this amount with a short term note, funded from the business' cash flow. Grace had only to wait 30 days for her $20,000 down payment. To protect Grace, John offered her a mortgage on his house, but she still resisted. John tried everything to convince her. "Aren't you getting everything you want? I'm paying your price. All I'm asking of you is to wait 30 days for your money. It's fully secured," he reminded her.

A victim of "seller's block" Grace suddenly blew up. She quickly rose, poked her finger in John's face and shouted, "Young man, who do you think you are? If you think you're going to buy my business without investing a cent of your own, you're crazy." Seller's block prevented Grace from accepting a perfectly rational deal that satisfied her every objective. The idea alone that the buyer was putting up no cash was more than Grace could accept.

A couple of weeks later I ran into Grace's attorney who confided that while driving Grace home from the meeting she insisted that, "only a fool would sell to a buyer with no money of his own to invest." After all, when she bought the business ten years earlier, she needed a $30,000 down payment.

I reminded Grace's lawyer that John was investing $20,000 represented by a valid mortgage on his house with plenty of equity. If

Grace didn't need the $20,000 immediately, what did she have to lose? After a few moments he said, "She has nothing to lose. But with Grace it's the principle of the thing." That's just what I wanted to hear. I said, "Would your client Grace lend my client John $20,000, secured by his house, if he hands her $20,000 at the closing?" He called Grace, discussed it with her for several minutes, and called to say we had a deal.

The subsequent exchange of $20,000 checks represented one of the most ridiculous deals I've ever witnessed. Both Grace and John ended up with exactly what they would have had under John's proposal, but Grace added an unnecessary step of exchanging checks to overcome seller's block.

Seller's block can be as simple as a man's being ashamed to admit to his wife or friends that he gave up his business to someone with no money invested. Some sellers think about the hard-earned cash they originally invested in their business, resenting the fact that you negotiated a smarter deal. Whatever the case, you must recognize seller's block for what it is. Be patient. A well-structured and logical no cash deal eventually can erode seller's block.

Here are a few simple arguments you can raise when you encounter seller's block:

- Ask the seller what he wanted from the deal. Isn't he getting it? Turn the deal into the reality that the seller is obtaining just what he wanted. Why should it matter to him whether the money is coming from you?

- If the seller is financing the deal, show him how he's protected. Remind him of his security and what his options are if you default. Once he's convinced he has little risk and you have considerable liability, resistance usually drops.

- Show him that you are investing. It may not be your own money on the line, but what about your personal guarantees and what you stand to lose on default? This demonstrates a financial commitment on your part that should nullify any thoughts you're trying to steal his business or get something for nothing.

- Finally, show the seller your plans for the business. Let him know what time and effort you will spend to build and improve it. Once convinced that you mean business, he'll be in a better frame of mind to give you his.

Once your position is effectively set forth you'll no longer look like Dillinger. Instead the seller will see you for what you are—a sincere buyer who is smart enough to satisfy his needs without spending a dime of his own.

SELL YOURSELF

Why do some salespeople consistently outsell others? How do some business people pull off deals others can't? The successful businessperson, like the successful salesperson, sells himself or herself as well as the deal.

Your business terms and all the "hocus-pocus" with numbers may make sense, but if the seller has trouble relating to you personally, your job will be twice as difficult. You must handle people properly to build the confidence and trust vital to most business deals, and particularly deals where the seller must extend substantial financing. Chemistry between people can make or break a deal. You must learn to adapt your unique personality to the seller's. Remember, sellers are only people with the same likes, dislikes, prejudices and concerns as you. Some sellers may become lifelong friends, while others will never give you the time of day.

Regardless of the seller's temperment, you can learn to appear more credible and thus reduce seller resistance. Use common sense and cater to the psyche of the seller. Harvey can show you how not to win friends. He thought he was a skillful negotiator, but it turned out he didn't know the first thing about handling people. Harvey wanted to buy a typical gas station for sale by a nice enough guy to whom the business represented years of hard work. Harvey knew he could make the station far more profitable, but he didn't have the down payment the seller was looking for. Harvey had seen the gas station but had not personally met the seller because earlier negotiations were conducted between their lawyers by telephone. The day of the transfer arrived and all the legal papers were in order. Only the buyer's and seller's signatures were needed. What could be easier? In walked Harvey. The seller and his wife greeted him with customary cordialities but Harvey decided it was time to impress everyone with his managerial brilliance. Turning to the seller, he said, "The first thing I'm going to do is paint that dump of yours. And how did you survive without opening on Sundays?" On and on Harvey stormed, trying to prove what a great station owner he would be by knocking the seller's ability. After listening to Harvey's insulting comments, the seller got up and quietly walked out leaving Harvey to his old job sorting mail at the post office. The world is full of Harveys. They seldom learn diplomacy. Those who understand human nature don't need lessons from a book. Those who refuse to understand it cannot learn it from all the books in the world.

Contrast Harvey's approach with Mark's. Mark understands people. He never discusses or negotiates a deal until he has formed the closest possible relationship with the seller. Once the bond of confidence and trust exists, everything else falls into place. For years Mark owned a small Cape Cod restaurant. Although he was relatively new to the business, he had already enjoyed modest success. Before long Mark discovered a larger and more prosperous restaurant for sale for which the seller wanted $300,000 with $100,000 down. Mark first met the seller at the seller's restaurant, engaging him in constructive and pleasant conversation concerning their mutual business interests. They compared menus, costs, customers and suppliers. Mark gave the seller the recipe for his own restaurant's best selling dessert. At Mark's invitation the seller toured Mark's operation the following week. They never discussed a business deal. Instead, Mark asked the seller's advice on classic restaurant problems, allowing the seller to demonstrate his broad knowledge. After a couple of months Mark and the seller became fast friends. When Mark finally presented his no cash down deal, the seller instantly agreed and Mark soon owned his second restaurant with 100 percent financing. Mark's story proves an important point. When two people like and trust each other, they can work out the most beneficial and creative terms.

Business deals are much like romances, and the best have as their foundation a "courting" period. It's people getting to know each other, building a like, trust and understanding of each other.

In this book I refer to the negotiating table. That's only a figure of speech, for that conference table in a lawyer's or accountant's office is absolutely the worst place to negotiate. Smart buyers avoid this austere environment, and instead try to build relationships slowly and gradually in an atmosphere more conducive to favorable negotiation. That's why the IRS allows tax deductions for business entertainment. They know that more deals are concluded in fancy restaurants than in business offices.

So sell yourself before you try to sell the deal. Once the seller sees you as more than just another buyer, that down payment can become the most unimportant part of the deal.

KNOW THE BARGAINING BASICS

Every deal has hundreds of variables to negotiate. To win one you sometimes have to forfeit another. That's what makes the negotiating game so fascinating. Like tennis, the winner simply scores more points than his opponent.

To readers of this book the most vital variable is the down payment, so no cash down terms must be the one point you never sacrifice. Give up anything else if you must, but never budge on this one item.

Consider the vast numbers of points open for negotiation in the typical business deal:

- Price
- Business assets to be sold
- Duration of financing
- Interest on notes
- Security for notes
- Personal guarantees on notes
- Seller's agreements not to compete
- Assumed liabilities
- Brokerage commissions
- Closing dates
- Leases (if the seller is the landlord)

Since this list of negotiable points just scratches the surface, rely on your attorney who will have most of the other important questions at his fingertips.

Turning to the most important point, a seller may demand a down payment but will probably be willing to concede the point for other concessions of equal or greater value to him. Let's take a test run. A seller offers his business for $100,000 with $20,000 down. How much will you have to give away to get it for nothing down? Start with price. Perhaps you offer $89,000 with $10,000 down.(Don't worry about the $10,000; you're not signing agreements yet.) The

seller counters with $95,000 with $15,000 down. Prog
switch to financing terms. Now the seller will accept
over seven years at 12 percent interest. You chip away. You'll
agree to the seller's terms if he reduces the down payment to
$10,000 and increases the note to $85,000. He agrees, but you're not
through. You say you won't sign a personal guarantee on the note.
The seller will have to accept your corporation's note so you incur
no personal liability in the event of default. Predictably, the seller
balks. You mull it over, saying you'll provide your personal guarantee if he accepts $5,0000 down and drops the interest to ten
percent. He goes along with the $5,000 down payment but holds
out for 12 percent interest. You concede. Finally, you tell him he
has to agree not to compete with you within ten miles and for ten
years. You're adamant on the point. The seller argues that's too
restrictive, so you reply, "Okay, make it five miles instead of ten,
but only if we can shave $2,500 off the price and down payment,
and I can pay the remaining $2,500 for the down payment within 30
days after closing."

That scenario portrays how typical negotiations proceed. It may
extend over weeks, or even months, or it may instead consist of a
few telephone calls or letters. Regardless of how it's achieved, the
essentials remain the same. Be prepared for a give and take, but
always keep your eye on the one important point: no cash down.

TEN RULES FOR SUCCESSFUL NEGOTIATIONS

Negotiating a business acquisition follows the same basic strategies as negotiating any other transaction. However, the stakes
are typically greater. How can you improve your negotiating
techniques?

Investigate the seller's position. How motivated is this seller? Why
does he really want to sell? What are his problems and pressure
points? Remember, you bargain from your opponent's position,

not your own. Do your homework and investigate the seller as thoroughly as you do the business.

Listen—don't talk. When you listen you pick up valuable clues. When you talk you tip your hand. Encourage the seller to explain his situation. Ask questions. Draw your opponent out. You'll not only receive information useful in negotiating a better deal but helpful to improve your relationship.

Divide and conquer by addressing multiple issues one at a time. Where multiple issues exist or where multiple problems exist, separate them and discuss and resolve each individually. Larger problems become more manageable when divided into their smaller component parts and each part can then be considered individually. But bear in mind that you cannot commit yourself on any one point unless you reach agreement on all other points, as an acceptable deal requires striking a favorable balance on all points.

Address easy issues first and put problem issues off until last. Don't get stalled on one particular issue or on one aspect of the deal which is the most difficult to resolve. Set areas of disagreement aside and address more easily resolved issues first. Hopefully when you and the seller return to the problem issues you already will have resolved most other items. At that point in the negotiation process an earlier obstacle will take on a different perspective and be resolved more easily.

Work with the seller to create a joint solution. Encourage the seller to participate in the proposed solution. Draw him into the process. Work with him to identify the problem. Ask his advice. Listen to his opinions and suggestions. Literally work together with the seller so that both parties can feel an ownership in the solution.

Put yourself in the seller's position. Consider the seller's point of view. Does your proposition satisfy his needs, goals and objectives? Where does it fall short? What are the alternatives to satisfy those needs and thus create an acceptable deal for the seller as well as for yourself?

Develop multiple solutions. Once you have identified issues to be resolved, determine how you can resolve the problems efficiently and economically. Walk into negotiations with all the possible alternatives in mind, but don't rely on your solutions alone. Ask the seller for his ideas on the processes for resolving issues you cannot resolve between you. Neither you nor the seller should be limited to your own solutions. Brainstorm with advisors and associates until all the possible solutions are explored and discussed.

Deal with the decision maker. Don't engage in two step negotiations where your opponent later clears every point with a partner, attorney, spouse or other alter ego. Find out in advance whether your opponent shares your authority to make a deal and if not insist that the decision makers be present at negotiations.

Be patient. Negotiating a business acquisition can often take months and the process can't be accelerated without paying a steep price. Conversely, the patience to extend negotiations can often create a much more favorable deal. Make the element of time work for you, not against you.

Be prepared to take a walk. Don't become emotionally committed to a prospective acquisition. You defined your limits on acceptable terms before you started negotiating and if an acceptable deal cannot be reached, be prepared to walk away. Until you are handed the keys the business isn't yours. In fact, it may never becomes yours. This advice applies equally to sellers. Just as there are many other businesses, there are many other buyers.

SALVAGING COLLAPSED NEGOTIATIONS

Negotiations frequently collapse when the parties remain too far apart on issues. How can you revive negotiations without weakening your bargaining position? Always break-off negotiations on a friendly note. The fact that you couldn't reach agreement shouldn't create a hostile relationship between you and the seller. Leave the door open to re-open negotiations at a later date. Both you and the seller may agree to reconsider certain points with the passage of time. The business may have improved or deteriorated or you may conceive a new approach to a troublesome issue. Bargaining positions do change.

Involve your attorney or accountant to break a negotiating stalemate. Direct negotiations between the parties may not have been successful, but if your advisors negotiate with the seller's advisors they may find ways to break the stalemate.

Don't stand on principle alone. If you have to give in on one or two small points to make the deal, don't let ego stand in your way. If the business deal is basically sound and reasonably fair, a few extra dollars is a negligible concession over the long term.

Seasoned negotiators are indeed a joy to behold. They throw appropriate glances at the right time, pause for dramatic effect, and light their pipe or cigarette at the perfect moment. Their voices rise and fall with persuasive inflection, and all the while they barter away meaningless points in exchange for crucial ones. Not everyone, of course, can play the negotiation game as effectively, but if you stay with these rules you'll be well on your way to a no cash down deal.

MAKE IT A WIN-WIN DEAL

Whoever heard of paying a seller more than he asks for his business? Such a strategy can create precisely that win-win situation under which you win no cash down terms. Put yourself in a seller's shoes. Pretend you want to offer your business for $100,000 with a $40,000 down payment, with you financing the balance. Assume you don't need cash from the sale and will accept $90,000 with $30,000 down from the right buyer.

How would you react if a convincing buyer simply put it on the line and offered you $100,000 with nothing down? You would essentially "loan" the buyer the $30,000 at a fair interest rate. When all is said and done, you will receive $10,000 more for your business than you were willing to accept plus interest on the $30,000 loan. Not a bad trade-off!

Now, look at the same deal from the buyer's point of view. Yes, you're paying $10,000 more than if you had the $30,000 down payment, but consider how insignificant that $10,000 can be over your long term ownership of your business. And if the business is indeed worth $90,000, it is worth $100,000. Yet that same $10,000 can be a powerful motivator to induce the seller to strike a no cash down deal.

A fair number of no cash down deals come about because the buyer agreed to pay a premium price. One example involved a small chain of dry cleaning stores that recently changed hands in my town. George asked $250,000 with $125,000 down. For five months the buyer Ed negotiated with the seller. Finally, George agreed to a $225,000 price with $100,000 down. Ed never confessed that he didn't have the $100,000 down payment. As long as George believed Ed enjoyed strong financial backing, he would continue to negotiate, but slick negotiations, like good comedy, require artful timing.

One day George and Ed were playing golf to celebrate their "deal." At the eighth tee, Ed turned to George and asked, "George, how do you plan to invest the $100,000 down payment I'm going to give you?" George replied, "Who knows? I suppose I'll stick it in a money market account or bank certificates paying 8 percent interest." Ed timed it perfectly. Casually he asked George if he'd instead consider investing the $100,000 in a solid and secure business deal at 12 percent payable over seven years. In addition, the borrower would pay George a $15,000 finder's fee. Of course George was interested, for it would pay far better dividends than conventional investments. The rhetorical nature of the question, of course, gave Ed an "out" if George wasn't interested. Ed moved in for the kill. "George, I'm that borrower. For me to buy your business I'd have to borrow the $100,000 down payment on those same terms from a relative. I'd rather give you the benefit of the deal." Then Ed delivered his clincher, "And what could be safer than lending against your own business?"

Soon Ed acquired the six store chain earning profits of $100,000 a year, or $700,000 over the seven year term. Think about it. In exchange, Ed paid what amounts to a $2,000 a year premium for seven years. Wouldn't you willingly pay a few extra dollars to own a business that will land 50 times as much in your own pocket? The message is that if you are to successfully negotiate no cash down terms you must often bring to the bargaining table a dose of generosity.

THE "WALK AWAY" AND OTHER NASTY TRICKS

Most people honestly believe everything they hear. If a buyer tells you she's going to buy your business and hand you her $10,000 check at the closing next Wednesday afternoon, you'll probably believe her. Nor do I suggest you shouldn't unless of course, you're dealing with a strange breed of negotiating scoundrels I call "Walk Away Artists."

The "Walk Away Artist" doesn't do anything that can land her in jail, but she does often know how to land herself in a business of her own without investing a cent. How does she operate?

First, she negotiates the lowest possible down payment, then encourages the seller to make irreversible plans in anticipation of the sale. The "Walk Away Artist's" scheme is always to set up the seller so it's difficult, for him to back out of the deal. Administering the coup de grace, she threatens to walk away at the closing, announcing she has a last minute problem. Her uncle from Peoria was going to loan her the down payment, but he died suddenly. Full of regret, the buyer offers a short term note in place of the expected cash down payment; otherwise, she'll have to walk away from the deal. What can the seller do? Not only is he all "psyched up" about selling but has plans dependent on the sale going through. His wife can't wait for their long overdue vacation, his employees threw a farewell party the night before, and he's incurred $5,000 in legal expenses to bring the deal this far.

I can tell you about one "Walk Away Artist" that landed three no cash deals using that technique. In one memorable case he purchased an appliance store, making his agreement conditional upon negotiating an acceptable lease. He even promised a $20,000 down payment. To the seller everything looked great until the day of the closing, when the "Walk Away Artist" complained, "The landlord saddled me with a horrendous three year lease instead of the ten year lease I wanted. I don't see how I can go through with the deal if I have to pay you $20,000 down. The deal just isn't attractive enough! I hate to do this, but the only way I can see my way to complete the deal in light of that lousy lease is if you add $20,000 to your note and waive the down payment." One more unwary seller snagged!

Despite variations of the theme, the "Walk Away Artist" always plays by the same tune. The agreement is conditional upon some external factor—a lease, other financing or perhaps the accountant's approval of the books. This allows you the legal right to terminate the agreement and walk away from the deal if you cannot satisfy the contingency.

CEMENTING THE DEAL

Just as the "Walk Away Artist" can play havoc with an unsuspecting seller, so too a seller may decide to dump you for a more affluent buyer. There is a considerable difference between reaching a handshake agreement and a legally binding agreement. Between the two events the deal can easily fall apart.

The seller may withdraw from the deal once approached by another buyer with a more generous offer. He may perhaps develop his own anxieties about selling for any number of reasons. And both the buyer and seller typically receive armchair advice from well intentioned friends and relatives on why they shouldn't buy or sell. Considering Murphy's Law that all that can go wrong in life usually does, it takes a determined buyer and seller to close a deal. Keep in mind these two essential strategies to keep a hard fought deal together:

1. Insist on binding agreements within ten days of reaching verbal agreement. The longer you delay the less chance you have to cement the deal, so don't allow either attorney to stall.

2. Don't spread the word that the business has been acquired until binding agreements have been signed. As a buyer you don't want to invite last minute bids from competitive buyers. The seller will not want you to reveal to his employees, suppliers, etc. that the business is sold until the event actually occurs.

No matter how hard you and the seller may negotiate, it is important that you each leave the negotiating table with mutual trust and confidence. This advice is particularly vital if you are to maintain an on-going relationship, such as when the seller agrees to finance you or perhaps is the landlord under your lease. There are many instances where you will need the seller's cooperation and small battles unfairly fought can prove enormously costly later.

KEY POINTS TO REMEMBER

1. Always negotiate from the seller's position.

2. Seller's pull predictable plays. Never allow a seller to intimidate or rush you into a deal.

3. Take your time when negotiating and think each step through objectively.

4. Test the water. What terms has the seller agreed to with other buyers? Use these as a springboard for an even better deal for yourself.

5. Seller's naturally resist no cash down terms. Learn to overcome this resistance.

6. Build a good relationship with the seller based on mutual confidence and trust. It can pay big dividends later.

13

Closing Your No Cash Down Deal

HOW TO STRUCTURE THE TRANSACTION

Before final agreement can be reached, decide upon the method of transfer, as the structure of the transaction involves important legal, financial and tax issues. For the smaller business the sale can be accomplished by either of two methods. When the seller operates as a sole proprietorship or as a partnership, the sale must be handled as a *sale of assets*. Under a transfer of assets, the seller conveys to the buyer title to the assets acquired. The buyer typically sets up a new corporation to accept title, entering into new leases and contracts with employees, customers and suppliers.

When the business is incorporated, the transfer can still be achieved through a sale of assets but it can also be through a *sale of corporate stock*. Essentially, the ownership of the existing corporation changes with the new stockholders (buyers) electing new officers and directors to manage the existing corporation.

There can be modified approaches as when the corporation redeems, or buys, the original stockholders' stock for an agreed price. The buyer simultaneously acquires new shares in the corporation and becomes its new and sole stockholder. The redemption sale is commonly used when the selling stockholders receive a note and want to secure the purchase price by a mortgage on business assets. In all other respects the redemption sale presents similar advantages and disadvantages as a direct stock sale.

Seldom does one factor alone control the method of transfer. However, one consideration generally outweighs other factors and supports a particular approach. What factors should you consider in deciding whether to buy assets or corporate shares?

Liability Protection

A primary consideration is protection against unknown or contingent liabilities of the seller. A purchase of assets would better insulate you from the seller's liabilities, provided assets were verified to be clear of liens and encumbrances and there was strict compliance with the Bulk Sales Act, which requires advance notice of the sale to the seller's creditors. Assuming the sale is for fair consideration and does not constitute a fraudulent transfer, a buyer would have no further concern over the seller's liabilities. This broad protection argues strongly for an asset sale and in many instances a buyer's attorney will insist on this form for this reason alone.

The concern over undisclosed liabilities is far greater under a stock sale since undisclosed creditors can later assert claims against the acquired corporation. The extent of concern will, of course, depend on the alternative forms of protection available to the buyer under a stock sale.

Typically, the buyer will rely on his accountant's opinion as to whether the seller's corporation appears "clean," with a solvent financial condition, adequate accounting records and evidence that obligations are currently paid in an orderly manner. Once satisfied the likelihood of an undisclosed liability is small and the recourse remedies adequate, the purchase of shares can be safely considered.

Leases

The lease on the business location can be another very practical and important consideration. Under a sale of assets, the buyer will be required to obtain a new lease, unless the seller has the right to assign its lease. Conversely, with a purchase of shares of stock, generally the lease remains intact and no new lease or lease assignment is required. If there is a favorable lease in place, it will be advantageous to acquire the corporation rather than assets to avoid negotiating a new lease. In an era when rents are rapidly escalating, a rental increase on a new lease can be significant. Oftentimes the buyer will be required to renegotiate a new lease anyway, because the existing lease is near expiration. In this situation the lease will be unimportant in structuring the sale.

Financing

The financing can also determine whether a sale of assets or of shares should be used. If the corporation has high debt, the debt can be credited to the purchase price. Although the debt can be assumed under a transfer of assets, it is more easily accomplished through a stock sale.

When the assets of the corporation are secured by security agreements or other encumbrances and these debts are to be assumed by the buyer as part of the purchase price, creditor approval for the transfer will be required. The creditor may insist upon full payment or allow the transfer only with new and less favorable financing terms. Under these circumstances a sale of stock would allow existing financing to remain intact.

Contract Rights

The corporation may hold certain contract rights such as franchises, distributorship agreements or supplier contracts which are not assignable without the consent of the other party. The acquisition of corporate stock will leave these important contracts intact whereas an asset transfer will require approval to assign these contract rights, often available only on less favorable terms.

Employee Benefit Plans

The compatibility of the selling corporation's employee benefit plans with the buying corporation's benefit plans may affect the method of transfer selected for the transaction. If the selling corporation's plans are substantially more expensive than the buyer's plans, it may be worthwhile for the buyer to maintain the acquisition as a subsidiary.

Credit Rating

The corporation's credit rating can either be an advantage or disadvantage when acquiring assets. With the purchase of shares the buyer can obtain the continued benefit of a favorable rating. A corporation newly created by the buyer will start with very little credit available.

Conversely, a buyer may do better to rely on a new corporation with no credit rating rather than take over one with an adverse rating. This can be an important issue, particularly when relying on credit to compensate for lack of working capital.

Corporate Charters and Licenses

Another time when a stock transaction is preferable is when preservation of a corporate charter is important. For example, when the seller corporation holds a banking or insurance charter, a convincing case can be made that the parties should consider only a stock sale.

Partial Sales

If the parties contemplate a sale of only a portion of the business, it is logical to plan on a sale of particular assets, retaining the intact corporation for continued operation by the seller.

Stockholder Approvals

If the selling corporation is owned by a number of stockholders, the sale of stock can only be accomplished with the agreement of all stockholders, assuming the buyer wants 100% ownership, which is generally the case with small businesses. When some stockholders refuse to sell their shares, a sale of assets may be the only alternative. In these instances, the seller and buyer each share the responsibility to make certain the corporation has authority to sell and the sale is proper, to avoid litigation by dissenting minority stockholders.

Weighing the numerous factors to determine the final method of acquisition is rarely easy. The problem is further magnified by the fact that the buyer may prefer one method of acquisition and the seller another. Many deals fall apart only because the parties disagree on the method of transfer, despite agreement on other terms.

PREPARING THE AGREEMENT

The purchase and sales agreement does more than put in writing what you have agreed upon. Corporate, tax and many other problems may have been overlooked in earlier negotiations and arise only when the contract is prepared. More importantly, the contract defines the rights and obligations of the parties after the sale is completed.

A contract to buy or sell a business, like any important legal document, must be specifically designed to the transaction. Like the deals themselves, no two contracts are identical. You will need a carefully prepared agreement to meet your special needs, so follow these points.

Don't play lawyer. Buying or selling a business requires professional assistance. You will need your attorney to prepare the agreement to protect you; and never sign an offer or agreement unless approved by your attorney.

Work closely with your attorney. A well-prepared agreement is a collaborative effort between attorney and client. Your attorney knows the law but doesn't necessarily know the intricacies of your business, the special conditions you require or other legal safeguards needed for your business.

Put it in writing. The rule is that if it isn't in writing it isn't enforceable. All terms of agreement as well as later modifications should be in writing and approved by your attorney.

CONTRACT TERMS FOR AN ASSET DEAL

Buying the sellers assets is the most common type transaction for the smaller firm. For maximum protection the agreement should cover the following points:

The Parties to the Agreement

The agreement should include all parties to the agreement. Besides the corporate seller and buyer, principals of the respective companies should individually join in the agreement if personally bound an indemnifications, notes or non compete agreements. Business brokers or finders due a commission should also sign for purposes of assenting to their commission agreements.

Assets to be Sold

The contract must accurately specify the specific assets to be sold, as later disputes may center on this issue. Seldom will the deal include all assets of the business, requiring the parties to itemize between those sold and those retained by the seller. Which of these assets will and will not be sold?

- Cash on hand
- Accounts receivable
- Notes receivable
- Securities or interests in other businesses
- Prepaid deposits and utilities
- Tax rebates
- Insurance claims
- Lawsuit claims
- Inventory
- Furniture and fixtures

- Equipment
- Motor vehicles
- Leasehold improvements
- Real estate
- Good will
- Business name
- Patents
- Trademarks
- Copyrights
- Customers lists
- Trade secrets
- Franchise or distributorship rights
- Licenses and permits
- Transfer of telephone numbers

Typically the seller will retain the liquid assets such as cash, receivables, prepaid expenses and securities such as stocks and bonds. Real estate may also be retained by the seller as a passive investment.

Often the sale will include only inventory, furniture, fixtures, equipment, name and good will as the essential operating assets, although the division of assets will always be the heart of the agreement.

Items Excluded from Sale

Certain items used in the business may not be owned by the seller and will neither be sold nor retained by the seller. These include items loaned to the business, leased property, consigned goods and similar items to be reclaimed by a third party.

Listing these items disclaims any implied warranty of title. The agreement should provide that the buyer will return these items to their owners. Wherever possible, the seller should return such property prior to closing, unless the buyer makes arrangements to retain possession.

The Purchase Price

The purchase price can be based upon one of several formulas. The simplest form is a *fixed price*, where the purchase price is a fixed dollar amount established prior to contract. A *formula price* is used when you have agreed how the price is to be arrived at but you cannot determine it before closing. An example might be a price based upon the value of actual inventory, outstanding receivables and assumed liabilities existing at time of closing. You must specify the procedures for adjusting the price, the method for determining the value of each item on which the price is based and the acceptable price range. A contingent price formula is determined by the earnings (often called an "earnout"), sales volume or commissions of the acquired business for a specified period following the closing. The price becomes payable at certain intervals or in full at the end of the period. A contingent price should clearly define the method of computation and provide for an accounting to the seller. A contingent price may be combined with a fixed or formula price.

How the Purchase Price Is Paid

Fixed or formula prices may be paid in a lump-sum payment at closing or installment payments paid over a period of time after closing. In the latter case, the agreement usually calls for a down payment at closing with the balance financed. When a formula price is used, state whether the adjustments will change the down payment or the amount financed. When it will change the financed amount, will it extend or contract the installment period, so that payments will remain the same? On installment contracts, define the terms of financing, guarantees and the security for the note. Each of the financing documents should be prepared and approved at time of contract to avoid later dispute.

Deposits paid prior to closing would, of course, be taken as a credit against the total down payment. Brokers usually hold the deposit, although in the absence of brokers or an escrow bank, the attorney for the seller may hold the deposit in escrow. Where the deposit is sizeable, place the deposit in an interest bearing account, with interest to follow principal. The escrow agents should be parties to the agreement and obliged to release the escrowed deposit at closing. Define procedures in the event of a dispute. The parties may also agree whether the buyer will forfeit all or part of the deposit as liquidated damages in the event of breach, thus avoiding further claims and liability.

How the Price Is Allocated

The allocation of the purchase price among the various assets being acquired is essential for tax purposes. Attempt to allocate as much of the price as possible to the depreciable assets. The seller, however, will realize a taxable gain if these assets have been depreciated below the allocated price. In most instances, however, the seller will plan either a three month or 12 month liquidation of his corporation so as to treat the sale as one taxable transaction to avoid adverse tax consequences to the stockholders of the selling company.

Allocating price to assets has more than tax significance. If an asset is misrepresented, the allocated price may be decisive in determining damages. Insurance companies also base losses on the allocated amount.

Handling Liabilities

If the assets are to be sold free and clear of seller's liabilities, the agreement should so specify. Take all required steps to protect yourself from liabilities. This includes compliance with the Bulk Sales Act (with notice of the intended sale to creditors), the acceptance of indemnifications from both the seller and its principals, and the right to withhold note payments should creditor claims arise.

Contracts usually provide that the seller may use sales proceeds to discharge liens or encumbrances. Coordinate payment to lienholders with receipt of appropriate discharges.

Liabilities may be assumed by the buyer and credited toward the purchase price. The contract should specify the amount of assumed liabilities. While the specific liabilities to be assumed are usually not known until closing, the contract should define the type and maximum amount of liability. At closing the seller will provide a list of liabilities to be assumed, which becomes part of the contract.

Where liabilities are to be assumed, you may want the right to compromise or settle liabilities without price adjustment provided the compromise does not create further liability to the seller. This is a particularly desirable provision when liabilities are excessive.

The seller, of course, also wants protection on assumed liabilities, including indemnification by the buyer company and its principals. The contract may also require payment to creditors within a specified time, with proof of payment. Further, the seller may require a pledge of the stock or some other collateral to insure payment by the buyer.

Oftentimes the parties will elect a split approach with the buyer assuming certain liabilities and the seller retaining and paying others. The seller may want to pay directly liabilities for which there may be personal liability, such as guaranteed debts and tax obligations.

Representations and Warranties

Representations and warranties in the contract can support a later claim of misrepresentation, fraud or deceit. Where the seller is a corporation to be liquidated, or one with negligible assets, the seller's principals should join in the warranties.

Seller's Warranties

A comprehensive checklist of seller warranties include:

- Seller has good and marketable title.
- Assets are sold free and clear of liens and encumbrances.
- Seller has full authority to sell and transfer the assets.
- Seller, as a corporate entity, is in good standing.
- The seller's financial statements present fairly and accurately the financial position of the company as of its date and there are no material adverse changes thereafter.
- Contract rights and leases to be assigned are as represented and in good standing.
- There is no material litigation pending against the company.
- All licenses and permits required to conduct the business are in good standing.
- There are no liabilities other than as represented.
- The use of seller's name does not infringe on the name of any other party.
- All equipment and fixtures are in good working order.

The parties may elect to cover certain assets by warranty provisions. For example, the seller may warrant inventory levels or the face value of collectible accounts receivable at time of takeover. As a practical matter the seller cannot know in advance of closing their actual values and therefore the warranty may only state a range.

The seller should also warrant that certain documents, such as financial statements, tax returns, leases and contracts to be assigned, are as represented. Wherever practical, these documents should be attached to the contract as exhibits.

The agreement should further specify which warranties remain enforceable after the closing and which are satisfied upon closing. The buyer will ordinarily insist that all warranties survive except those that can be verified at closing. An example of the latter may be the warranty that the equipment is in good working order.

Buyer's Warranties

In a cash acquisition, buyer's warranties are generally limited to those relating to its authority to consummate the transactions under the contract of sale. Where the seller is to provide financing, the warranty should include representations as to the buyer's financial condition. Buyer's warranties can protect the seller in the event the purchase is not completed. The buyer, for example, should warrant it will not use the seller's trade secrets, induce employees to leave the seller's employ and not disclose confidential information.

To insure that the buyer will not compete unfairly with the seller if the purchase is cancelled, the buyer may agree not to compete or not to lease the premises unless through acquisition of the business.

Conditions

Conditions make performance contingent upon certain events, allowing for the termination of the contract if all the conditions are not satisfied. Unlike warranties, which are generally within the control of the parties, conditions ordinarily depend upon a third party.

Most conditions are imposed by the buyer. Essentially you must consider every event upon which the deal depends. Consider this checklist:

- The seller's warranties and representations shall remain accurate and true at closing.
- There is no materially adverse change in seller's financial performance prior to closing.
- The seller has performed all its affirmative and negative obligations.
- The seller provided all required documents contemplated by the agreement at closing.
- All required opinion letters are obtained.
- An assignment of lease or new lease on terms acceptable to buyer is obtained.
- Satisfactory financing for the transaction is obtained.
- Required approvals by governmental agencies are obtained.
- Licenses and permits can be transferred.

This list, of course, exemplifies only the more common conditions. The possible conditions are limited only by the needs of the particular deal.

The conditions should be reasonable and sufficiently specific to determine whether it has been satisfied. For example, a condition for financing on terms satisfactory to the buyer will easily allow the buyer to avoid performance by rejecting even the most favorable financing. A better approach is to specify the required financing. The contract may also require the parties to expend "best efforts" to satisfy their respective conditions.

When the contract imposes conditions over which the seller has no control (financing, satisfactory leases, etc.), the seller must weigh whether the buyer can satisfy the conditions. The seller certainly should not rely on a sale until all conditions have been satisfied. The practical approach is for the seller to set a time for the buyer to satisfy the conditions. On that date the buyer should either confirm satisfaction of the conditions or terminate the contract with a return of deposit. Oftentimes, the parties may agree to extend the date for performance, but this should be agreed to only when the seller is convinced there is satisfactory progress. The seller may require the buyer to forfeit a part of the deposit if the condition is not satisfied by the extended date.

Allowed Activities

What are the required and prohibited acts by either party pending the closing or thereafter? Most covenants are to be performed by the seller and relate to the operation of the business until closing. These covenants are designed to prevent the seller from impairing the good will or adversely affecting the financial or legal structure of the business. The covenants may require the seller to maintain business hours, inventory, credit, service and pricing policies, as necessary to insure customer retention.

Covenants can also apply to acts to be performed at closing. Normally the agreement will specify the respective documents to be delivered by the buyer and seller, including the delivery of books and records relating to the conduct of the business.

A covenant not to compete may be particularly important. In negotiating the covenant not to compete, specify each of the parties required to execute the covenant. Where employees are expected not to compete, obtain their signatures in advance of the closing. The covenant not to compete should specify the prohibited activities and impose reasonable time and geographic limitations. The remedies for breach should also be carefully stated. The seller may want notice of breach and an opportunity to cure. Thereafter the buyer will want injunctive relief in addition to legal remedies for damages. The covenant may also say whether the buyer will have the right to curtail future payments due the seller in the event of breach. Reciprocally, the seller should be released from the covenant upon default by the buyer of any note payments due the seller.

Casualty to the Business

Contemplate the possibility of casualty to the assets prior to closing. A common contract provision is to require the seller to maintain adequate insurance and, upon casualty, to assign the claim or insurance proceeds to the buyer. Usually the buyer has the option to terminate the agreement. Minor casualty (casualty to less than 5% of the total value of the assets to be sold) may be an exception. Here the buyer should accept the insurance proceeds, an adjustment to price, or a replacement of the assets.

Casualty to the premises should give the buyer the same rights as casualty to assets. This is particularly important when casualty would terminate the lease or cause business interruption. The parties may agree to extend the closing for a reasonable time to allow the seller to restore the premises to its prior condition.

If the business is located within a shopping center or depends on a larger nearby business to draw traffic, extend the casualty provision to other tenants or areas of the shopping center.

Paying Brokers

Brokers or finders entitled to a commission should be parties to the agreement. Their participation is necessary to confirm the commission arrangement and their obligations as escrow agents where they hold deposits. Oftentimes co-brokers are involved, where one broker provided the business listing and the other the buyer.

While brokers are entitled to a commission upon producing a buyer ready, willing and able to buy on the offered terms or such substitute terms as the seller may accept, the seller may condition payment on an actual closing. This would avoid a broker's claim against the seller if for any reason the sale does not occur.

The contract should also provide for sharing of the deposit in the event of buyer breach. Customarily, the proceeds are evenly divided between seller and broker; however, this remains a matter of agreement. Similarly, the broker may bargain to participate in any recovery against the buyer for damages.

Closing Adjustments

Most asset transfers require closing adjustments between seller and buyer. Common adjustment items include rent, payroll, insurance, utilities, service contracts, license and permit fees and taxes.

Prior to agreement, the parties should review allocable items with their attorneys. The agreement should identify each item subject to adjustment and the adjustment formula when a pro-rated allocation is not suitable. The adjustments should also reflect the possibility that goods ordered by the seller prior to closing may be received by the buyer after closing and therefore not tabulated in the inventory or price. The buyer should then have the option to reject or pay for the goods.

Typically, the parties will not have all the amounts to adjust at time of closing. The contract may provide for escrowing a sufficient portion of the purchase price to satisfy adjustments due either the seller or buyer.

The Closing Date

Buyers and sellers are typically anxious to close on the transaction, but often unrealistic in their assessment of the time required to complete the legal work, obtain financing and satisfy other conditions. Plan a realistic closing date and provide for flexibility when the closing is necessarily extended for reasons beyond the control of either party.

Unquestionably, it is best to close as rapidly as possible, consistent with the parties objectives. Because so many problems can develop during the pre-closing stage, the time span should be shortened as much as possible.

On occasion the parties will prefer a delayed closing. For example, the parties may reach agreement in October but negotiate a closing in January for tax purposes or perhaps to allow the seller the benefit of the high selling season. Frequently, the concession to allow one party or another to capture the peak season sales may influence greatly price or other terms, and may even be a sufficient buyer concession to win no cash down terms.

Unless strict performance is required for some compelling reason, it is best to build flexibility into the closing date, allowing for an automatic extension of 15 to 30 days. In scheduling the closing, some thought should be given to the most convenient closing date. It is usually best to schedule the closing for the commencement of a new business period, such as the first business day of a month, to ease the calculation of adjustments and simplify accounting.

While it is true that a scheduled closing date is at best only a target, the parties should execute formal extensions when extensions are required.

CONTRACT TERMS FOR A STOCK DEAL

Many of the contract terms that apply to asset transfers also apply to stock transfer agreements. However, the priorities are somewhat different. The asset transfer may be far less complex, since the buyer's primary concern is the assurance of clear title and continuity of the business in a reasonably stable manner pending the closing. Because a stock transfer contemplates the takeover of the seller's corporation, the buyer's priorities are expanded to include every facet of the corporate structure.

The following points are essential to any stock transfer agreement.

The Stock to Be Transferred

The agreement must specify the stock interest being transferred with certain warranties relating to the shares of stock, including the following:

- The shares will represent at the time of closing a stated percentage ownership of the corporation, all classes of stock inclusive.

- The seller has and shall deliver good title to said shares free of encumbrances, pledge or other liens.

- The shares are fully paid and nonassessable.

- There are no outstanding proxies or other assignment of voting rights.

- Any restrictions on transfer imposed by the by-laws or otherwise have been waived, allowing for transfer.

The Purchase Price

Seldom are shares of the closely held corporation sold for a fixed price. Generally, the formula price is used reflecting the net worth of the corporation at closing. Although many of the asset values such as capital assets and goodwill may have a stipulated value, cash, accounts receivable, inventory, and existing debts will cause variations in the price. As with asset transfers, the agreement must include the method for determining each at time of closing.

Larger corporations are oftentimes sold for the "book value" of the shares at time of closing or based on audited financial statements at a stipulated date. This approach has little application to the smaller firm whose assets, including goodwill, are more accurately valued as under an asset transfer.

Warranties

The most important provisions in the stock agreement are the warranties relating to the legal, financial and business affairs of the corporation. The buyer will have these warranties only to rely upon if misrepresentations are discovered.

A checklist of common warranties include:

- The corporation is in good standing (and in all jurisdictions if a foreign corporation).

- The corporation has good title to all the assets or properties used in connection with the business (except for those confirmed as nonowned).

- All required federal, state and local tax returns have been filed and all monies due paid and there are no known audits or notices of audit pending.

- All contracts (principal contracts to be specifically identified) are in good standing and not in default or threat of termination.

- All leases are in good standing, without modification or amendment.

- There are no known proceedings against the corporation by any governmental body or agency.

- The corporation is not a party to any litigation (except as may be delineated).

- There are no liens or encumbrances against any asset of the corporation (except as may be delineated).

- The corporation is not a party to any contract not subject to termination at will without penalty (except as may be delineated).

- The corporation has and shall maintain insurance (as specified).

- The corporation has no bonus, profit sharing or pension plan (except as specified).

- The financial statements annexed to the agreement accurately and fairly represent the financial condition of the corporation as dated and there have been no material adverse changes since.

This list certainly is not all inclusive and many other warranties can be included. The buyer's accountant and attorney probably will identify other warranties appropriate to the deal. Considerable care is needed to obtain the broadest possible protection.

Two very important additional warranties refer to liabilities and accounts receivable at time of closing, for both are the basis for determining the purchase price. A list of existing liabilities is usually prepared by the seller for the closing and included as an exhibit to the contract. Nonlisted liabilities, or liabilities in excess of stated amounts, constitute a breach of warranty. Under a breach, the remedies are normally indemnification, right to setoff against notes due the seller and claims for money damages.

The term "liabilities" under the warranty must be carefully defined and should include accounts payable, notes payable, expenses payable, taxes accrued to date, rent and occupancy costs accrued to date, loans notes either secured or unsecured, accrued wages and any other debt or obligation, whether disputed or undisputed, liquidated or unliquidated, contingent or noncontingent and not withstanding whether past due, current or due at a future time and notwithstanding whether known or unknown.

The seller also will want protection on indemnified liabilities covered by the warranty. The seller, for example, should have no liability for contingent liabilities adequately insured against. The seller may want to limit his liability to either the buyer's investment or proceeds derived from the sale. While not unreasonable, the limitations of liability remain an item for negotiation. At the very least the seller will want notice of an indemnified liability and the right to defend and settle the claim before the buyer may use self-help to pay the debt and then seek recourse against the seller.

The warranty on accounts receivable and other obligations due the corporation are handled in a manner similar to liabilities. The closing documents will generally reflect the existing receivables, providing for recourse against the seller if receivables remain uncollected beyond a specified time period. Under this warranty the buyer will convey to the seller title to the uncollected receivables in exchange for payment. The seller may instead allow a credit against future installments due under a note. Another common approach is for the seller to escrow a reserve against uncollected receivables.

Since the buyer ordinarily will rely upon certain asset and liability levels to arrive at the price for the shares, it would be wise to incorporate a further warranty as to an acceptable range. For example, a depletion of inventory and receivables prior to closing might have a serious impact on future cash flow or the ability of the buyer to finance the acquisition. Make certain the business is as healthy when you buy it as when you first negotiate the deal.

Covenants

The affirmative and negative covenants under a stock transfer also are much the same as those found in asset transactions. Under stock transfers, however, the covenants will necessarily be expanded to protect the buyer from major changes in the financial or legal structure of the corporation to be acquired.

Common covenants provide that until closing the corporation will not undertake:

- New indebtedness
- New mortgages
- Extraordinary improvements
- Extraordinary purchases
- Extraordinary disposition of assets
- Defaults on contracts
- Extraordinary contracts
- Distribution or redemption of shares
- Issuance of new shares
- New compensation plans
- Charter or by-law amendments

Personally Guaranteed Debts

There are numerous corporate obligations on which the selling stockholder may have personal liability. Often the seller is unaware of issued guarantees, only to learn of it long after the sale when the corporation may be in default. The seller therefore must identify the various personal obligations that will require termination, prior payment or indemnification under the contract.

Any corporate obligation may be subject to guaranty. Loans due lending institutions invariably require the personal guarantees of the stockholders. The same is true of leases on the premises, equipment leases or other long term or major obligations. It cannot be taken for granted that vendor obligations are without personal guarantees. Increasingly, suppliers to the small business firm demand guarantees. In many instances these might have been issued years earlier when the business was started. For this reason the seller will want the right to notify vendors that any personal guarantees on future debts are to be terminated upon the closing date. The seller should also investigate the existence of personal guarantees on such commonly overlooked items as utility accounts, money orders, and any fiduciary accounts. The selling stockholder, as principal officer of the corporation, also may have statutory liability on federal and state withholding taxes collected from employees, sales and meal taxes, unpaid payroll and, in many states, unemployment compensation payments.

HOW TO ESCAPE LIABILITY

You never know what might go wrong after you sign the contract. You may discover fatal problems with the business or a better opportunity may be found, or you may simply want to abandon the deal for personal reasons. There are times when you want to safely walk away from even no cash down deals.

For each of these reasons you always want an escape route should you want to wiggle out of the contract. Try these steps.

Use your escape clauses. Your agreement should be conditional on several factors such as a satisfactory lease, approval of the seller's books by your accountant, etc. These unilateral conditions can be a convenient escape route. Why lock yourself in?

Keep your deposit to a minimum. Never put down a larger deposit than you are willing to lose. Brokers and sellers will push for as large a down payment as possible but a deposit in the range of $1000 to $5000 is adequate for most small business transactions. And always specify the seller may keep the deposit as liquidated damages should you default. Without this clause the buyer may have a claim against you for substantially greater damages.

Buy through your corporation. Incorporate before you sign the contract, and the corporation rather than you should be named as the buyer. With a corporation you will be shielded from personal liability should you decide to default.

KEY POINTS TO REMEMBER

1. Select the type transaction that will be most favorable to your situation.

2. Your contract must specify terms to protect you.

3. No contract should be signed without your attorney's prior approval.

4. Draft the contract so you can walk away if you must.

14

Pyramid Your No Cash Down Deal

How would you like to start with one wall furnishing store grossing $300,000 annually and within three years have a prosperous mini-empire of seven stores ringing sales of $2,800,000? The story becomes even more interesting when you discover that each of the seven stores was acquired with absolutely no cash down. That can be done by pyramiding, parlaying your business, using it as leverage to put you into more and bigger deals to expand your wealth.

With your first business successfully underway, you enjoy certain advantages that can propel you right along. Cash flow is now available to you. Creditors will help more readily once you are a proven customer. Banks and other lenders accept you as more than an idea person and listen seriously to you. Prospective partners can examine what you have done and not what you might do. In short, you have a track record and momentum. With your first business you've marshalled assets, power and influence. To multiply your wealth, you must strike while the iron is hot and you look like a winner.

BUT WHO NEEDS IT?

That's far from a rhetorical question. Ray Kroc, the farsighted founder of the stunningly successful McDonald's hamburger chain, was delighted each time they changed their signs to announce still another billion hamburgers sold. "No, it's not because of the money involved," said Kroc, "but because of the tremendous satisfaction in having built something so big and dynamic." Still I doubt Ray Kroc's lifestyle would have change much if McDonald's was only one-tenth its enormous size.

My neighbor Walter personifies a miniature Ray Kroc. He doesn't flip hamburgers, but at last count he owns 15 thriving businesses, from a car dealership to restaurants to a bicycle rental shop in a local resort town. Walter's bank account is his secret, but I'm sure he too has surpassed the point at which more money would significantly change his lifestyle. But does that slow Walter down? No. He keeps chasing success more and more. Recently Walter confided he's negotiating to buy a large motel in a neighboring state that would add $100,000 to his present six figure income.

You may not have met Ray Kroc, but you certainly know other Walters. They're easy to spot, for their life is wheeling and dealing, collecting businesses like squirrels collect nuts.

Ask any "Walter" what really makes him run. The surprising answer is that money alone almost never motivates them. Money is simply the yardstick by which they measure success. The joy of having achieved a major goal is reward enough.

Some Walters are driven by ego, the need for personal satisfaction, power or perhaps the sheer thrill of helping something grow.

Statistically such people as Walter are rare. The vast majority of us instead fall into the "who needs it?" category. You hear the rationalizations. "A Chevrolet will travel anywhere a Mercedes can." "How many steaks a day can you eat?" "Why kill yourself?" "You only live once." "Besides, I'd rather play poker with the boys than take on more business headaches."

I do not suggest you cancel your Saturday golf game to go after another deal, but in this chapter I will show those willing Walters how to expand their success, even if it is only for the sheer joy and thrill of it.

BIGGER CAN BE BETTER

There are plenty of good reasons for fixing your sights on a bigger operation and expanding your existing base. Expansion does not have to change your lifestyle or turn you into a workaholic, nor does it require a "wheeler-dealer" mentality. The fact is, bigger can not only be better, it even can be easier. Consider what a larger empire can do for you.

Increase security through diversification. Why put all your eggs in one basket? Your business may give you your paycheck, but what happens if it suddenly stops? It frequently and unexpectedly happens. Fire, unexpected competition, bankruptcy or a fatal labor strike could occur at any time. Unfortunately, an owner of a small business has security only as long as she is in business. With thousands of companies failing every year for one reason or another, it doesn't offer all that much protection. Why not multiply your businesses and diversify your income sources?

Improve profits through leverage. Your existing business can benefit financially from expansion. Think of the added purchasing power which can translate into lower prices, higher volume and greater profits. Such a strategy can help you compete with large chains. Many businesses expand just to survive in the competitive jungle.

Strengthened management. Growth can allow you to develop the management team you need to succeed. Regardless of your business, you'll need people who are expert in all areas of management. Modern management and the attack of big business on small mom and pop operators have all but killed the "one man show." A small business cannot afford a diverse number of highly skilled specialists on a payroll, but a big business can.

Reduce pressure on you. This may be the number one reason to expand. Contrary to what you might think, bigger does not necessarily mean more work or more pressure. A larger endeavor doesn't necessarily require that you work harder, just that you work smarter. With a strong management team to help manage your business you may find that you can spend even less time with your business and stop being married to your work.

Lincoln supposedly freed the slaves, but one acquaintance of mine evidently didn't realize this. About 15 years ago Joe bought a small but successful insurance agency. Like so many small business owners Joe reported to work daily and couldn't bring himself to take a vacation. Even a week away from the business for needed surgery was out of the question. He was the proverbial "indispensable man" without whose constant presence the business would immediately fall apart. Joe was chained to his own success.

Over the years I asked Joe why he didn't expand and build a staff that would allow him to enjoy life more. Joe always offered the same tired excuse. "Who needs more headaches?" Joe clung to the myth that bigger means more problems, never considering that just the opposite could be true.

Quite by accident, Joe picked up a combination insurance agency and real estate office in an adjacent town. The owner, an old friend of his, suddenly died and his widow handed Joe the keys to the business at an attractive price. Joe immediately hired a bright college graduate to oversee both his businesses. This talented woman not only relieved Joe of many of the tedious day to day matters that kept him chained to his desk, she even improved his businesses by bringing fresh ideas and the objectivity of a newcomer.

Joe was thrilled. For the first time in 22 years he vacationed for more than a few days and finally began to enjoy life. Today Joe owns five insurance agencies with numerous other business interests. Joe wisely developed a first class management staff to run everything efficiently in his absence. When he does work, he does so as a decision-maker, using his head instead of his strong back. Joe now enjoys the lifestyle so many dream about but so few achieve. And it all became possible because expansion offered Joe the support he needed to achieve what he always believed he had to do for himself.

WHERE DO YOU GO FROM HERE?

Suppose you've dived into the entrepreneurial waters and emerged with a business of your own. The hardest part was conquering doubts about your management capability while relinquishing the security of a steady paycheck. Since you haven't drowned, expansion should be easy. Why not? You not only have your feet wet, you're already swimming. All you have to do is learn a few additional strokes to become a true champion.

But before you enter deeper water you first have to know where you are now and where you want to go. A word of caution. Even the most carefully planned courses are full of interesting detours that can provide opportunities. Who knows where any given business will end up years from now? No crystal ball can give you the answer. That unpredictability is one of the things that makes business so exciting.

We can only wonder whether Ray Kroc visualized his present McDonald's empire when he hung his sign on his first stand. Did you ever hear of Radio Shack, part of the Tandy Corporation, with over 5,000 stores dotting America? Thirty years ago their first hi-fi shop was a crowded little store hidden amongst the skyscrapers of downtown Boston. One of their first employees, a radio buff high school classmate of mine, told me that when Radio Shack started the business they anticipated only three or four stores.

Don't waste much time looking ahead five, ten or 15 years. Long range planning is useful, but things rarely turn out the way you plan. Take one step at a time. You'll instinctively know the next right move when the time arrives.

ALWAYS MULTIPLY A WINNER

The key to rapid expansion is to parlay one successful business into a bevy of others using the same formula. Ten years ago the Clauson brothers opened their first Quick Stop automotive tune up center in the outskirts of Seattle. Despite heavy competition, sales were brisk. The operation required startup capital of over $100,000 borrowed from banks and a couple of confident relatives and by taking in a partner. And so the Clausons opened the doors with nary a penny of their own. Flushed with early success, they quickly repaid their debts and found their business worth in excess of $200,000 on the open market.

The Clausons each drew a respectable $60,000 salary, but they wanted more, so they expanded by opening several more tune up centers. Trading on their equity and track record they were able to borrow $175,000 from a local bank to open a second unit and convert a defunct gas station into a third unit. With three operations, increased sales and profits soon mushroomed into even more equity. Today the Clausons own 15 automotive centers and are happy millionaires.

Observe the pyramid pattern of growth. Borrow against equity; open more units or expand the present business with the borrowed funds; pay the loans through increased cash flow and thus build even more equity to finance future expansion and growth.

On my way to my office each morning I often stop at a local luncheonette famous for its delicious coffee. The owner successfully operated his luncheonette for about ten years following a stint in the army. And Carl runs his busy restaurant so well he could probably sell it tomorrow for over $150,000. Sitting on $150,000 in equity, Carl nevertheless slaved day in and day out working behind the counter exactly as he had for the past ten years. All he had to look forward to was many more years of the same.

Carl finally saw the light and decided to unleash the equity in his business to create greater wealth. True his coffee shop provided a solid income, but by tapping his $150,000 equity he easily raised the funds needed to make a down payment on a far larger restaurant which generated larger profits and allowed Carl to build his equity and wealth at a far faster rate. Carl tripled his income and can look forward to over a million dollars net worth within a few years.

For Carl, trading up to a much larger operation within the same industry was a perfect strategy. The Clausons developed their business with a string of additional units following a strategy of horizontal expansion.

Unlike Carl, who expanded by trading up to a more successful operation, many other entrepreneurs employ "vertical" expansion to build their fortune. This type of expansion plugs you into every level of distribution and it oftentimes can be a brilliant growth strategy. David, as one good example, entered the business world after working years as a sales representative for a business forms distributor. The owner, approaching retirement age, agreed to a gradual takeover of ownership by David with the purchase price paid from a portion of David's sales commissions. After three long, hard years, David owned the growing company outright. Sales leaped under his management to over $2 million a year. That's when David decided it was time to expand. He wisely purchased a printing company so he could print his own forms for the distributing company. Another two years elapsed and David found a small paper supply firm for sale. A logical acquisition, the paper company could sell to his printing firm, and the printing firm in turn could print the forms for the distributing company. David now owns three companies, each at a different point in the distribution channel. David always capitalized on the equity of his existing businesses, borrowing on a short term basis to finance the down payment of his next acquisition, while the seller provided most of the financing. Each business paid its own purchase price from its own profits, creating a mini-empire for David in the process.

Diversification may be even more challenging than trading up or expanding within the same industry. Imagine starting your day visiting your chain of appliance stores, then journeying to your car dealership for lunch, finally stopping at the headquarters of your sporting goods chain in midafternoon. Before heading home you check your movie theatre to see that everything is ship-shape.

Sound like a hectic schedule and a bit more than you would like to handle? Not if you're like Hartford's Ken Wilson. Business is his thing. He would suffer chronic boredom if forced to spend his days overseeing just one type business. To Ken, different challenges, problems and opportunities offer the spicy mix that promises success. Ken remembers growing up poor and watching his father get wiped out when his small chain of jewelry stores failed during the depression. Ken learned from his father's bitter experience and thereafter refused to rely on just one type of business for security.

What makes Ken's story even more exciting is that he created his conglomerate starting without a dime of his own. Still, Ken knew precisely how to claw his way up the ladder. Ken's first business, a small appliance store, was taken over for its debts only. Ken bailed it out by settling with creditors for 30 cents on the dollar. Then with some imaginative marketing he built it into a $1 million a year moneymaker. His second appliance store was plenty solvent but Ken still waltzed in with no cash down. Borrowing $30,000 from the available cash of his first store Ken coupled it with seller financing of $60,000 and the assumption of some existing debts to reach the price of $140,000. The car dealership came even easier. The seller confidently turned it over to him with 100 percent financing based on Ken's financial strength alone. Today, Ken sells over 1600 Chevrolets a year.

The movie theatre was a high flyer. It was available for $90,000 but Ken scooped it for $75,000 borrowed from a local bank while Ken enticed the previous owner with a good job.

Ken needs no cash to expand. He now has credit, borrowing power and a signature on a note that means something. All he has to do is find more businesses and sellers who don't need money up front, but need only the security that the buyer is financially strong enough to justify 100 percent financing.

PYRAMID EQUITY INTO REAL WEALTH

What is your present business worth? Surprisingly few business people evaluate their net worth and fewer still understand how to parlay their net worth into a larger, more successful business. Before you launch more no cash down adventures, add up your business assets. What are they worth on the open market? Remember, goodwill may be your most valuable asset. Now subtract your business liabilities from your total assets to find your net worth or equity. This represents your "wealth" invested in the business. Think about it as hard cash that should be working hard for you. The balance sheet your accountant hands you at the end of the fiscal year does not accurately reflect your equity or real worth because it includes equipment and fixtures at depreciated rather than market value, and disregards goodwill and other intangible but valuable assets that may represent the lion's share of your wealth.

Assume for the moment that you accurately calculate your business net worth at $100,000. Now ask yourself two questions:

1. Is that $100,000 working as hard as it can for you? What profit does it really return to you? Is it building all the wealth it is capable of building?

2. What could that same $100,000 earn for you if invested elsewhere?

Small business owners are unaccustomed to thinking about their businesses in so objective a way. I periodically conduct management seminars at local colleges. At a recent seminar I suggested participants bring their financial statements so we could go through precisely that exercise. One woman owned a large fabric store with a net worth of over $100,000. We put Selma's business to the acid test. Selma volunteered that all she could manage to take out of the business was $15,000 in salary and $5,000 in net profits, despite the fact the business was fully paid for and had little debt. To Selma, $20,000 was a satisfactory return on a $100,000 investment. While I hated to disillusion her, the fact remains that if she got a job in another fabric shop she would still receive a $15,000 salary. Therefore her $100,000 investment was really earning only a $5,000 profit, or a paltry 5 percent return on her investment. Selma obviously could sell out, throw the $100,000 into a money market account and watch it earn $10,000 without lifting a finger and with absolutely no risk. Selma was hardly overwhelmed with the idea of selling out. But once we identified her inadequate return on investment, I asked what she intended to do about it. "Gee," she replied. "What can I do? I don't want to sell out. I enjoy working for myself. What can I do to earn more money from my business?" The answer is use existing equity to build more sales and profits.

Selma reduced inventory in her fabric shop from $80,000 to a more appropriate $50,000. Sales and profits remained at the same level without the excess inventory, and now Selma had $30,000 in cash for further investment. She also changed her costly policy of always paying C.O.D. for merchandise and now buys on 30 day terms. Her average trade payables of $20,000 now can work for her without cutting into operating profits. With this $50,000 additional cash in her hands Selma was still showing the same miserly $5,000 profit but had enough capital to open a second shop in a large suburban mall. Selma invested $10,000 of the $50,000 for a small down payment on her fixtures and to cover rent and working capital. Her loyal suppliers agreed to stock the new store with $40,000 in inventory with favorable long term, low interest credit terms. This second store promises at least a $15,000 profit in its first year and considerably higher profits once established.

Eventually Selma opened two more stores in other mall locations using the same leverage techniques. At the helm of her growing chain, stores three and four will likely produce a combined profit of $25,000 for Selma. With $20,000 remaining on her original $50,000, Selma diversified. She invested $20,000 setting up a small distributorship to import Danish fabrics for which she obtained exclusive New England rights. This proved to be a smart move because the distributing company now earns pretax profits of $50,000 on sales of nearly $600,000.

Remember the $5,000 profit that Selma once earned on her $100,000? Look at how she leveraged precisely the same net worth into an annual profit of over $100,000. Of course Selma works harder than ever, and she will continue to do so for the next two or three years, but she doesn't mind. Buoyed by whopping annual profits, she knows she can eventually sell her growing company and pocket considerable wealth. More importantly, Selma's having the time of her life and has several additional acquisitions in her sights.

USE YOUR CREDIT POWER TO EXPAND

Remember how Selma raised $20,000 when her suppliers extended just one month's trade credit? I highlight that one maneuver because it is probably the quickest, easiest and least expensive way to raise expansion capital. It's also the most common way.

Properly handled, trade credit can allow you to expand without investing a dime. I learned the power of trade credit many years ago when a partner and I embarked on building a chain of retail pharmacies. Since my partner had a proven track record operating his own pharmacy, I knew he had what it takes to make money. My job was to leverage our limited capital into a fast growth company.

For starters, we scraped together $30,000, purchasing our first pharmacy for $85,000 with the seller financing $55,000. Knowing then what I know today I could have easily kept our $30,000 in the bank and instead applied no cash down techniques to buy the business.

Once we had our first pharmacy underway, we decided to leverage trade payables into the capital we needed for further acquisitions. A safe rule of thumb in most businesses is to operate with 30 days trade credit on the books. Since we purchased about $360,000 in merchandise a year, we could build liabilities to $30,000 and still remain financially strong. Within our first few weeks we had $30,000 tucked in our pockets, rather than in our suppliers'.

With the capital accumulated from our first store we immediately purchased a second store for $36,000 with $12,000 down, again with the balance financed by the seller. Since this new operation purchased $240,000 a year, we could safely tap it for $20,000 for further expansion. Now we had $18,000 in cash remaining from the first store plus $20,000 from the second and began to scout for more pharmacies to buy.

Anxious to expand we quickly invested in two more pharmacies, acquired with far less cash than the business would provide us. Our objectives were always the same:

- Use surplus cash flow from prior acquisitions to finance down payments on new acquisitions.

- Ascertain that the down payment is less than the amount of cash you can pull out of the business by safely building liabilities.

- Require the seller to finance the balance of the purchase price.

With this technique we soon had 13 stores generating over $5 million per year and we did it all with only $30,000. But looking back we could have achieved it with absolutely nothing down. When my partner wanted to cut back on his work because of ill health, we sold the stores, but from our experience I learned a valuable lesson. Once you have one business you can use it to leverage your way into your next deal and can continuously repeat the process to go as far as your management skills and ambition allow.

THINK MINI-CONGLOMERATE

When American Express or IT&T find a business they want to acquire, they simply swap pieces of paper, exchanging their shares of stock for shares in the acquired company. But what works for IT&T doesn't necessarily apply to Dan's Donut Shops, unless you happen to be Dan Collins, who found plenty of takers for the shares of his bustling Chicago donut emporium. In just over two years Dan turned his one small donut shop into a thriving chain of 23 successful shops grossing $8 million annually.

Dan inherited his first donut shop from his father, and soon saw an opportunity to buy another a few miles away. The seller asked $10,000 down and would finance the $25,000 balance. Unfortunately, Dan didn't have $10,000, so he instead proposed an interesting deal. Dan would set up a new corporation called Dan's Donut Shops, Inc. as a holding company which would own all the shares of both Dan's and the seller's shop. Dan, in turn, would own 90 percent of the shares of the holding corporation and the seller would receive 10 percent in place of the $10,000 down payment. The seller would still finance the $25,000 balance. Dan convinced the seller he could build a successful chain and persuaded him to accept stock in the new enterprise. Dan's mini-conglomerate was launched!

Dan next bargained eight percent ownership in the holding company for a down payment on a $50,000 coffee shop in a downtown office building. As Dan expanded, he always adhered to the same approach: exchange a small ownership share in the holding company for a down payment on a new acquisition with the balance of the acquisition's price paid from its own future profits.

Today Dan still owns 52 percent of the shares of his mini-conglomerate, while the sellers who demonstrated their confidence in Dan own the other 48 percent. Dan reports the net worth of the business to be over $2 million, with Dan's personal net worth well over $1 million. And Dan was the guy who only two years earlier couldn't raise $10,000 for a down payment! No, you don't have to play in the big leagues to build your own mini-conglomerate; just follow Dan's method:

1. Create a holding company. This is nothing more than a corporation that owns the shares of individual operating corporations.

2. Transfer the stock ownership in your existing business to the holding company in exchange for the shares of the holding company.

3. Find other businesses where the seller may be willing to substitute a down payment for a few shares of your holding company. Your selling point is always the same: You have what it takes to make the holding company grow and grow.

The few shares the seller accepts may soon be worth far more than what would have been his down payment.

4. Pay the amount financed on each acquisition from its own profits. Be careful. Don't borrow from one company to pay for another. This can create a costly domino effect should you pick up a loser along the way. Each business must stand on its own financial feet.

5. Hold on to at least 51 percent of the shares. You started out as the boss and that's what you want to stay!

Do these financial machinations sound too difficult? In truth, it is one of the simplest concepts for expansion. Nor is it "pie-in-the-sky" theory, for it's done all the time. You just may not have heard about all those little pieces of paper changing hands and making millionaires.

TURN A NAME INTO A MONEY-MAKING FRANCHISE SYSTEM

You may be a brilliant operator but still oppose expansion because you don't want the headaches that come from managing a bevy of businesses. If that is so, but you still want the wealth that bigness can bring, franchising may be your answer.

Before you can consider franchising you need one indispensable ingredient: a business with a highly successful name, reputation, service or product that lifts it above the competitive crowd. Franchising can be the perfect way to expand for several reasons:

- Properly organized, you can establish a large network of franchised businesses without any investment on your part.

- You by-pass the headaches of managing large numbers of company-owned operations. Your efforts are limited to selling

franchises and providing general business direction and supervision to your growing cadre of franchisees.

- Your income is assured because it comes not only from the
  sales of franchises but from royalties that pour in day after
  day.

Think back on how it all began for Ray Kroc and his McDonald's
franchise empire. It was not long ago that McDonald's was a
solitary hamburger stand in San Bernardino, California. Colonel
Saunders started his "Finger Lickin'" franchise chain when he was
in his 60s.

Look around. Observe the number of small regional franchise
networks springing up in virtually every type of business. If your
business is unique, highly profitable and has a good track record,
why not duplicate it in other locations? Better yet, why not have
others capitalize it, manage it and still pay you for the privilege?
You may not end up another Ray Kroc, but franchising can work
wonders for your bank account.

AVOID THE GROWING PAINS

Before you leap into an expansion program, take a hard look at
some of the most common mistakes that can bring your venture
tumbling down around your ears.

Evaluate your own strengths. Do you have what it takes to manage
multiple operations? This requires the ability to delegate and motivate. You must be able to work through other people, an ability
that requires far different skills than are needed for the smaller one
man business.

Watch cash flow. Every acquisition has to stand on its own feet
without draining cash from existing operations. Never acquire
new businesses unless they can be self supporting.

Don't build on quicksand. Make certain your existing operations are solid, running smoothly and in good financial health before you expand. Keep your organization on a firm financial footing.

Develop a management team. You can't be everywhere and do everything at once. A capable management team will help you manage when you're no longer a one man show.

Limit overhead. Forget fancy offices and big expense accounts. Don't let your ego dim your judgment. Watch every dime, even when you're worth millions.

Protect yourself. Set up each business as a separate corporation. If one goes sour it won't bankrupt you or your remaining organization.

Consider logistics. Confine yourself at first to one geographic area. Forget businesses in distant locations where they cannot be adequately supervised.

Don't let growth problems discourage you. Growing pains are natural; and every business suffers from them. The trick is to be prepared for them.

Grow with no cash down. You can expand quickly with little or no cash if you master the techniques. The few dollars you may need can easily come from your existing business.

KEY POINTS TO REMEMBER

1. It's easier to expand on no cash down terms than it is to start from scratch.

2. Use trade credit to raise the growth capital you need.

3. There are many ways to grow a successful business. Adopt a growth strategy suitable for your business.

4. You can build a mini-conglomerate through the sale of shares in your corporation.

5. What's in a name? It may be the start of a powerful franchise system.

6. Growth has its pitfalls as well as opportunities. Proceed carefully.

15

Sell for No Cash Down

I'd never sell a business to a buyer with a hefty down payment. In fact, if I were looking to sell I'd probably work even harder than the buyer to find a way to have him take over my business with absolutely no investment on his part. And my motivation is hardly for charitable purposes—unless I could be considered the charity.

Does this sound illogical? I don't think so. In fact, selling a business for no cash down is by far the most logical way to sell a business— at least if you're a seller who wants to go against convention and put plenty more dollars in your pocket in the process. In this chapter I'll show you how you can do precisely that.

So far I have aimed most things in this book at buyers. Every case illustrated yet another method by which a successful buyer can get into business without cash. Now I'll show you, if you're that smart seller, why you should help him reach his objective. You've already learned that in the game of business, both sellers and buyers *can* win. Here you will see how both *will* win.

For starters, imagine yourself ready to sell that prosperous business you have spent years building. Now it's time to cash in your chips. I suggest you have only two basic objectives:

1. Sell as quickly as possible.
2. Sell for as much money as possible.

The simple truth is that the best way to satisfy both of these objectives is to sell with no cash down terms.

CASH DEMANDS BRING SLOW SALES

Time and time again you have observed a perfectly saleable business with a fair price tag sit idly on the market waiting for a buyer. Chances are it's a seller demanding too high a down payment. The sad truth is, most businesses either don't sell at all or sell too slowly because the seller needlessly narrowed the number of possible buyers by demanding a large down payment. But what if one of those precious few buyers who happens to have the money decides not to buy your business?

To stimulate a fast sale you must expand the buyer market dramatically by including those without substantial cash, who nevertheless could be good, qualified buyers. Obviously many more people are available to buy without high cash requirements. That's the thought process that turns quick sales!

Consider one frustrated seller who had a superette for sale for over a year but just couldn't consummate a deal. The business grossed $500,000 annually and consistently showed a respectable net profit. Cal was asking $150,000 with $50,000 down. Business brokers and others within the industry insisted the price was reasonable considering prices for comparable stores. Still, Cal couldn't dig up a buyer even though he faithfully advertised each week in his metropolitan newspaper, exhausted the efforts of seven local business brokers and even touted the business to competitors in his trade association.

There was, of course, plenty of active buyer interest, with Cal receiving inquiries from 30 people, but the story was always the same. The down payment threw up a big stumbling block. Not one of the 30 interested buyers could or would invest the $50,000 Cal stubbornly demanded.

At this point I suggested that Cal place the following ad in the newspaper: "Superette. NO CASH DOWN. Sales $500,000. Price only $200,000 on good terms to responsible buyer." That $17 ad prompted over 400 phone calls. Notice we didn't offer the business for $150,000 but for $200,000. Why? If the number one concern of buyers is the down payment, the price becomes secondary provided the business can comfortably pay the price.

After we screened the many phone calls, we set up appointments for the 12 buyers who displayed the strongest backgrounds and interest. Within three weeks we sold Cal's superette to a young man who had worked as a manager for a large grocery chain. He had impeccable credentials which easily offset his lack of cash. He finally agreed to pay $190,000 with nothing down and assumed $25,000 in outstanding trade liabilities towards the price, financing the $165,000 balance over five years at 18 percent interest. What was Cal's score-card on the deal?

Yes, Cal sacrificed a $50,000 down payment with which he would have paid his own liabilities, thus walking away with only $25,000 in his pocket. But don't feel bad for Cal. He originally was willing to take back a $100,000 note for five years at 12 percent interest. Instead, he'll receive $165,000 at 18 percent, and will come out many thousands of dollars ahead.

Equally important, Cal now enjoys his retirement playing golf every day at his Arizona country club. He says, "It sure beats stacking cans of peas on the shelf while hoping somebody will walk in and write me a $50,000 check.''

While there aren't many buyers who can raise $50,000 or more for a down payment on a small business, especially wage earners buying their first small business, the problem grows even more acute if the business requires special skills and appeals to only a narrow range of buyers. A superette will normally attract the largest number of buyers regardless of terms, because it falls within that broad range of businesses that almost anyone can operate without special training, experience or education. And it's appropriate for either men or women. Yet, despite its wide appeal, Cal still couldn't find a buyer with $50,000 in a city with over one million people. What would the odds of finding such a buyer be in Horseshoe, Wyoming?

Consider a business requiring a more specialized background. What if Cal were selling a pharmacy instead? For example, at any given time there are fewer than a handful of young pharmacists in Boston willing to buy a small drugstore. A seller of such a business explores no cash down possibilities or discovers he may not sell at all.

ACCEPT LESS NOW FOR MUCH MORE LATER

Cal's story showed you how no cash down can get you on the golf course sooner, but don't miss its important second message: take less now in exchange for much more later. Buyers will pay a premium for no cash down terms. If you are a no cash down buyer expect the seller to make up for it on the other end, whether through a higher price, higher interest rates or some other concession. Astute buyers realize they have to give up bargaining points for no cash down terms, but try to sacrifice as few as possible. The seller, on the other hand, will want to strike a bonanza for his generosity, and as a seller you can strike a bonanza if you play it right. As with every deal, playing it right depends on knowing your adversary and a few negotiating tricks.

Buyers will frequently buy most any business on any terms at almost any price if they can get in with little or no money of their own and pay the balance from the cash flow of the business. Even unprofitable businesses are grabbed up by no cash down buyers. I once saw a seller forgo a small down payment for a selling price triple the original asking price!

Why? The down payment is a Buyer's most immediate concern and the one overwhelming stumbling block if she has no money. In contrast, buyers often view price as only so many dollars a month to pay the seller. Once the buyer is satisfied the business can make those payments and provide a healthy income to boot, price becomes a far less important issue than the question of down payment.

What about interest rates? Similarly, while the sharp buyer with money in her pocket will zero in on interest rates as a key bargaining item, the no cash down buyer will consider interest only an an extension of price.

I know from experience that a "cash" buyer can bargain very low interest rates from a seller and these hard-bargain rates can be as low as one-half of bank rates. But can you see a buyer with nary a penny in his pocket anxious to buy a business driving a hard bargain to save a few points on interest?

Remember, the buyer's objective is to eliminate his stumbling block, the down payment, while the seller's chief concern is to sell on terms that will ultimately put the largest amount of dollars in his pocket. The two objectives can nicely coexist.

Just as Cal understood the psychology of no cash down buyers, so did Fillmore, a legendary "horse trader" from Omaha who started out in real estate. He bought older homes at low prices, paying quick cash to desperate sellers, then placing the houses right back on the market for a quick 30 to 50 percent profit. Whenever he sold, however, Fillmore would generously offer attractive no cash down terms. Before he turned 35, Fillmore had earned profits of several million, represented by the many mortgages he held on the homes sold. Earning high interest on his profit, Fillmore figures he could afford to wait for his fortune to roll in. Theorizing that this approach could work as well on business deals, "no cash down Fillmore" set out to make his second fortune. On his first deal he picked up a small general store on the outskirts of town. The seller's husband had recently died and the bereaved widow was anxious to sell as quickly as possible for ready cash. The store was for sale for $40,000, but Fillmore didn't care about the asking price. Upon meeting the bereaved widow, Fillmore opted he "might" be interested but he'd only pay $25,000 cash. Desperate for fast money, the anxious widow snapped it up. Of course, with his millions, Fillmore had no intention of operating a tiny general store. One week later, Fillmore ran an ad in the newspaper offering the business for sale for $50,000 and with only $5,000 down.

Buyers flocked to the deal. Several didn't have $5,000, but those were exactly the ones Fillmore most wanted. To one highly motivated buyer, he countered, "Young man, if you can't come up with $5,000 I can't sell to you." He slowly stuffed his pipe with fresh tobacco, looked up and continued. "However, since I think you would do a fine job with the business, I'll tell you what I'll do. Make the price $57,000, and pay it off over five years at current bank rates and it's yours."

Think about it. Fillmore bought a business on Tuesday for $25,000 cash and sold it the following Monday for a $32,000 profit. The buyer didn't fare too badly either. The store was the starting point of a successful career that made him wealthy. So what if he paid a few more dollars for his first business? Over a period of years the business made him rich.

This could be the most important lesson in your life. You can sell a business for huge dollars if you forget the small dollars up front. It can be the best investment you ever make!

THE BEST INVESTMENT YOU'LL EVER MAKE

What constitutes a fair return on an investment? Of course you will consider such factors as liquidity, safety and taxes, and it will also depend on the nature of the investment. But suppose you invest in the business you're selling. What return should satisfy you?

Having sold over 40 businesses for no cash down, Fillmore contends a good return is 300 percent, excluding interest. Here's how he justifies such whopping returns.

"If I have a business that would typically sell for $50,000 with $10,000 down, I figure I can boost the price to $70,000 and peddle it any day of the week with no down payment. Since I'm lending the buyer $10,000, and since it's the only way he can get the business, he'll readily agree to a 40 percent higher price. I not only get back my $10,000, I receive another $20,000 in the process. And the buyer's interest payments on the entire $70,000 give me a healthy bonus!"

Intrigued with Fillmore's ideas, I tried my hand at it when I came across a small machine shop for sale. It was a perfect setup. The seller was anxious to sell for only $35,000 cash. I signed a three day option to buy, but before I took title to it I sold it after one phone call to an old college classmate looking for a similar opportunity. I went into my spiel. "I have a super machine shop for sale for only $60,000 with absolutely no cash down." Within two days my classmate was in business and I was back at my desk with his $60,000 secured note earning me 16 percent interest.

Was my spectacular venture beginner's luck? I don't think so. I may not do as well on every deal, but it beats almost any other investment I have ever made. I have done many such deals since, picking up a business for a few dollars and selling it for a giant profit on paper. Many of my colleagues have successfully followed in my path.

Next week, for example, I'm going to complete a small deal for a client just learning his no cash down lessons. Just three months ago he bought a run-down cheese and fruit shop for only $23,000. It was a tiny store with hardly any inventory, and my client did absolutely nothing to improve the business. How is he selling it? For $75,000 payable over three years—nearly a five-fold return on his investment! The best part is he never invested $23,000 to buy it in the first place because he assumed $20,000 in payables. His new buyer agreed to assume the same trade payables, offering my client nearly a $50,000 profit for his few dollars invested. Could he have done as well had he looked for a buyer with a large down payment? I doubt it.

Earning big no cash down dividends is only half the equation. Consider that the average business sale requires a 25 percent down payment. On a $100,000 deal with a $25,000 down payment you stuff perhaps only $10,000 into your wallet after liabilities that typically may approximate $15,000.

Unless you're desperate for $10,000 cash, why not latch onto a buyer with no cash, sell her the business for $125,000 and have her assume the liabilities? That one strategy would give you a hefty $25,000 bonus over several years instead of a meager $10,000 today.

BUT I NEED CASH NOW

If that's your predicament, then it's easily solved. You can walk away from a no cash down sale with as much money as you would receive from a sale requiring a hefty down payment, and that can indeed be plenty of cash! Just don't expect it to come out of the buyer's pocket.

Remember Fillmore and his $57,000 general store? True, Fillmore walked away from that deal with nothing but $57,000 worth of paper, plus future interest, but he could have exercised other options to generate immediate cash. For instance, he could have proposed that the buyer obtain a $30,000 loan on the business from a bank, with Fillmore accepting a second mortgage on business assets for $27,000. If the buyer didn't have an adequate credit rating to swing the $30,000 loan, Fillmore could have guaranteed it. Would it have mattered to the buyer? Of course not. He would still be paying $57,000 on the same terms, but he would just break it into two separate loans. The point is that Fillmore would have received $30,000 cash plus a $27,000 note at closing.

Or look instead at a business selling for $100,000 with $25,000 down. Assume you agreed to hold a note for the $75,000 balance and could anticipate receiving $10,000 from the $25,000 down payment after paying $15,000 to creditors. Why not instead urge the buyer to borrow $50,000 against the business with you accepting a note for the balance? Remember, on the original deal you would have sold for a net price of $85,000 based on $100,000 less $15,000 in assumed payables. Why not parlay more generous terms into a far more generous price?

Perhaps you would be able to sell for as much as $125,000 if attractively financed as follows:

$ 50,000	Mortgage from bank
60,000	Note to you
15,000	Liabilities to be assumed
$125,000	Purchase price

Look at the scorecard. You actually increased your walk away money from $10,000 to $50,000, plus you made an extra $25,000 based on the increased price. Equally important, the buyer gets your business without spending a dime of his own.

Use your imagination. Don't be a psychological slave to those few dollars down. There are countless ways to package a deal to maximize your profits once you learn to focus on the big dollars later rather than the small change today.

A PROMISE IS NOT A PAYMENT

But, you argue, how can you possibly sell a business for no cash down without knowing for certain you will ever get paid? Many sellers demand a hefty down payment only because they mistakenly believe a down payment somehow proves a buyer is a person of substance and a good credit candidate thus reducing the risk in collecting the balance owed.

Others cautiously say, "I need a down payment to at least cover the value of the inventory." It all comes down to the same thing: The seller clings to the belief that a reasonable down payment provides that security.

Of course, you can't blame sellers for this attitude. A promise is not a payment, and the woods are full of birds who'll promise anything to get their hands on your business then let you whistle for a check to arrive in the mail.

But say Fillmore had bargained for a $10,000 down payment on his little country store. To what extent would that have assured him he would ever collect the $47,000 balance? Not much.

What could go wrong? Everything. The buyer could perhaps back up a truck and move the inventory and fixtures to Wyoming. Such things happen. Where is Fillmore's security then?

Maybe the buyer is not a crook, but simply belongs to the fraternity of "Lousy Business People," who are as common as sparrows in springtime. Then you may instead see the inventory slowly but surely dwindle as losses cut into credit and cash flow. Good will vanishes as customers patronize competitors. Finally, the business folds with Fillmore holding his $47,000 note and nary a chance of collecting.

Unfortunately, unless you sell your business for cash, you always incur the risk of not collecting the balance. So if security is your number one concern, perhaps you should consider an all cash sale; but unless you have an unusual deal you'll pay a steep price for avoiding the risk of high leverage financing. You'll get a much lower selling price and undoubtedly face considerable difficulty finding a buyer with so much cash. A down payment then actually plays a very small role in reducing risk. The key to safe financing is knowing how to protect yourself.

FORMULAS FOR AIRTIGHT DEALS

I asked "no cash down Fillmore" to tell us his views on the risk involved in turning the keys to the business over for little or no cash in return. Fillmore offered a compelling philosophy. "When I finance a business, one of two things happens. Either the buyer fulfills his obligations and makes all the payments, or I foreclose, taking back the business, often selling it again for additional profits. Sometimes I get an even better price the second time around."

That sounded reasonable, but I voiced other concerns. "What if the buyer starts with $50,000 in inventory but it's down to $25,000 by the time you foreclose? Isn't the business worth $25,000 less?" That question required yet another pipeful of tobacco. "Sure," Fillmore proclaimed, "but it never happens to me. I tie up the buyer so I can foreclose even if he looks at me the wrong way, let alone drains my inventory or otherwise reduces the value of the collateral. It's all in the paperwork and how well you screen and monitor the buyer. That, not the down payment, guarantees you'll get paid one way or the other."

Set up your deal so you can't lose. Either you get your payments or you get the business back with the collateral intact. That's the only way to operate if you're financing any part of the purchase price.

I promised to stay away from legal jargon that your lawyer will handle, but successful entrepreneurs nevertheless must know a little law if they are to have the self-protection vital on leveraged financing deals.

Examine these methods for securing the price. Fillmore calls them the "can't lose formulas." Secure the buyer's note with a mortgage (security agreement) on all the business' assets. Should the buyer default, you can foreclose and quickly take over the assets without assuming the buyer's outstanding liabilities. This protection is so elementary few attorneys overlook it, but other "can't lose" methods are less well known and may be overlooked.

Require the buyer to maintain inventory at specified levels. As Fillmore explains, "It's no good if I give the buyer $50,000 in inventory and he runs it down to $25,000. I stick a clause in my mortgage that forces the buyer to maintain a specific level of inventory. If it dips below that level I can immediately foreclose." Standard mortgage forms do not contain this vital safeguard. Tell your lawyer about it, and he'll agree that it makes sense.

Take an "assignment of lease" as further collateral. This can be the most important weapon in your self-protection arsenal. It is an agreement between landlord, seller and buyer that lets the seller step in and take over the buyer's lease if the buyer defaults on his note to the seller. If location is an important asset, Fillmore always demands it. He puts it into perspective in this discussion about his $57,000 general store. "Let's suppose the buyer defaults. With my security agreement (mortgage) I can foreclose and take over the inventory and fixtures and sell them to someone else. But what are these same assets worth if I can't give the new buyer a lease? When selling the business again I want a viable ongoing business. I don't want to auction the business. Otherwise, I can't get top dollar to recoup what's owed to me." Good Ol' Fillmore with his fourth grade education should be teaching law at Harvard.

The instant default clause is also a favorite of people like Fillmore. The standard note provides that the seller cannot foreclose or take back the business as long as payments come on time. Fillmore told me of one experience that forced him to invent the "instant default" clause. He sold a hobby shop for $75,000 (after buying it for $42,000 one month earlier). Since it was a no cash sale Fillmore accepted a secured note for the full $75,000, a clause requiring the buyer to maintain inventory at $40,000, and an assignment of the lease. When the business was sold it grossed $300,000 a year. Unfortunately, the buyer didn't tend to business and sales skidded downhill. Fillmore nervously watched the business on the skids, but could do nothing because the buyer made all his payments on time and maintained a $40,000 inventory. If the buyer eventually went belly-up, Fillmore would end up with only a ruined business.

Sure enough, two years after Fillmore sold the business the payments stopped. The business was destroyed to the point where Fillmore could get only $40,000 for it; and since he was still owed a balance of $48,000 on his original $75,000 note, he "lost" $8,000 on the deal. (Actually, Fillmore didn't lose at all because his profits on the deal were simply reduced from $33,000 to $25,000.)

But Fillmore learned an important lesson. He now writes into all his notes a provision that allows him to foreclose at any time he deems himself insecure. "Now," says Fillmore, "When I see a buyer doing anything that can hurt the business, I can step right in and take it back. That's real protection."

Of course Fillmore doesn't overlook the other common methods for increasing security. He'll try to obtain a mortgage on the buyer's house or car, and he'll bargain for as many guarantees on the note as possible.

Fillmore continues to laugh at conventional sellers. "They'll sell a business for $100,000, accept $25,000 down, and think they have it made. But they don't really protect themselves. When the business flops, they pick up a few more dollars but still face a whopping loss. Not me. It's not what's up front that counts—it's setting up the deal so you get it all, no matter what happens. I like 'airtight' deals with no leaks."

I agree with Fillmore. Don't delude yourself into thinking that the down payment is any guarantee that you'll see the rest of your money. Well drafted legal documents and your intelligent and constant supervision of the business are considerably more important if you really want to collect the full price.

Nor can you be too careful about who you sell to. I have nothing against Rolex watches. They are among the world's finest timepieces. But they don't really care whose wrists they adorn. I first met a phony buyer sporting a $10,000 Presidential Rolex ten years ago. He was negotiating to buy my client's motorcycle dealership, angling for no cash down terms on a $125,000 purchase price. We were blinded by the glare of his phony "Rolex" watch, his Brooks Brothers suit and Hathaway shirt. "Mr. Solid's" image was further fortified by the new Jaguar parked outside my office and a deep tan recently obtained at what could only be his Palm Beach villa. Who wouldn't be impressed? He looked impeccable, spoke "money" and oozed success. Anyone should gladly accept his promissory note for any amount with few further questions. We fell for it. Two months after taking over and ripping off the dealership, "Mr. Solid" declared personal bankruptcy with liabilities in excess of $2.8 million. His only declared asset was one fake "Rolex" watch.

I tell this story to underscore a most important point. As a seller you want payment, not promises. When you're gambling that your buyer can make the business work, check him or her out. Probe into the prospective buyer's work record, personal credit, work habits and lifestyle. You need a conscientious and sincere buyer, not a fast-buck artist.

FROM NO CASH TO COMFORTABLE RETIREMENT IN FIVE YEARS

Get in with little or no cash, build the business and sell on no cash terms and you could see enough money coming in to keep you in style for a lifetime. That's what Bob Everett did with his Black Angus Steakhouse attracting hungry diners for miles around Nashville, Tennessee.

Bob bought the small steak and beer restaurant in 1971 for $150,000 without a dime of his own, using creative financing to get the keys. The seller agreed to finance $100,000 with the remaining $50,000 financed by $20,000 in assumed seller's debts and a short term $30,000 loan from the company's meat supplier. Bob since expanded the restaurant twice, added an upstairs "function room" for parties and boasted the best steak in the south. Sales steadily increased from $400,000 to over $1 million by 1976, at which point Bob, who now owned the business free and clear, decided to sell. Bob correctly figured it was worth $400,000 with a conventional $100,000 to $150,000 down payment with the balance to be financed by Bob.

But Bob wisely decided to make it available instead to a responsible no cash down buyer—his loyal night manager with whom he had worked side by side for years in building the business. Bob structured the deal to suit his own retirement needs, selling the restaurant for $550,000 with no cash down, payable over ten years at 15 percent interest. Bob now has it made. He comfortably lives on nearly $100,000 a year in interest payments, reinvesting the principal in new deals to keep his entrepreneurial juices flowing.

Bob knew how to get started without capital, and he knew how to increase his wealth by selling to somebody else without capital. As he confesses, "If I didn't have the imagination and courage to find ways to overcome my empty wallet, I'd still be a short-order cook working for somebody else for $300 a week. That's what you need—courage and determination to make it come true for yourself!"

KEY POINTS TO REMEMBER

1. You want to sell as quickly as possible and for as much as possible. No cash down deals accomplish both those objectives.

2. Don't limit your market. Encourage buyers without cash.

3. Buyers are down payment conscious. Give up a few dollars now for much more later.

4. Reinvest your down payment. It could earn you as much as 300 percent interest.

5. You can sell for no cash down and still walk away with plenty of money.

6. Sell your business on airtight terms to guarantee your payments.

7. Your best security is a no nonsense buyer.

8. Buy for no cash down and sell on the same terms. It can make you wealthy.

Index